Cultural Offensive

Cultural Offensive

America's Impact on British Art Since 1945

John A. Walker

Pluto Press
LONDON • STERLING, VIRGINIA

First published 1998 by Pluto Press
345 Archway Road, London N6 5AA
and 22883 Quicksilver Drive, Sterling,
VA20166–2012, USA

British Library Cataloguing in Publication Data
A catalogue record for this book is available
from the British Library

ISBN 0 7453 1321 3 hbk

Library of Congress Cataloging in Publication Data
Walker, John Albert, 1938–
        Cultural offensive : America's impact on British art since 1945/
    John A. Walker.
        p. cm.
    Includes bibliographical references.
    ISBN 0–7453–1321–3 (hbk.)
    1. Art, British—American influences. 2. Art, Modern—20th
    century—Great Britain. I. Title.
    N6768.W25 1998
    709'.41'09045—dc21   98–22146
                                                    CIP

Designed, typeset and produced for Pluto Press by
Chase Production Services, Chadlington, OX7 3LN
Printed in the EC by TJ International, Padstow

Contents

Acknowledgements

For information, comments and help, thanks are due to Art &
Language, Terry Atkinson, Professor John Ball, Clive Barker, John
Boty, Prunella Clough, Magda Cordell-McHale, Roderick Coyne,
Barry Curtis, Alan Davie, Nick de Ville, Toni del Renzio, Caroline
Edwards, David Enthoven, Bryan Ferry, Adrian Glew (of the Tate
Gallery Archive), Mel Gooding, Althea Greenan (of the Women's Art
Library), Richard Hamilton, Michael Hazzledine, Janet Henderson,
Gordon House, Allen Jones, Peter Kennard, Max Kozloff, Gerald
Laing, Mrs S.M. Lanyon, Mark Lancaster, Marco Livingstone, Nigel
McKernaghan, Helen and Tony Messenger, Sanna Moore, Lisa
Moran, Christine Mulloy, Linda Myers, Paul Overy, Kate Paul, Peter
Phillips, Clive Phillpot, Kenneth Prater, John Beldon Scott, Alex
Seago, Colin Self, Sylvia Sleigh/Alloway, Peter Smithson, Mary Spear,
Chris Stephens, Mark Stringer (of the J.M. Richards Collection,
Middlesex University), Stephen Stuart-Smith, Michelle Thomas,
Harriet Vyner, Sue Watling, Tom Watt, Hugh Wilford, Malcolm
Yorke, and to the British Council, the Reference Center of the
United States Information Service, the American Embassy, London,
the library staff of Middlesex University, Cat Hill campus and
Westminster Central Reference Library.

I am also grateful to Middlesex University for a research grant which
provided relief from teaching in order to finalise the text and to Anne
Beech for her encouragement and editorial skills, as well as Derek
Manley for his assistance with picture research and his helpful
comments on the text.

Thanks also to all the agencies, artists, galleries, museums and
photographers who kindly supplied images for illustration purposes.
Great efforts have been made to trace and acknowledge copyright
holders, but if there are any who have been missed, the publishers
would be glad to hear from them so that corrections can be made in any
future editions.

Introduction

'Americanism' – one dictionary definition of this word is: 'devotion to or preference for the United States and its institutions.'

There are many Britons who have never visited the United States of America in a physical sense but, of course, they have been there thousands of times in their imaginations. Those who are British[1] by birth, education and lived experience, nevertheless feel partly American because so much of their culture has originated there: American jazz, rock'n'roll, MTV, novels, poems, plays, American-style architecture, paintings and sculptures; aircraft like the Boeing 777, manufacturers such as the Ford Motor Company with factories based in Britain, designed products like IBM computers, Kodak and Polaroid cameras, Remington electric razors, Hoover vacuum cleaners; Coca-Cola and Pepsi drinks, Levi 501 jeans, Harley-Davidson motorcycles, Camel and Lucky Strike cigarettes, Colgate toothpaste, Kellogg cereals, Campbell's soups, Nike trainers, Wrigley's chewing gum, fast-food franchises such as McDonalds and Kentucky Fried Chicken; comics like *Superman* and *Spiderman*, magazines like *Life*, *Playboy*, *Reader's Digest*, *Time* and *Scientific American*, and, above all, American movies and television series which have infiltrated and colonised the British psyche. While British children may regret the lack of a Disneyland in the United Kingdom, there is one in northern France a few hours' travel away. British holidaymakers in search of sunshine are now as likely to travel to Florida as they are to Spain.

America's effect upon Britain's everyday life and culture – an instance of what social scientists term 'transculturation' – in all its forms would be a huge subject to explore.[2] The scope of this book is narrower because it concentrates upon the fine arts. Its central aims are to document and clarify the impact of America, American art, criticism and mass culture upon British visual art and criticism mainly during the 1950s and 1960s, in the hope of adding to historical knowledge and contributing to the British people's self-understanding.[3] Writing in 1987 Andrew Brighton observed:

> The USA has been a constant and formative element in the British art world for the last twenty-five years, and a history of postwar British art must address the rise, and now the decline, of its influence.[4]

Art historians routinely discuss the influence of one artist upon another. This book is certainly a study of influence, but we need to elaborate the concept because the responses of artists to foreign art and places are complex and multifarious. (An earlier version of the book title *The Americanisation of British Art* was abandoned because it suggested a one-way process involving a supine victim.) Michael Baxandall has described influence as 'the curse of art criticism' and has argued that the common sense idea that artist A influences or acts upon artist B, should be reversed because, in reality, artist B acts upon the work of artist A.[5]

Baxandall went on to list the variety of ways in which such acts occur: 'draw on, resort to, appropriate from, adapt, misunderstand, refer to, engage with, react to, quote, assimilate, copy, paraphrase, make a variation on, ape, emulate, parody, distort, simplify, develop, subvert, transform ...' Thus, while one artist may respond in a submissive manner by adopting and imitating a foreign style, another may react by strengthening their native characteristics; another may selectively appropriate certain elements of the foreign style and then incorporate them into their own work in such a way as to generate a new synthesis; another may be energised and stimulated to experiment in order to push foreign ideas further or in new directions. This means that close attention needs to be paid to exactly how British artists behaved when they were exposed to American visual culture and America itself.

American art, mass and material culture became known to the British in four ways: (1) via the importation into Europe of American art works, books, films, magazines and other manufactured goods; (2) via British artists and critics making visits to, or residing in, the United States; (3) via American artists and critics paying visits to, or residing in, Britain; (4) via American companies investing in British industry or establishing factories and franchises in Britain.

During the period under review, transportation and communication systems increased massively. Thousands of people now fly back and forth across the Atlantic daily, whereas in the 1940s most travelled by sea on liners. After the satellite Telstar was placed into orbit in July 1962, live television transmissions from the United States to and from Europe became possible for the first time. Those British readers who lived through the 1960s will vividly recall the television reports about the assassination of President Kennedy in 1963 shortly after the event. Information, news, goods and people now travel at high speeds around the world and America is thus much closer to Britain at the end of the twentieth century than it was in 1945. However, the rest of the world is also closer.

Britain emerged from the Second World War victorious but exhausted, damaged and in debt to the tune of £3,000 billion. It had only been able to prosecute the war because of a Lend-Lease financial arrangement provided by the United States and Mutual Aid from Canada which ceased when Japan was defeated. In 1948 Britain became dependent on Marshall Aid, the European Recovery Programme funded by the United States.[6]

Many British homes, factories and cathedrals had been destroyed or damaged by bombing. Existing industries and transportation systems desperately needed investment to renew them. The British Empire, which had once been a source of strength, was now a financial liability owing to the costs of maintaining bases, troops and fleets overseas. Two years of national service had to be imposed on two million British young men between 1947 and 1960 in order to support the nation's military commitments at home and to fight wars in Cyprus, Kenya, Korea and Malaysia. Some budding artists resented the loss of time that national service represented. David Hockney, a conscientious objector, had to spend two years working as a hospital orderly.

Gradually it became clear that Britain was no longer a world power of the first rank, that it had to dismantle its Empire and reduce its military expenditure. Adjustment to Britain's relative decline proved difficult for a people accustomed to thinking of themselves as the nation that 'ruled the waves' and 'carried the white man's burden'. As a group of islands close to the continent of Europe, geographically speaking Britain's future was logically connected to that of Western Europe rather than that of North America or the far flung Commonwealth but, of course, the opportunity to join the European Economic Community in 1958 was not taken (Britain did not join until 1973). The history of Britain's colonisation of North

America, the alliances during two world wars and the shared English language meant that Britain felt it had 'a special relationship' with America which ought to be maintained.

Another reason for the willingness of the British to absorb American culture was, of course, the fact that much of it had originated in Europe: many leading 'American' filmstars and directors – such as Charlie Chaplin, Ida Lupino and Alfred Hitchcock – were originally British. Leading European architects, art historians, artists and designers also emigrated to the United States as adults. George Steiner has gone further, and offended many American thinkers in the process, by arguing that American culture is a branch and continuation – indeed a kind of museum – of European culture rather than something significantly new and different.[7] Steiner's views are surely flawed because American artists *have* contributed something new. Furthermore, the roots of American culture have not just been European – they have been African, native-American Indian and Oriental as well. America's size, wealth and power means that it attracts, and sometimes actively seeks out, talented people from all corners of the globe.

Britain can be viewed, therefore, as a nation pulled in opposite directions. Even in the 1990s, long after Britain joined the EEC/Common Market, the British seem reluctant to commit themselves wholeheartedly to Europe for fear of losing more of their sovereignty and national identity. Of course, there was a positive dimension to the 'pig in the middle' situation: Britain was a place where European and American cultures intersected and cross-fertilised.

Once the Second World War ended and it was possible to travel to the continent of Europe again, many British artists took the opportunity to visit Paris and/or the Mediterranean coast. Chapter 1, therefore, considers Eduardo Paolozzi's extended stay in Paris which, paradoxically, brought him into contact with Americans and American imagery. It also examines Herbert Read's relations with America and Americans.

As the foremost example of capitalism triumphant, America posed the greatest threat to the communist Soviet bloc and, consequently, during the 1950s there was an ideological struggle between East and West for the hearts and minds of Europeans. Many of those who lived through the Cold War period were unaware of the precise nature of the struggle and only discovered later on that the Central Intelligence Agency (founded in 1947) and other powerful forces within the ruling elite of America had been involved in the covert promotion of American art and the funding of certain British magazines, institutions and sculpture competitions.[8]

Culture, it would appear, was not simply a realm of innocent pleasure. These matters are addressed briefly in Chapters 2 and 3 which examine the history of the Institute of Contemporary Arts, the Independent Group and the impact that exhibitions of Abstract Expressionism had on British artists and critics during the 1950s.

Chapter 4 considers the efforts by younger British painters and sculptors who were indebted to American Abstract Expressionism to go beyond it during the following decade. It also examines the work of British Pop artists who reacted against abstraction by adopting representation. During the 1950s and 1960s the mass media proliferated and expanded, and played a more important role in people's lives. Much media imagery was American in origin. For British Pop artists, American mass culture was the equivalent of nature and therefore a prime source of iconography.

From the late 1950s onwards younger British artists and art students began to make trips to the United States rather than to France or Italy. Some of them remained for years or even made their homes there. Chapter 5 describes their experiences and the impact the reality of America and American art had upon their work.

In the mid-1960s 'swinging' London became a fashionable city noted for its visual arts, Pop design and music. (Patrick Heron, the British painter and critic, even went so far as to write an article entitled 'The Ascendancy of London in the 1960s'.) As a result a number of American artists were tempted to pay short visits or even to take up residence in Britain. Their response to it and their contributions to British culture are the subjects of Chapter 6.

The twentieth century has been called, by Henry Luce, 'the American Century' in recognition of the power and dominance wielded by the United States. Certainly, the United States emerged from the Second World War as the richest nation on Earth – no other country could match its military might, economic and political power. It was more or less inevitable, therefore, that America's art and culture should come to dominate Europe and other parts of the non-communist world. This is not to say that there was not criticism and resistance to this instance of cultural imperialism.[9] Often there was outright hostility on the part of individuals, organisations and European nation states (especially France). Virtually every non-American has an ambivalent, love/hate relationship towards American culture because it can be crass as well as marvellous, and because it can damage or even destroy native cultures, languages and industries. Chapter 7 considers

Nigel Henderson (1917–84), an amateur cameraman of upper-class origins, photographed one such shop – located in Hackney, a poor district in the East End of London – some time between 1949 and 1952. This photograph is a vivid reminder of the penetration of American mass culture into British, proletarian life: the top of the window is full of American crime, detective, pin-up and film magazines while on the pavement below stands a hand-painted board which announces 'Stop! here for American comics, biggest selection in East London'; a second sign for ice cream lollies is accompanied by a crude depiction of Mickey Mouse's head; a third displays several Pepsi-Cola bottle tops.

The newsagent's window is so replete with imagery, products and lettering that one cannot see the shop's interior. Unwittingly, the shopkeeper had produced a huge collage – similar to the pinboards crowded with images that certain British artists were so fond of generating at the time – in which American and British signs vie for the attention of passers-by. Such newsagents were a familiar sight to the people who were later to be labelled 'Pop artists'.

Another place where American mass culture was available to working- and middle-class Britons was, of course, the cinema. Before the spread of television in the 1950s caused a decline in cinema attendance, 30 million Britons used to visit 4,500 cinemas (some people went two or three times a week) to view the two feature films shown per programme, plus trailers and Pathe News, and to listen to organ playing during the interval. Cinemas were far more numerous in the 1940s than they are today. Despite a quota system designed to protect the indigenous film industry from being overwhelmed or even destroyed by Hollywood, most of the films screened were American in origin and so certain visions of the American way of life were conveyed to British viewers, most of whom had no way of checking their veracity.

The interest which many British artists were to take in American culture, as Robert Kudielka has observed, 'was not based on personal experience' because 'very few artists ... had actually been to the United States. America was a fantasy *of* mass media *via* mass media.[1] Even before the Second World War – in 1927 – an editorial in the *Daily Express* had noted:

> The bulk of picture goers are Americanised to an extent that makes them regard the British film as a foreign film. They talk America, think America, dream America; we have several million people, mostly women, who, to all intents and purposes, are temporary American citizens.[2]

Via the contents of American movies a British child would learn far more about the history of the Wild West, the behaviour of private detectives, the police and criminal gangs in the major cities than they would about, say, the history of Europe. The effect of films on the feelings and imaginations of children is incalculable. Michael Sandle (b. 1936), the British sculptor, has acknowledged how the private fantasies and fears that followed watching Hollywood movies as a child fuelled the imagination that inspired the sculpture he made as an adult.[3]

American vernacular or mass culture was thus much more available to the British than either American or European modern art. Access to the latter usually depended upon an art school education. It also helped to live in London and to be a member of the Institute of Contemporary Arts: some provincial towns had no art galleries at all. At that time, books, magazines and catalogues about the work of living artists were few and far between. And to see what little existed one needed access to an art school library or specialist London bookshops such as Tiranti and Zwemmer.

One European city where new American art could be viewed in the late 1940s was Venice. This was because of the Biennale exhibitions held there and the presence of the American collector, Peggy Guggenheim. She had bought a Palazzo on the Grand Canal and turned it into a museum. As we shall discover, a number of British architects, painters and critics first encountered Abstract Expressionist canvases in Venice.

As mentioned in the Introduction, during the late 1940s a number of British artists travelled to Paris because they assumed it would resume its pre-1939 position as the world's art capital and that the School of Paris – a galaxy of foreign and French artists: Picasso, Braque, Matisse, Brancusi, Giacometti, et al – would continue to be the cutting edge of artistic innovation. However, once it became clear that America was now the dominant world power and that in Abstract Expressionism it had developed an art movement comparable in ambition and quality to any previous European movement, it dawned on European artists and critics that New York had supplanted Paris as the world's art capital. To some degree the shift of power across the Atlantic occurred before and during the Second World War when so many artists, especially the Surrealists, fled to America. Clement Greenberg (1909–94), an American critic who was to become extremely influential in the 1950s and 1960s, was later to argue that New York did not become the world's art capital by rejecting Paris but by assimilating its achievements and then transcending them.

There is an amusing painting by the American artist Mark Tansey (b. 1949) which records the transfer of power. Entitled *Triumph of the New York School* (1984), it depicts members of the two schools dressed in military uniforms assembled for a surrender ceremony. André Breton, the 'Pope' of Surrealism, signs the surrender document for the School of Paris in front of Greenberg, the representative of the victorious New York School.

Even in Paris during the late 1940s it was not possible to escape the presence of America because there were ex-GIs and American artists living there. Eduardo Paolozzi (b. 1924), a Scottish-born sculptor, collagist, film-maker and printmaker of Italian immigrant parents, was one of the British artists who went to Paris – in 1947 – and remained for two years. William Gear and William Turnbull, two other Scottish artists, were also in Paris at roughly the same time. Gear's abstractions were indebted to the School of Paris but his wife Charlotte was an American and it was thanks to her that a selection of his gouaches were shown at the Betty Parsons Gallery, New York in the autumn of 1949. At the time, Parsons was Jackson Pollock's dealer.

Paolozzi had grown up in Leith which was then a rough district of Edinburgh. His parents ran ice cream and sweet shops so his social circumstances were of working or lower middle class. Naturally he was exposed to mass cultural influences: he drew footballers, aeroplanes and film stars, copied and collected cigarette cards, and enjoyed American Western and gangster movies screened in local cinemas. He also read comics and pulp magazines full of science fiction stories and tales of air battles. His propensity to collect mass culture material and his fascination with the conjunction of fantasy and machines and technology can therefore be dated to his childhood. The adult Paolozzi was to write:

> It is conceivable that in 1958 a higher order of imagination exists in a SF pulp produced on the outskirts of LA than in the little magazines of today. Also, it might be possible that sensations of a difficult-to-describe nature be expended at the showing of a low-budget horror film. Does the modern artist consider this?[4]

What was valued by the staff in British art schools during the 1940s were the fine arts, the masterpieces of European 'high' culture and subjects like the nude. 'Low' or mass culture was despised, and

students were expected to abandon or suppress any enthusiasm they might have had for it. At that time it was not envisaged that such material might become the content of fine art. Paolozzi – who attended art schools in Edinburgh, London and Oxford (1943–47) – was only one of many British art students who experienced this clash of cultures and tastes. The more adventurous students also tended to identify with modern rather than historic art and this was another bone of contention with tutors because many of them were suspicious of all artistic developments since Post-Impressionism.

In Paris Paolozzi became acquainted with Arp, Brancusi, Dubuffet, Giacometti, Léger and Tzara. He learnt about Dada and Surrealism, in particular the work of Duchamp and Ernst. But while he familiarised himself with modern art, he also made crude collages in scrapbooks from issues of American magazines he was given by some of the wives of ex-GIs whom he met. On their discharge from the armed forces, GIs were given grants to study equalling the number of years that they had served. There were also a number of American artists staying for short or long periods in Paris.

At the time Paolozzi's collages were not intended as works of art in their own right, but simply as reference and inspiration sources. In the 1970s Paolozzi explained that his attitude to the raw material had been 'ironic' and 'rather surrealist'.[5] When Paolozzi showed them to others, their reaction was generally one of amusement. Nevertheless, in retrospect, a plausible claim can be made for Paolozzi being the founder, or at least a key precursor, of Pop art.

Let us consider the contents of some of Paolozzi's early collages: *I was a Rich Man's Plaything* (1947) consists of the cover of the magazine *Intimate Confessions* with a smiling semi-naked female on the front, to which has been added the exclamation 'Pop!' emerging from a hand-held gun, a slice of cherry pie and the emblem 'Real Gold' derived from the label on a tin of Californian fruit juice. Below is a cigarette card illustrating an American bomber with the slogan 'Keep 'Em Flying!', plus the image of a Coca-Cola bottle and a circular advertisement stating 'Serve Coca-Cola at Home'. Thus, in this loose assembly of images we find the themes of sex, gun culture, military power and junk food and drink. It is left to the viewer to connect them but they certainly serve as an array of the common stereotypes Europeans had of the American way of life.

Another collage, *Meet the People* (1948), features the head of the film and television star Lucille Ball, the Disney cartoon character

2. Eduardo Paolozzi, *Real Gold*, 1949.
Collage on paper from the *Bunk* series, 28 x 40.6 cm. London: artist's
collection. © Eduardo Paolozzi 1998. All rights reserved DACS.

Minnie Mouse, a tin of tuna fish, a overhead shot of a fizzy drink and a
sumptuous plate of fruit; all superimposed on a colourful, abstract,
wavy pattern. A third collage – *Sack-O-Sauce*, (1948) – represents the
collision of European modern art and American mass culture: the
ground upon which the cut-out collage elements – which include
Mickey Mouse – are pasted is a reproduction of a Miró painting
extracted from a copy of *Verve* that Paolozzi had been given in 1947.

Other collages are dense compilations of images depicting new
American cars, motorcycles, roast meat, tinned spam, cameras, kettles,
radios, lipstick, housewives in lavishly appointed kitchens, atomic technology, science fiction and striptease scenes. Paolozzi makes no attempt
to provide a critique of these images or any explanation as to how and
why Americans came to enjoy such material wealth, he simply gathers
and presents them. His aim had been 'to find a kind of connection
between those found images and one's actual experience, to make them
into an icon, or a totem, that added up as different types of symbol'.[6]

When Paolozzi returned to live in London in 1949 he bought
reduced-price copies of *Colliers* and *The Saturday Evening Post* from
newsagents on the Charing Cross Road. The abundance depicted in the
advertising pictures they contained was in stark contrast to his own

straightened circumstances. Later Paolozzi explained that, for him and his friends:

> The American magazine represented a catalogue of an exotic society, bountiful and generous, where the event of selling tinned pears was transformed into multicoloured dreams, where sensuality and virility combined to form, in our view, an art form more subtle and fulfilling than the orthodox choice of either the Tate Gallery or the Royal Academy.[7]

It signified, therefore, an 'alternative' to 'official' British culture. Robert Kudielka was later to argue that the American dream, as perceived in Britain via the mass media, 'made it possible to *name* what seemed to be wrong with English culture: insular complacency, carefully cultivated amateurism, indulgence in private allusions, and the inclination towards pastoral romanticism.'[8] 'Pastoral romanticism' was a reference to Neo-Romanticism, the art movement fashionable in Britain during the 1940s. Isolated from Paris and the continent of Europe because of the Second World War, many British artists had resorted to national, landscape and visionary traditions associated with such figures as Samuel Palmer and William Blake. Paolozzi, in contrast, sought inspiration from modern art, the urban environment, mass media and technology.

Once in London again Paolozzi, along with some of his close friends, joined the newly founded Institute of Contemporary Arts (ICA) and during the 1950s they contributed to the debates and exhibitions that took place there.

The ICA, Sir Herbert Read and his American Trips

The ICA, an important British cultural organisation, was established in the late 1940s by a group of people which included the critic Herbert Read, the patron Roland Penrose, the publisher Peter Gregory and the wealthy collector of modern art and financial backer of *Horizon* magazine Peter Watson. Their aim was to provide London with a centre for the promotion of modern and contemporary, avant-garde art. The ICA's first home was at 17 Dover Street – a gallery was opened there in December 1950. Later, in 1967, it transferred to more spacious premises in Nash House, The Mall.

Since the ICA was (and remains) a private organisation, its income was precarious and derived from a variety of sources: membership fees, grants from the Arts Council, entrance charges, sponsorship from businesses, auctions of works of art donated by artists, and gifts from wealthy individuals. Some Americans were among the latter. Peggy Guggenheim, for example, made a small donation, while John D. Rockefeller once gave $2,500 to Read when he was visiting New York. Eventually, Read became willing to accept money for the ICA from any source 'so long as it didn't stink'.

By the mid-1940s Read (1893–1968) was established as Britain's leading champion of modern art.[9] The artists he admired most were Henry Moore, Barbara Hepworth, Ben Nicholson and Naum Gabo. Picasso was too extreme for his taste. Read was also a poet, lecturer, cultural bureaucrat and author; his writing output was prodigious. He accepted a knighthood for his services to literature in 1953 – a somewhat strange decision for a man who claimed to be an anarchist. The necessity to earn money prompted him to travel abroad a great deal. Another reason was to escape the austerity of life in Britain in the aftermath of the Second World War.

During the period 1946–65 Read visited the United States several times (he travelled by sea on the liner *Queen Mary* and by air) and sometimes he stayed for several months. He went there in response to invitations to lecture, to receive honours and to perform editorial duties for the publishers Routledge. Besides New York, he visited cities and university campuses across America and even made one trip to Vancouver in Canada. In contrast to Paolozzi, Read was thus in a position to compare the reality of America with its media representations.

Read's first American trip took place from March to May 1946. New York struck him as a city in which 'the machine and all its values has conquered man'.[10] As a result of his visits he naturally became acquainted with many North American curators, rich patrons and collectors, writers and scholars but he does not seem to have met that many American artists and critics. However, in 1946 he was shown a painting by Jackson Pollock (his muted reaction will be described in Chapter 3). Eventually Read concluded that the friendships bestowed by Americans were 'superficial, warm but skin-deep'. 'Sentiments', he once remarked, were 'as fluid as the cash'.

Read was impressed by the significantly higher standard of living in the United States compared to the one in Britain but he also noted that the extremes of wealth and poverty were greater. On an internal flight, he admired the speed and comfort of a Constellation aircraft. Lunch was served on board by stewardesses who were so attractive that they reminded him of Hollywood movie stars. However, he judged the general standard of intelligence of the population to be lower than that of Europeans and he thought that the Americans would never understand artists and intellectuals. As an anarchist and pacifist, he was critical of American capitalism and its military aggressiveness. Even its vaunted democracy failed to impress him.[11]

Corporate sponsorship of the arts also aroused his suspicions even though he had been friendly with Peggy Guggenheim, the American patroness of modern art, since the 1930s. (Guggenheim had aided Read financially before the Second World War and she owned a small dog which she had named 'Sir Herbert' even before Read himself was knighted!) He also received personal travel and living subsidies from the American Bollingen Foundation.

By 1951 the material benefits of life in the United States that Read continued to appreciate were: 'American plumbing, unlimited supplies of orange juice and the telephone operators', but what he disliked about American college campuses were the crowds of undergraduates dressed in tight jeans, with crew-cut hairstyles and ape-like slouches. In 1953 he was also disturbed by the virulent anti-communism of Senator Joe McCarthy then visible on American television.

According to Read's biographer James King, once, when the critic returned from a long stay in 'the wilderness' of America, he experienced 'subtle pleasure'. England appeared to him like 'a walled garden' which had 'a quality of freshness' that the United States lacked.

It is clear that Read benefited from his contacts with Americans and his visits to the United States, but it is equally clear that there were many aspects of America which he found unattractive, which prevented him from migrating there permanently and precluded wholehearted admiration. By the time he went to the United States, his political ideas and preferences in art were well established; his attachment to British and European modern art was already too deeply entrenched for exposure to American art to change it.

Another British writer who visited the United States and was more enthusiastic about new American art in the late 1940s was Denys Sutton (1917–91), the future editor of *Apollo*. He studied at Yale in 1949 and on his return wrote an article entitled 'The Challenge of American Art' which was published in *Horizon*.[12] This was an early British appreciation of the work of Baziotes, Calder, Graves, Pollock, Rothko, David Smith and Tobey. Two years earlier Greenberg's article 'The Present Prospects of American Painting and Sculpture' had appeared in the October 1947 issue of *Horizon*. Hence British readers of this journal received advanced notice of the art from across the Atlantic which was to have such a potent effect during the 1950s.

2
The ICA, the IG and America During the 1950s

During the 1950s influential Americans used the ICA – as they did travelling exhibitions of Abstract Expressionism, *Encounter* magazine and Radio Free Europe – to promote the American economic and political system at the expense of that of the Soviet bloc.[1] In 1951 Pat Dolan, an American public relations expert, offered to raise money and obtain corporate sponsorship for the ICA both in Britain and the United States by using a member of the British Royal Family as a figurehead. Penrose found the idea attractive but Read was hesitant because he feared that any links with big business would threaten the ICA's independence. Dolan, apparently, hinted that the ICA's exhibitions could not afford to be too radical. In the event, an American director of public relations – Anthony Kloman, who was related to the architect Philip Johnson – was appointed in 1951.

According to James King, American influences behind the scenes at the ICA meant that 'by 1952 Soviet artists and speakers were not welcome at the ICA because their presence would make it unlikely that any financial help would be forthcoming from American sources'.[2]

From the outset, the ICA was happy to display examples of recent American art. In July–August 1950, for example, a show called *American Symbolic Realism* was mounted, accompanied by a catalogue paid for by the American impresario and ballet director, Lincoln Kirstein. A series of shows of American art followed: drawings by Saul Steinberg; photos from *Life* magazine funded by Time-Life; paintings by Jackson Pollock and Sam Francis featured in the 1953 *Opposing Forces* show; a Mark Tobey retrospective in 1955. American speakers such as Alfred H. Barr, Thomas B. Hess, Philip Johnson, Ben Shahn and Meyer Shapiro were also invited to deliver lectures.

Kloman returned from one trip home with a proposal for an international sculpture competition on the theme of the Unknown Political Prisoner.[3] At the time this subject was thought 'universal' although it now seems obvious that the competition was a Cold War propaganda exercise designed to embarrass communist regimes. The prize money on offer (which included a £1,000 management fee for the ICA) was £16,000 and was supplied, it later emerged, by John Hay Whitney, oil millionaire, publisher of the *International Herald Tribune* and a trustee of the Museum of Modern Art, New York.

The British sculptor Reg Butler won the top prize in March 1953 with a semi-abstract design: a cage-like structure made from wire mounted on a stone base with some standing figures. It has been argued by scholars such as Anne Massey and Robert Burstow that Kloman acted as a go-between for the ICA and Whitney, that Whitney in turn served as a front man for the CIA and that the competition was one of many covert cultural operations mounted at that time. It was originally intended to build the winning design as a huge public monument in West Berlin overlooking the East, however it was never erected because the funding mysteriously dried up. The political climate of confrontation diminished somewhat after Stalin's death in 1953 and, so Burstow claims, the hidden American sponsors of the competition were also put off by the modernism of Butler's design.[4]

In addition to Kloman's trans-Atlantic connections, there were close links between the ICA and the United States Information Service (USIS) located in the American Embassy, London. The USIS was a division of the United States Information Agency (USIA) based in Washington DC, which was responsible for arranging exhibitions of American art abroad. Employed at the embassy was a cultural affairs officer – Mrs Stroup Austin – who made a donation to the ICA in 1954. In the following year Stefan Munsing (1915–94) was appointed assistant cultural affairs officer and he was to prove even more helpful to the ICA.[5]

The Independent Group (IG)

Ironically, while Read was guarded about American influence, younger members of the ICA, that is those who constituted the IG, welcomed it even though many of them were politically sympathetic to the Left. (The Americans were willing to support left-wingers abroad providing they were not communists.) This example demonstrates that in the struggle between two generations one often finds the culture of a foreign country useful as a weapon.

The IG was an informal think-tank which met intermittently between 1952 and 1955. The adjective 'independent' was intended to signify a degree of autonomy from the host institution, in particular a distance from the aesthetic principles and artistic tastes of Read and Penrose. But it also meant that the members of the group were highly individualistic. Participants included: Lawrence Alloway, Reyner Banham, Magda and Frank Cordell, Toni del Renzio, Richard and Terry Hamilton, Geoffrey Holroyd, John McHale, Nigel Henderson, Eduardo Paolozzi, Colin St John Wilson, Alison and Peter Smithson, James Stirling and William Turnbull. Thus the IG represented a cross-section of the visual arts, theory and criticism.

Its aim was to consider the implications of science, new technology and the mass media for art and society at the midpoint of the twentieth century. Topics discussed included: the machine aesthetic, Action painting, American car styling and horror comics, consumer goods, fashion and communication theory. Images from American mass circulation magazines, advertising, the cinema and science fiction were viewed and the term 'Pop art' was used – by Alloway – to designate contemporary popular or mass culture. (It was only later, after the IG had ceased to meet, that Richard Hamilton began to make Pop art from the raw material of popular culture.)

Because IG meetings were attended by a small number of people (perhaps 20 on average), their deliberations were not widely known. Nevertheless, their ideas did reach a bigger audience by feeding into other ICA events and via the various exhibitions that members of the IG were involved in mounting at the ICA and the Whitechapel Gallery during the 1950s. Furthermore, the subsequent influence of the main IG participants was immense: in the decades that followed most of them became leading figures in their respective professions.

In later years some critics made the contentious claim that the members of the IG were the 'fathers' of British Pop art. This gendered description ignored the contribution of the 'mothers' of Pop and it was problematical on other grounds too, for example, the IG's interests were far wider than popular culture and one 'father' of Pop art, Peter Blake, had nothing to do with the IG. During the period 1985–97, art and design historians re-examined the history of the IG in great detail and exhibitions devoted to it were held both in Britain and the United States.[6]

Bunk: Paolozzi's Image Show

By 1952 Paolozzi's archive of American magazines included copies of *Cover Girls Models*, *Hi-Ho* comics, *Radio Electronics*, *Popular Mechanics*, *Amazing Stories*, *Thrilling Wonder Stories*, *Science Fiction*, *Time* and *Life*. In April 1952 Richard Lannoy asked him to give a presentation of images at what many scholars regard as the first IG meeting. This presentation – called *Bunk* after one of his collages – of illustrations from books and magazines, together with his own collages, projected via an epidiascope which was so hot that it scorched the paper, has since become legendary in the annals of the IG.

Paolozzi was nervous and spoke little. Because the content of the presentation was not argued in a logical, linear way – instead, according to Nigel Henderson, it was connected in a lateral way (a collage exemplifies the simultaneous coexistence of disparate elements) – the small audience was disconcerted and Paolozzi recalls that the reaction was 'disbelief and hilarity'. Turnbull – who had himself pinned popular images to the walls of his studio – had, of course, seen Paolozzi's collages in Paris so they were no surprise to him. He considered that the main function of such collections of images was to randomise one's thinking, to break down logical patterns of thought.

What those who were present at the *Bunk* lecture chiefly remember is the visual impact of the sequence of mainly American images. The images had a particular resonance for British viewers because of their contrast with the shortages in Britain during the late 1940s and early 1950s (rationing continued on certain items up until 1954). Banham later recalled:

> We goggled at the graphics and the colour-work in adverts for appliances that were almost inconceivable in power-short Britain, and food ads so luscious you wanted to eat them. Remember we had spent our teenage years surviving the horrors and deprivations of a six-year war. For us, the fruits of peace had to be tangible, preferably edible. Those ads ... looked like Paradise Regained.[7]

Thus it was not only the content of the advertising images that impressed Paolozzi and Banham but also their high-quality photography and graphic design.

Despite Paolozzi's fascination with popular culture, his sculpture – his principal medium – did not reflect that interest for some time and never to the same extent as it did in the case of Richard Hamilton's paintings of the late 1950s. The screenprints that Paolozzi executed during the 1960s are the works most clearly indebted to the 'multi-evocative' imagery of his early scrapbooks. It was not until 1972 that a facsimile edition of the *Bunk* collages was produced with the assistance of the printer Christopher Betambeau of Advanced Graphics and published by Snail Chemicals.[8]

Paolozzi did not visit the United States until 1968 when he was a visiting professor at the University of California, Berkeley. Uwe M. Schneede reports:

> ... his curiosity about the strange new environment was in no way directed towards museums and galleries. Nor was he interested in the fascinating landscape. Instead, he visited Disneyland, the Paramount Studios in Hollywood, the computer centre at the University of California, the waxworks in San Francisco and Los Angeles, the particle accelerator at Stanford and the Douglas Aircraft Company in Santa Monica.[9]

It is evident, therefore, that Paolozzi's early interest in American mass culture and technology did persist well into the 1960s.

Some other members of the IG will now be considered – beginning with the architects – who either visited America or whose iconography was derived from American sources.

The Architects Stirling and Holroyd

James Stirling (1924–92), who hailed originally from Glasgow, became one of Britain's leading and controversial modern and post-modern architects but he built more abroad than at home. From 1945 to 1950 he trained at Liverpool University's School of Architecture. In 1949, while still a student, he travelled to America on an exchange scheme for the purpose of learning as much as possible about modern American architecture and industrial design.

During the 1950s Stirling participated in some IG debates. He recalls:

> There was considerable fascination with American popular culture in IG circles and I contributed somehow to this since I had visited America in

> 1949 ... I went to New York where I worked in an architecture office
> [O'Connor and Kilham] for six months and visited Boston, Chicago,
> Philadelphia, San Franciso and Los Angeles. I recall my amazement, coming
> from Europe soon after the war, on seeing the bright chrome buildings and
> spotless pavements of New York. People forget how clean and bright and
> shiny New York was back then. Also I was surprised that all the cities I
> visited were quite amazingly different. In Los Angeles I visited Charles and
> Ray Eames at home on the cliff edge in Santa Monica and went to the
> factories where his designs were being produced.[10]

After his return to Britain Stirling gave an informal talk and slide show
at the home of the abstract artist Adrian Heath. Amongst those present
were Alloway, Theo Crosby, del Renzio, Paolozzi and Colin St John
Wilson. Paolozzi remembers photographs of Frank Lloyd Wright's
California house being viewed and he claims that the seeds of the 1956
This is Tomorrow exhibition were sown at this gathering.[11]

Images of American architecture and cityscapes were to remain
potent for several members of the IG, but many British architects
still looked as much to the continent of Europe because of the
powerful influence that Le Corbusier exerted. The situation was
complicated by the fact that leading European architects and
artist-designers such as Breuer, Gropius, Mies van der Rohe and
Moholy-Nagy had emigrated to the United States. So, many new
'American' buildings were designed by ex-Europeans or were not
exclusively American because they conformed to the conventions of
the International Style. Colin Rowe – an influential British historian
who spent many years lecturing in the United States believes,
however, that Stirling did learn something from American architecture, namely, 'a gratifying simplicity'.[12]

Stirling was to return to America during the early and late 1960s as a
visiting critic and a professor at Yale University. Speaking in 1980 he
recalled:

> I found the asymmetric 'turn of the century' timber shingle houses of even a
> town like New Haven an eye opener and more interesting than Saarinen or
> SOM [Skidmore, Owings and Merrill] – the current heroes. Though I do
> confess I was impressed by a limited period of Frank Lloyd Wright's
> production – particularly the concrete block houses around Los Angeles.
> During my first visits to the US I was also aware of the incredibly high
> finish and *way out* aspect of New York art deco buildings – such as the

Chrysler tower among others. In the whole of Europe it seemed to me we had nothing to come near to them.[13]

Those in charge of American universities clearly respected Stirling's architectural abilities because he was commissioned to design an extension to the School of Architecture at Rice University, Texas, a theatre for Cornell University at Ithaca, a new building for the Fogg Museum for Harvard University, Cambridge, Massachusetts, and a new building for Columbia University in New York.

Some young British architects who visited America during the 1950s were seeking an alternative to what Geoffrey Holroyd called 'the universalist model of the 1920s' associated with the architecture and theories of Le Corbusier.[14] This was certainly Holroyd's motivation when he and his wife travelled to the United States in the summer of 1952 to spend a year studying at Harvard University. The following April they visited Chicago to view buildings by Sullivan, Wright and Mies, and to visit the Illinois Institute of Design directed by Moholy-Nagy. In August they drove across the Rockies to San Franciso and Los Angeles to see the work of Charles and Ray Eames. They then spent a year working for several architectural practices in Chicago including that of Skidmore, Owings and Merrill. At the Art Institute of Chicago in October 1953 they attended a screening of the film, *A Communications Primer*, made by Charles Eames and George Nelson, plus a 'slide carnival' of symbolic objects. Holroyd reports:

> Through these and other American influences, I learned a way of seeing architecture as part of a general cultural situation focused on daily life and experience ... I returned to London in the summer of 1954, impressed by Charles Eames's visual intuitions of a design theory based on assemblages of signs and symbols.[15]

The Eameses helped to bring about a shift of emphasis within design from form to meaning, from structure to signification.

Holroyd brought back with him such influential American books as Norbert Weiner's *The Human Use of Human Beings* and Suzanne Langer's *Philosophy in a New Key*. Architecture and design were being rethought by the IG in terms of the then developing theories of communication, information and semiotics.

Two American Designers: The Eameses

The achievements of the husband and wife team of Charles (1907–78) and Ray (1912–88) Eames, which began in 1940, merit a brief description because they excited the interest of so many members of the IG. The work of the Eameses encompassed research into structure and materials, the design of architecture, products, graphics, home and office interiors, furniture, toys, storage units and exhibitions. They also produced multi-screen projections and films. During the 1950s they became famous for several of their creations: their 1949, rectilinear, steel-framed, off the peg (standardised parts) 'Case Study House' (also known simply as the 'Eames House'), situated in Santa Monica; their mass-produced chairs made from either moulded plywood, wire mesh or plastic (a photograph of four IG members posing in the middle of a

3. Nigel Henderson, *Peter Smithson, Eduardo Paolozzi, Alison Smithson and Nigel Henderson in an East End Street with two chairs by the Eameses*, 1956.
Photo taken for *This is Tomorrow*'s poster and catalogue but not used.
Gelatin silver print, 20.3 x 25.4 cm. Estate of the artist.
Photo: reproduced courtesy of Janet Henderson.

Hackney street shows Nigel Henderson sitting in one of the Eameses' 'organic' plastic chairs and Peter Smithson using a different type), as well as their luxurious, swivel or tilt 'lounge chair and ottoman' made from rosewood, leather and steel in 1956. Many of their designs were commissioned and manufactured by the Herman Miller Furniture Company.

Charles and Ray were keen to disseminate their ideas via visits abroad, spells of teaching, reports and visual aids such as multimedia presentations and films (some of which were sponsored by commercial companies). The latter, of course, could be viewed around the world. Their 1953 *A Communications Primer*, a reflection on the nature of human communication, was, in fact, screened at the ICA in March 1955. In April of the following year a discussion took place, chaired by Alloway, about the Eameses' output entitled 'The Toys and Films of Charles Eames'. (The Eameses' 1951 'The Toy' was a 'collapsible giant constructor-display kit' which children or adults assembled themselves.) In 1959 Charles came to London and delivered a lecture at the Royal Institute of British Architects in which he stressed the designer's dependency on current information and the need for feedback mechanisms.

Along with Alloway and del Renzio, Holroyd sought to apply some of the Eameses' ideas to the Group Twelve's 'tackboard' exhibit of the 1956 *This is Tomorrow* exhibition. Holroyd has claimed that the Eameses had 'a profound influence on the Smithsons'. Certainly, the Eameses were 'guru' designers whom every member of the IG who journeyed to the United States wanted to meet.

Another Briton who was influenced by their work and ideas was the young designer Terence Conran (b. 1931) who was to found Habitat in 1964. Conran studied at the Central School of Art and Design in the late 1940s and he became aware of the Eameses' furniture design as well as that of Florence Knoll through the magazine *Arts and Architecture* which was taken by the school's library. Conran also became close friends with his tutor Paolozzi and through him met two other members of the IG, Henderson and Turnbull.

In 1966 an issue of *Architectural Design* was devoted to the Eameses which included articles by Holroyd and the Smithsons.[16] When Charles died in 1978, Peter Smithson wrote a tribute for the *RIBA Journal*. Pat Kirkham, the author of a major study of the American couple, sums up their mission as an attempt to 'humanise the modern'.[17]

the Seagram Building being erected in New York at that time, designed by Mies and Philip Johnson, and Johnson's own 'see-through' glass house at New Canaan, but the many mediocre modern buildings he saw were dismissed as 'aluminium folk art'. Their 'squareness and symmetry', he surmised, satisfied 'a deep American folk-need'. Some years later the British artist Patrick Heron was also to complain about the symmetrical compositions of so much American abstract painting.

The most exciting landscape Peter encountered was the New Jersey Flats:

> a dream-world of refineries and factories and marshlands, criss-crossed with Skyways. This is the supra-image of the American urban landscape – the urban excreta squeezed out from the old city over the last fifty years ... [26]

As a European, what Peter valued most about America were its designed products, many of which had a short-term use: 'The magnificent magazines, advertising and packaging; the refrigerators and the motor cars.' In fact, one of his major aesthetic experiences was provided by the design, fixtures and fittings of a washroom in a Madison Avenue building:

> It is quite impossible to communicate the feeling one had of a new sort of solidity, wealth and power in this quite unextraordinary American lavatory. And everything was out of a catalogue.[27]

In the design of automobiles, industrial goods, heavy earth-moving equipment and freight trains Peter felt American values were communicated 'through an imagery created without self-consciousness'. He detected the same feeling in the paintings of Pollock but, as far as Peter was concerned, American architecture had not yet produced anyone comparable in stature to Pollock.

Writing in retrospect about their contribution to the IG, the Smithsons explained their relationship to America as follows:

> We always considered ourselves very English ... we have always been oriented towards Europe and never deviated, reacting to aspirations beamed out of America that we saw would be irresistible, but also, recognising these as part of a wider threat to Europe's cultural identity.[28]

If this self-description is accepted as accurate, then it would appear that, of all the members of the IG, the Smithsons were the most sceptical in their attitude to the United States despite their respect for Pollock, American industrial design and the Eameses, and the fact that they were the proud owners of a war surplus US Army jeep.

McHale, Hamilton and *This is Tomorrow*

John McHale (1922–78) was a many-sided intellectual: a collagist, film-maker, educator, exhibition designer and organiser, author and theorist.[29] Born in Glasgow, McHale was educated in England and the United States. He obtained a Ph.D in sociology and brought a witty and analytical mind to the study of modern society. He was fascinated by robots, cyborgs, science, technology, futurology, ecology, mass communication systems, the icons of popular culture and their relationship with the traditional visual arts. In 1955 McHale convened – together with Alloway – a series of IG meetings in order to discuss aspects of popular culture. Among the American sources of ideas they drew upon were *Scientific American*, Norbert Weiner's writings on cybernetics, Claude Shannon's text on information theory and von Neumann's on game theory.

A Yale University scholarship enabled McHale to live in the United States from August 1955 to July 1956. His ostensive reason for going there was to study colour theory and industrial materials with the ex-Bauhaus master Josef Albers (1888–1976, a German artist who emigrated to America in the 1930s and who became an American citizen in 1939), but McHale's experience of the United States confirmed his shift of interest from European modernism towards American mass culture and consumerism. With other students he made expeditions to roadside diners and photographed them with big, bulbous automobiles parked outside.

While in America McHale became acquainted with the French Dadaist Marcel Duchamp from whom he obtained the optical discs which were used in the perception section of the 'Fun House' exhibit – designed with Richard Hamilton and John Voelcker – for the Whitechapel's *This is Tomorrow* show of 1956. He also met Buckminster Fuller, the radical American designer famous for his geodesic domes and 'Dymaxion House'. Later, in 1961, McHale mounted an exhibition about Fuller at the USIS Gallery in the American Embassy, London, and in 1963 he published a monograph about Fuller.

McHale's American sojourn was to become legendary because of a
black wooden box full of popular magazines and Elvis Presley records
that he brought back with him. Hamilton, McHale himself and Magda
Cordell (McHale's future wife) were all to plunder this treasure trove.
McHale made a collage on the theme of machine-made America for the
cover of *Architectural Review* (May 1957, a special issue devoted to
'Machine-Made America') which depicted a robot-like figure composed
of fragmentary images of spark plugs, mechanical parts and tubing,
ticker tape, television sets, food, etc. He also wrote a two-page article
entitled 'Marginalia' for the periodical. Much of the latter's architectural content was concerned with curtain walling, the glass and metal
cladding that was then becoming fashionable for office buildings.

4. John McHale, *Personage Symbolising Machine-Made America*, 1957.
Collage as featured on the cover of *Architectural Review*, May 1957.
Photo: reproduced courtesy of Magda Cordell-McHale and
the J.M. Richards Library, Middlesex University.

The continuing attraction of America was such that at least three ex-members of the IG, namely, Alloway, McHale and Magda Cordell, emigrated there during the 1960s. They were joined, during the 1970s, by Reyner Banham.

McHale's contemporary at the IG, Richard Hamilton (b. 1922), a Londoner, developed an early interest in drawing and painting but it took him many years of training to achieve his goal of becoming an artist. During the Second World War he was employed as a 'jig and tool' draughtsman for the Design Unit Group and Electrical & Musical Industries (EMI), where he gained some insight into the worlds of industry and commerce. In the late 1940s he read Siegfried Giedion's *Mechanisation Takes Command* (1948), a contribution to 'anonymous history' that stressed the role of mechanisation and technology in the history of design rather than the part played by great designers. Giedion was a European scholar who had emigrated to the United States, so many of his examples were American. His lavishly illustrated book was an inspiration to many members of the IG. Simultaneously, Hamilton was avidly consuming Hollywood films in London's cinemas.

During the early 1950s Hamilton devised and designed exhibitions for the ICA, and he was a keen contributor to IG discussions. American car design and styling was one topic in particular which fascinated him and Banham. (An interest in cars was a family tradition for Hamilton – his father had been a driver for Henley's car showroom.) Marshall McLuhan's analyses of American advertisements – *The Mechanical Bride: Folklore of Industrial Man* (1951) – was another stimulus. McLuhan discussed the way in which car advertising conflated the bodies of automobiles and women, and this was later to become a crucial theme of Hamilton's Pop art.

His paintings dating from 1951 to 1954 contained no explicit mass media material but one of them concerned with relative movement – a speeding car viewed from a moving train – evoked chase scenes from Hollywood movies. Beginning in 1956, Hamilton incorporated images derived from the mass media into his collages and from 1957 onwards into his paintings. Both were replete with American iconography taken mainly from American magazines such as *Life, Look, McCalls, Saturday Evening Post, Astounding Science Fiction, Scientific American* and *Mad* magazine. In some instances Hamilton borrowed images of objects from a variety of sources and then integrated them into a single, conventional, perspectival space, while in other instances he accentuated the contours of objects, distributed them across a white ground and then linked them in a way that suggested a shallow relief (sometimes he added actual relief elements).

It was from McHale's trunk of magazines that Hamilton constructed the small but now famous 1956 collage *Just What is it that Makes Today's Homes so Different, so Appealing?* It served as a poster and catalogue image for the *This is Tomorrow* exhibition. Hamilton had prepared a list of themes he wished to illustrate and he asked Magda Cordell and his own wife Terry to find them in the magazines. They were then incorporated into a domestic interior scene which showed a naked muscleman and pin-up woman – the Adam and Eve of the new consumer society – surrounded by products and mass communication media (a vacuum cleaner, a television, a telephone, a can of ham [a pun on Hamilton?], a tape recorder, a newspaper, a cinema, etc.) Much of the imagery was clearly American: a cinema frontage advertising *The Jazz Singer*, a heraldic symbol of the Ford motor company on a lampshade, a *Young Romance* comic framed like a painting (anticipating Roy Lichtenstein's comic-based paintings by some years). Instead of a ceiling, Hamilton's room features a view of part of the Earth taken from a rocket; the photograph was derived from a *Look* magazine article entitled 'A 100 Mile High Portrait of Earth'.

This is Tomorrow, an exhibition co-ordinated by Theo Crosby, attracted around 19,000 visitors. It was intended to illustrate the benefits of interdisciplinary collaborations between architects and artists. There were twelve groups, each consisting of an architect, a painter and a sculptor. Group Two – Hamilton, McHale and Voelcker (with the help of Magda Cordell and Terry Hamilton) – was responsible for the 'Fun House' exhibit located near the entrance to the Whitechapel. This stole the show because of its familiar, mass culture content: a huge image of Robby the Robot carrying a half-naked damsel in distress taken from the 1956 science fiction film *The Forbidden Planet* (borrowed from the frontage of the London Pavilion cinema in Piccadilly Circus. Robby also appeared 'in person' to open the show); a cut-out image of Marilyn Monroe with her skirt billowing up (a still derived from Billy Wilder's *The Seven Year Itch*); a huge, CinemaScope-shaped collage of American movie posters; and a jukebox playing the latest Pop music hits. A large beer bottle signified the drinking preferences of the British and a print of Van Gogh's *Sunflowers* – the original was in the National Gallery in London – indicated the importance of mechanical reproduction and the immense popularity of Van Gogh's painting.

The exhibit had two facets: imagery and perception. Although the intention of the second section was designed to upset people's perceptions of space and time and included dazzling patterns which anticipated the Op art of the 1960s, for many visitors and later commentators the imagery section dominated. It subsequently came to be regarded as the origin of British Pop art and as a forecast of 1960s' pop culture.

In a now famous letter sent to the Smithsons in January 1957, Hamilton listed what he thought were the main characteristics of popular culture. Transience and expendability were two of them but they were not ones that he was prepared to emulate as a painter. His intention was always to produce works of fine art with long-term appeal and high aesthetic value. Like the realists of the nineteenth century, he wanted to be 'of his times' and to find the epic and poetic in everyday subjects.

Hamilton's paintings based on American advertising imagery produced during the late 1950s were: *Hommage à Chrysler Corp* (1957), *Hers is a Lush Situation* (1958) and *$he* (1958–61). Their subjects comprised car design, the United Nations building in New York, women's lips and bras, housewives in kitchens with appliances and white goods such as as toasters and refrigerators.

Hamilton did not simply appropriate and reproduce American iconography in an unthinking way. He was a discriminating and knowing consumer who approached mass culture in a quasi-anthropological fashion. There was admiration for American design and mass culture but at the same time a certain critical distance. Hamilton wanted to learn as much about this material as possible in order to gain an understanding of production and consumption processes – he was as interested in the 'presentation techniques' of American ads as in their contents. In time, he thought, artists could contribute as producers rather than as consumers. (This did occur to some degree in the 1960s when he designed an album cover with a poster insert for the Beatles, the so-called 'White Album'.) It is evident from the articles Hamilton wrote at the same time as he painted that he researched and analysed his subject matter in considerable depth.[30] The title of his sex and car-styling painting *Hers is a Lush Situation*, for instance, derived from a review of new Buick cars written by Deborah Allen for *Industrial Design* in February 1955. A 1959 paper on technical innovations in the leisure industries entitled 'Glorious Technicolour, Breathtaking CinemaScope and Stereophonic Sound' (a line borrowed from a

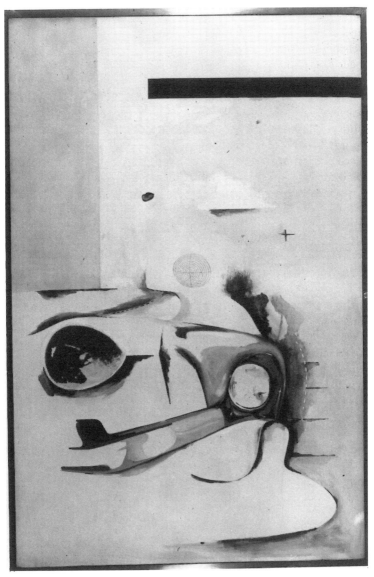

5. Richard Hamilton, *Hommage à Chrysler Corp,* **1957.**
Oil, metal foil and collage on panel, 122 x 81 cm. London: private collection.

Hollywood song) was given as a lecture in British art schools.[31] When Hamilton delivered lectures he even demonstrated new media technologies such as the Polaroid Land camera by taking snaps of the audiences.

Hamilton liked to tabulate his findings: he singled out key new products, special effects, technological innovations, styles and fashion trends, important American designers, and defined the specialist terms used in advertising and marketing. By any standards his articles are perceptive and substantial contributions to the literature of design history and cultural studies. Apparently, it was only after Hamilton's writings about his iconography and its sources appeared that critics and collectors began to take his Pop paintings seriously. In other words, their contents needed a scholarly, sociological gloss before they became acceptable. *Hommage à Chrysler Corp* was bought by E.J. Power, an electronics manufacturer and collector of contemporary art, whose wealth originated from the sale of television sets.

It should be remembered, however, that Hamilton's attentions were not exclusively focused on America because he was also interested in modern European art and design such as, for instance, the design of the Festival of Britain, the Bauhaus's Basic Design course, the German School of Design called Ulm, products made by the German company Braun and the work of Duchamp. Indeed, Duchamp's art was also an influence on those of Hamilton's Pop paintings which tackled American themes.

In spite of his fascination with America during the 1950s, Hamilton did not visit the United States until the following decade. His trip there will be described in Chapter 5.

Two Critics/Theorists: Alloway and Banham

Lawrence Alloway (1926–90) came from a cultured, middle-class London background – his father was a bookseller. A highly intelligent, intensely curious individual, Alloway was active within the ICA, the IG and the London art scene generally throughout the 1950s. He was a prolific art critic who also became a theorist of the relation between art and mass media, a historian of British abstract art and of British and American Pop art.

Besides reviewing, Alloway organised exhibitions, for example, the one entitled *Collages and Objects* (ICA, 1953). As already mentioned, he and McHale convened the last series of IG meetings which took place in 1955. He also collaborated with Holroyd and del Renzio to produce the Group Twelve exhibit for *This is Tomorrow*.

In an interview dated 1973 Alloway remarked: 'I've been pro-American ever since I can remember. Whether it was jazz, clothes, movies, painting, poetry.'[32] As a teenager in the 1940s he read and collected over 100 American science fiction magazines. He later sold them but began to read sci-fi literature again in the 1950s while he was reviewing books for the *Sunday Times* and studying the history of art. He gave two talks on the subject at the ICA. One of the things that intrigued him about the sci-fi genre was its stress on humans as users of tools and weapons. When Abstract Expressionist paintings were shown in London, Alloway responded with enthusiasm (see Chapter 3). During the 1950s, therefore, Alloway was open to the whole spectrum of American culture in both its 'high' and 'low' manifestations; indeed, one of his key achievements was to propose an alternative – the so-called 'long front of culture' – to that very hierarchical distinction.

As the decade progressed, Alloway became more and more a proselytiser of American culture. By 1957 he even looked like an American: his ginger hair was shaved in a severe crew cut. His 'Americanisation' was noted and deplored by Basil Taylor, art critic for the *Spectator* and art historian at the Royal College of Art, and others but, as the following defiant remark makes clear, Alloway was unrepentent:

> I have been accused ... of being Americanised and, since I am English, thus becoming a decadent islander, halfway between two cultures. I doubt that I have lost more by my taste for the American mass media (which are better than anyone else's) than have those older writers who look to the Mediterranean as the 'cradle of civilisation'.[33]

Even a fellow member of the IG – del Renzio, who was well informed about new European design – resented the 'blind acceptance of everything American as therefore good; and if there was a choice between an American and a European product, the American was automatically superior'. He added, 'Throughout the time I knew Alloway, I don't think he ever once even considered going to a foreign language film. I don't believe he ever said anything other than movie for a film.'[34]

Alloway was not bothered about Americanisation because he thought the communications and transportation revolutions had virtually abolished the division between 'centre' and 'periphery'. (In which case one wonders why he found it necessary to move from London to New York. One reason he gave was that of a dearth of suitable employment opportunities in Britain.) A few years later he and Sylvia Sleigh (b. 1917), his Welsh-born, painter-wife, became permanent residents of the United States.[35]

6. Cover of *Astounding Science Fiction,* **November 1953.**
Street and Street Publishing. © Dell Magazines, New York.

Alloway first crossed the Atlantic in 1958 with the aid of a State Department grant obtained via Munsing. In New York he met several painters but, because of his enthusiasm for American sci-fi, he was also keen to meet John W. Campbell Jr, the editor of *Astounding Science Fiction.* Campbell's Manhattan office overlooked the glass and marble rectangular slab of the United Nations building (1947–50, designed by Wallace K. Harrison and others), a photograph of which had appeared on the cover of the magazine in November 1953 along with the words 'Window to Tomorrow'. Alloway then visited California where he met another fan of this popular magazine, the designer Charles Eames.

An article written on his return to Britain, which was published in a journal read by architects, analysed and celebrated the American urban environment.[36] Alloway reported that he had visited a dozen American cities and that, while he had viewed important buildings by noted modern architects, 'the real city' was far more than a collection of permanent masterworks. It was a total, ever-changing environment, 'the model of maximised industrialisation ... a messy configuration' in which the past, present and future overlap. Architects, he contended, could never gain and keep control of 'all the factors in a city which exist in the dimensions of patched-up, expendable, and developing forms'.

Furthermore, he stressed the contribution of the people who lived and worked in cities, their restless mobility, their multiple, mutating roles and activities. 'Usage', he maintained, was always 'outpacing planning'. The inhabitants had their daily experience of the urban environment mediated and fed back to them via representations in magazine features, tourist postcards and crime movies. In addition to buildings, the city also consisted of traffic composed of luxurious American cars, the spectacle of advertisements and electric signs, and music emanating from stores packed with commodities ... In short, the American city exemplified the 'communications-saturated environment of the US'. He went on to praise Los Angeles – a city organised around the automobile normally criticised by European visitors – and Pop commercial architecture.

Alloway's article was intended to educate architects and planners, to point out the limited nature of their control over such an organic and anarchistic phenomenon as the modern city. It also sought to counteract the dismissive attitude of the British architectural establishment towards the American urban environment. (The December 1950 issue of *Architectural Review* had been devoted to 'The Mess that is Man-Made America'.) In fact, Alloway's article was a significant anticipation of the post-modern arguments found in Robert Venturi's influential 1966 text, *Complexity and Contradiction in Architecture*, and his (and others) 1972 book, *Learning from Las Vegas*.

When Reyner Banham (1922–88) recalled his childhood in Norwich, he claimed that the only 'live culture' around was from across the Atlantic:

> American pulps, things like *Mechanix Illustrated* and the comic books (we were all great Betty Boop fans), and the penny pictures on Saturday Mornings; I know the entire Chaplin canon back to front and most of the Buster Keatons ... [37]

Another remark indicates an early ability, which most of the IG members shared, to appreciate both 'high' and 'low' culture:

> I have a crystal clear memory of myself, aged sixteen, reading a copy of *Fantastic Stories* while waiting to go on in the school play, which was Fielding's *Tom Thumb the Great*, and deriving equal relish from the recherché literature I would shortly be performing and the equally far out pulp in my hand.[38]

During the Second World War, Norfolk hosted many Yanks serving in the US Eighth Army Air Force. Norwich was a city encircled by council houses, some of which, Banham remembers, served as brothels for the GIs. At a local theatre Banham witnessed a live performance by the Hollywood star James Stewart (1908–97) who was then in uniform.[39]

For a time in 1939 Banham trained to become a manager for the Bristol Aeroplane Company but, like so many British intellectuals, he preferred culture to industry: a decade later he studied the history of art at the Courtauld Institute in London. During the 1950s he wrote reviews for several London art and architecture journals. Later he undertook postgraduate work at the Courtauld where his thesis was supervised by Sir Nikolaus Pevsner. His research culminated in the book, *Theory and Design in the First Machine Age* (1960), which established his reputation as an expert on European modernism and a critic of simplistic histories of modern architecture.[40] (He argued for a more complex and inclusive history which encompassed Italian Futurism and De Stijl.) Banham subsequently became an exceptionally acute and prolific writer – of both journalistic and academic texts – for a variety of magazines on current architecture, product design, new technology and pop culture.[41]

Banham's interests were thus by no means confined to American subjects, but like other members of the IG he did have a special

affection for American design, especially automobile design. The latter
and 'Borax' styling were topics discussed by Banham and others at an
IG meeting held on 4 March 1955. In an article entitled 'Vehicles of
Desire' published in the same year, Banham argued that it is 'the
cunningly programmed minor changes that give one manufacturer an
edge over another, and the aesthetics of body styling are an integral part
of the battle for margins'.[42] After referring to 'the aesthetics of
expendability', he praises 'the dynamism of that extraordinary continuum of emotional-engineering-by-public-consent which enables the
automobile industry to create vehicles of palpably fulfilled desire'.

Clearly, Banham was conscious of the crucial role of styling in
relation to commercial success and competition in a free marketplace,
and the ability of the American designers to anticipate and satisfy the
consumers' needs rather than their own. After the Second World War
British automobile manufacturers quickly lost the competitive advan-
tage they had enjoyed owing to the defeats of Germany, Italy and
Japan. While British companies could not duplicate American cars for
the home market – there were no motorways until the M1 opened in
1959 – Banham was still offering them useful advice.

Later, in his 1976 paper 'Detroit Tin Revisited', Banham explained
why American car styling fascinated the IG and why it was such a
contentious issue in design circles.[43] American car styling during the
1950s, emanating mainly from Detroit, was highly innovative, imaginative, symbolic of speed and sex, and aggressively commercial. Designers used streamlining, the 'Flight Sweep Line', tail fins, the planned
obsolescence of annual model changes and powerful advertising campaigns to engage the dreams and desires of consumers. (Once a market
was saturated with products 'style obsolescence' had to be used to
persuade customers to trade in their old, but still viable, products for
new ones. This situation did not yet prevail in Britain.) 'Detroit',
Banham declared, 'was to cars in the fifties what Paris was to modern
art, say in 1910'. Its values were thus at odds with the ideals – 'good'
design, longevity, functionalism, no superfluous decoration – of the
modernist design establishment in Britain, that is, those pundits
associated with the Council of Industrial Design, *Architectural Review*
and *Design Magazine*. Consequently, American car styling was a stick
that Banham and his IG comrades used to beat their ideological
opponents with. In the 1950s, Banham complained, the British design
establishment dismissed American cars as 'vulgar trash' from a
position of distance and ignorance. He remarked: 'You don't have to

believe what it is trying to say, but the first step towards a proper evaluation of the product is to know what it is and what it is claiming to do.'

Banham admired the detailing of American cars and was sympathetic to the aesthetic of expendability and visual pleasure.[44] In a 1977 Arts Council film about the IG, *Fathers of Pop*, Banham was shown driving around London in a massive yellow Cadillac. He waxed lyrical about its heraldry, cascade of chromium, sensual lines and curves, and Cineramic, wrap-around windscreen. In short, he treated it like a major sculpture by providing a serious analysis of its aesthetic appeal, iconography and symbolism.

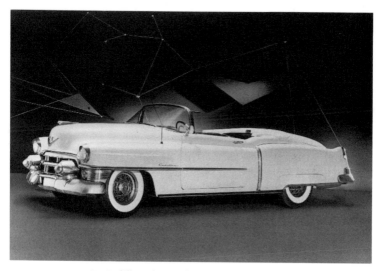

7. *Cadillac El Dorado Convertible, 1953.*
Photo: courtesy of Motoring Picture Library,
National Motor Museum, Beaulieu, Brockenhurst, Hants.

Besides cars, Banham was to write perceptively on a wide range of American subjects. The most relevant to the theme of this book was his 1974 paper 'Europe and American Design'.[45] It remains an illuminating comparison and historical study of changing European perceptions of American design and engineering. Banham concluded that Europeans could no longer view America as 'an exported European Utopia planted in virgin soil' or the model for their future. (Europeans tended to regard America's achievements and innovations in the fields of new technology, consumerism and mass entertainment as in advance of those of Europe, and they also tended to assume that sooner or later what happened there would, through importation or imitation, happen in Europe too; consequently, looking at contemporary America was like seeing their own future.) Instead they should accept it as 'a different culture with problems and possibilities that are not our fault and not our responsibility'. Even so, it was inevitable that America would remain 'part of the landscape of today'.

Banham had no direct experience of the United States until the early 1960s. Later on, in the 1970s, he emigrated to America and he died there in 1988.[46]

Conclusion

It should be clear by now that during the 1950s members of the IG were unusual in their willingness to study both 'high' and 'low' American culture, the fine as well as the applied arts. Alloway was particularly critical of hierarchical distinctions and value judgements, therefore he argued for 'a continuum' or 'long front of culture', or 'a general field of visual communication'. In other words, painting as a medium was not superior to film, they were simply different but co-equal.

In 1969 Banham explained why American culture was so bracing for the IG:

> It is important to realise how salutary a corrective to the sloppy provincialism of most London art of ten years ago US design could be. The gusto and professionalism of wide-screen movies or Detroit car-styling was a constant reproach to the Moore-ish yokelry of British sculpture or the affected Piperish gloom of British painting. To anyone with a scrap of sensibility or an eye for technique, the average Playtex or Maidenform ad in American *Vogue* was an instant deflater of the reputations of most artists then in Arts Council vogue.[47]

Summing up the significance and value of American culture to the IG in their struggle with their own, national culture David Robbins wrote in 1990:

> The modernist basis of the IG was an inter-textual project – the recuperation of the international avant-garde in the teeth of the dispiriting insularity

of British culture. The chief resource in this oppositional enterprise was the production of a text called 'America', drawn from a broad range of verbal and visual sources, from scholars like Norbert Wiener and Claude Shannon to 'Action painters' like Pollock to American magazines, movies, science fiction and technology. In this respect, the IG's total sphere of discourse, including exhibitions organised by its members, constitutes a remarkably overt instance of *Americanisme* – America as the ultra-modernist projection of a 'readymade' technological society unburdened by cultural baggage.[48]

However, admiration for America was not without its problems and tensions for IG members because of what Banham called their 'divided loyalties'. For example, he pointed out that those who had left-wing political convictions and CND affiliations, such as Richard and Terry Hamilton, experienced a contradiction, namely:

How to reconcile unavoidable admiration for the immense competence, resourcefulness and creative power of American commercial design with the equally unavoidable disgust at the system that was producing it ... how to maintain this discriminating admiration in the face of the conditioned-reflex atomic sabre-rattling of the Eisenhower regime?[49]

Del Renzio also recalled in 1984:

There was a vague leftish sympathy but it often seemed to be be swamped by a fierce 'Americanism', an admiration for American technology rather than conscious approval of American foreign policy; and the spectre of Cohn and Shine and McCarthyite witch-hunting was ever present. Some of us, too, had met some of the refugees from Hollywood [caused by anti-communist purges] and this tempered our attitudes.[50]

Clearly, the underlying issue was: could one have a dynamic, high quality art and design culture such as America's without also having a capitalist economy and the American political system? The brief but creative achievements of Russian Constructivist art and design imme-diately following the Bolshevik revolution suggest that one could, but if we consider the example of American advertising imagery – which Hamilton explored in depth – one cannot really imagine it flourishing outside the free market in commodities and services intrinsic to capitalism.

3
The Impact of Abstract Expressionism During the 1940s and 1950s

Abstract Expressionism (AE) – also known by a variety of other names, for example, American-Type Painting, New American Painting and Painterly Abstraction – was the first American art movement of the twentieth century that was acclaimed by many in Europe and recognised as comparable in aesthetic achievement to earlier modern movements such as Cubism and Surrealism. AE emerged primarily in New York during the 1940s and 1950s and its leading figures were: William Baziotes, James Brooks, Sam Francis, Arshile Gorky, Adolph Gottlieb, Phillip Guston, Grace Hartigan, Willem de Kooning, Franz Kline, Robert Motherwell, Barnett Newman, Jackson Pollock, Mark Rothko, Theodoros Stamos, Clyfford Still, Bradley Walker Tomlin and Jack Tworkov.

The label AE was unsatisfactory because some painters – de Kooning and Pollock in some of their works – employed figuration and artists such as Newman and Rothko also stressed the importance of subject matter. Furthermore, the artists could be grouped into two types: the Action or gestural painters (Pollock, de Kooning and Kline) and the colour-field painters (Newman, Rothko and Still).

External recognition for AE did not happen by chance: concerted efforts were made by wealthy and powerful American individuals and institutions to disseminate the movement abroad via group and solo exhibitions.[1] However, it should be acknowledged that they were also responding to requests from European museum curators for shows of contemporary American art. The key exhibitions that will be cited in this chapter are: *Opposing Forces* (ICA, 1953); *Modern Art in the United States* (Tate Gallery, 1956); *Abstract Impressionism* (Travelling show, 1958); *Jackson Pollock 1912–1956* (Whitechapel Art Gallery, 1958); and *The New American Painting* (Tate Gallery, 1959).

Also important were the articles and illustrations that appeared in American art journals and more popular magazines such as *Life*. New

York magazines such as *Art News*, *Art in America* and *Arts* were available in some British art school libraries and so information about new trends in American art was rapidly communicated across the Atlantic. *Art News* was virtually the house journal of AE. Harold Rosenberg's influential essay 'The American Action Painters' had appeared in its December 1952 issue. Significant too was an artists-at-work series: 'Pollock Paints a Picture', May 1951; 'Kline Paints ...', December 1952; 'De Kooning Paints ...', March 1953.

IG member del Renzio owned a copy of *Portfolio* which featured Hans Namuth's still photos of Pollock at work taken in 1950; one of which was included in the ICA show *Parallel of Life and Art* (September–October, 1953).[2] After seeing a Namuth photo in 1957, the British abstract painter Gillian Ayres was encouraged to paint pictures on the floor rather than on an easel. Namuth's 1951 documentary, a colour film showing Pollock in action, was eventually screened at the ICA in November 1958.

There was, of course, a European equivalent of AE, namely Tachisme or L'Art Informel or Art Autre. It included Hans Hartung, Georges Mathieu, Jean-Paul Riopelle (a Canadian), Pierre Soulages and Wols. Exhibitions featuring works by these artists took place in London during the 1950s and so the two tendencies were in contention and both vied for the attention of British viewers.[3] Tachisme did influence the practices of some young British painters, but on the whole it came to be perceived as a lesser movement when compared to AE.

Sam Francis (1923–94) was an American painter who spanned both tendencies because he was based in Paris from 1950 to 1962. His work appeared in exhibitions of Tachisme and AE (even though he hailed from California rather than New York).[4] Perhaps because Francis's paintings had something of the School of Paris's lyrical beauty about them and were less extreme than those by the New York painters, they seemed to have had a particular appeal to British artists and critics.

Read, Davie and Scott Encounter AE

Herbert Read was probably the first British critic to encounter the mature work of Pollock. In 1956 Read recalled:

> I remember, on my first trip to New York after the war, in the spring of 1946, being shown a large canvas by an artist I had then not heard of –

Jackson Pollock. Apart from its size – it was immense – it reminded me of the marbled patterns that we find on the end-papers of 18th and 19th century pattern books; and, indeed, the Jackson Pollock painting had been produced by similar methods – by dribbling and streaking varicoloured paints over a canvas laid flat over the floor.

Read was not terribly impressed. He remarked: 'The result I found decorative, but no more.'[5]

Alan Davie (b. 1920) a Scottish-born painter, poet, jewellery-maker and modern jazz musician was one of the first British artists to come across examples of AE. While visiting Venice in 1948 he saw a number of Pollocks, plus works by Gottlieb, de Kooning and Rothko, which were part of Peggy Guggenheim's private collection. By chance Guggenheim saw examples of Davie's work in a show held at the Galeria Sandri. Her first impression on glimpsing a Davie in the gallery's window was that it was a Pollock. (Thus it would seem that, independently, Davie had arrived at a similar style as Pollock. While touring Europe in the late 1940s Davie responded to the art and design of many cultures and periods and he also made experiments of his own.) The artist and the patron met and became friends. Guggenheim purchased Davie's *Music of the Autumn Landscape* and, later on, she bought several more of his paintings. At the time Davie was little known and for some years Guggenheim was virtually his only patron.[6]

The extent of Pollock's impact on Davie in 1948 and his influence on the latter's subsequent work is unclear. According to some Davie scholars, Pollock hardly rates a mention in Davie's journals. However, Alan Bowness reports that Davie was as interested in Pollock's 'symbolic-surrealist paintings of the early 1940s ... as in the drip pictures, which Pollock had only then begun to paint ... Pollock also provided a method of working, perhaps more important than any stylistic influence. He seemed to paint by instinct, exploiting the accidental and letting the picture take shape as he worked on it.'[7] Bowness also claims that Davie was particularly impressed by Pollock's departure from the easel painting tradition by placing canvases on the floor and working around their edges, dripping or pouring liquid pigment on to the surface rather than applying it with a brush. Davie too adopted this method of painting but he says it was a natural consequence of his desire to paint fast on a large scale.[8]

Furthermore, in a statement dated 1958, Davie rejected the label 'Action painter' and argued that the theory of Action painting was an invention of critics (Rosenberg, presumably) which did not adequately describe his creative procedures.[9] Whether the label was accurate or not, there is no disputing the fact that Davie subsequently became one of the few British, semi-abstract painters whose work rivalled the energy, improvisation and large size of American Action painting. He also shared with the American artists an interest in 'primitive' art and mythologies.

Davie's first visit to New York occurred in the spring of 1956. He met de Kooning, Kline and Rothko, and he spent a weekend with Pollock a few months before the latter's death. Davie recalls a bad atmosphere: the American artists were not working but drinking and brawling at the Cedar Bar (a favourite drinking hole of the AEs) and at parties. Bystanders, he says, encouraged Pollock to fight and even offered him a knife!

Davie was nominated for a Solomon Guggenheim Award and was given a one-man show at the Catherine Viviano Gallery in New York (March–April 1956). Pollock biographers claim that when he visited the show he was overheard mumbling about his influence on British painters. The exhibition was favourably reviewed in several newspapers and art magazines. It seems clear that, because Davie's work had close affinities with AE, it appealed to the Americans: both museums and private collectors acquired paintings. Financial and critical success in America obviously contributed to Davie's burgeoning international reputation. But when Davie was asked by the author in 1997 whether or not he considered himself to be an international, a British or a Scottish artist, he replied: 'I'm a Celtic artist.'

William Scott (1913–90), a painter of simplified, abstracted nudes, landscapes and kitchen table still lives, was the second British artist to encounter the AEs, but this time on their home ground. In 1953 he travelled to Alberta, Canada, in order to teach at a summer school organised by the Banff School of Fine Arts. In the early 1970s he recalled:

> I met a young generation from all over America and heard from them stories of the marvellous painting and painters of New York. I was already familiar with the work of Pollock, having seen one large work by him in London that summer, but others I had never heard of ... [in the late summer he visited New York] ... I was now invited to meet some of them by a gallery interested in my work in New York. [The critic James Johnson Sweeney had arranged for him to meet Martha Jackson who became Scott's American dealer.] I was taken to meet Jackson Pollock in Long Island and a number of other

painters were living there that summer, including de Kooning. Back in New York I met Rothko and I spent several evenings with Kline at the Cedar Bar. I was the first European painter apparently to visit Pollock, but Rothko and Kline, I gathered, were very Anglophile and very curious to hear about the art situation in England. I saw a large mixed exhibition of American art at the Museum of Modern Art, and I saw many works by artists whom I had heard of from the students in Canada.

My impression at first was bewilderment, it was not the originality of the works, but it was the scale, audacity and self-confidence ... My first impression of Rothko was his daring and beautiful colour and handling – the large empty shapes were the least part of his impressiveness. This had already been said by Europeans and I related his work more immediately to previous experience. Here was a metamorphosis of Nicholson and Turner. [10]

Scott returned home convinced that the Americans 'had made a great discovery and that the mood in England – a longing for a nice comfortable realist art would not last much longer'. By means of verbal descriptions and sketches he communicated his impressions to his painter friends Patrick Heron and Roger Hilton. Scott's loose style of brush and palette knife work, sensuous use of pigment and compositions that stressed the flatness of the canvas, had some affinities with the work of the Americans. Heron, however, was later to argue that it was not Scott who was influenced by them but he who influenced the Americans.[11] Scott himself commented:

My personal reaction was to discontinue my pursuit of abstract art and to try to put my earlier form of symbolic realism on a scale larger than the easel picture, with a new freedom gained from my American visit.

Despite the acknowledged influences of 'freedom' and 'scale', the overall effect of Scott's meetings with the AEs in New York was to confirm the fact that he belonged to a different pictorial tradition: 'I felt now that there was a Europeanism that I belonged to, and that many qualities of painting which were possessed by my friends might elude an American.' Since Scott was 40 years old in 1953 and his painting had long been steeped in the traditions of French art it was hardly surprising that he was not deflected from his path by exposure to the new American art.

The critic Ronald Alley also claims that 'the effect of his visit was to make his paintings more, not less, European'.[12] Yet Alley also remarks that 'enriched by what he had seen ... The forms began to swell, the colours became richer, and the brushwork more varied; he began to work with greater boldness and freedom.'

Scott was to cross the Atlantic again later in the decade. During the early 1950s examples of his work were displayed in mixed exhibitions in the United States but it was not until 1956 that he had his first one-man show in New York at the Martha Jackson Gallery. In 1959, the year in which he won the John Moore's Liverpool prize, he travelled to New York in order to attend a second one-man show at the Jackson Gallery.

Opposing Forces

Members of the ICA – especially the younger ones who constituted the IG and who were fascinated by all things American – were to develop a keen interest in AE. In January 1953 the ICA mounted an exhibition entitled *Opposing Forces* which was a variant of an earlier Parisian show – *Véhémences Confrontées* (Galerie Nina Dausset, March 1951) – which had been selected by the French dealer and theorist of Art Autre, Michel Tapié. The two shows were designed to contrast European Tachisme with American AE. At the ICA the Europeans were represented by Mathieu, Michaux, Riopelle and Serpan, and the Americans by Francis, Alfonso Ossorio and Pollock. A huge Pollock – *One (No. 31)* (1950) – took up an entire wall and dominated the exhibition.

According to the critic Robert Melville (1908–88), the Pollock was a 'heaving, undulating agglomerate', a 'majestic turmoil' which 'made Tapié's miscellany look ineffectual'; he later claimed that 'the only artist of consequence whose work was directly influenced by the ICA show was Magda Cordell'.[13] (Cordell [b. 1921] was a Hungarian-born painter married to the musician Frank Cordell, both of whom contributed to IG activities.) Heron was one British painter who saw the show. It was his first encounter with Pollock; however, he was more impressed by the work of Francis.

Later on, in December 1953, del Renzio delivered a talk entitled 'Non-Formal Painting'. In 1997 he recalled:

> It was very much a critical presentation of the famous Rosenberg Action painting piece plus an attempt to introduce Information Theory which presciently picked up on Norbert Weiner's citation of Mandelbrot to the effect that communication was a game in which two players were allied against a third and malevolent player called either entropy or the Devil![14]

**8. Installation shot of the *Opposing Forces* exhibition,
ICA Gallery, London, January–February 1953.**
Photo shows three Pollocks including on the left: *One (No. 31)* (1950).
Oil and enamel on canvas, 269 x 531 cm.
Now in the collection of the Museum of Modern Art, New York.
Source of photo: *Architectural Review*, Vol. 113 (April 1953), p. 273.

The theoretical and interdisciplinary ambitions of the IG are evident
from these remarks. Furthermore, del Renzio suggested that semiotic
theory, that is, Charles Sanders Peirce's (an American philosopher) trio
of signs – index, icon and symbol – would be useful for analysing
Pollock's paintings because they were assemblies of different types of
sign rather than images. Del Renzio also remembers ICA discussions
about recent art in which the critic David Sylvester contributed the term
'afocalism', by which was meant pictures which had several points of
focus distributed across the canvas rather than just one at a central
point.

Modern Art in the United States

January to February 1956 witnessed the first substantial showing of AE
paintings in London – at the Tate Gallery as part of the show *Modern
Art in the United States* (a selection of paintings, sculptures and prints

from the collections of the Museum of Modern Art, New York). On display were such major works as Gorky's *Agony* (1947), de Kooning's *Woman, 1* (1950–52) and Pollock's *Number 1* (1948). However, the Tate show was a broad survey of various tendencies within American art, including realist ones; only the final room was devoted to AE.

The year 1956, which also saw the death of Pollock in a car crash, was the year in which American rock'n'roll had a tremendous impact on British teenagers, the year in which the student magazine of the Royal College published an 'Americana' issue (*ARK*, No. 19), the year of John Osborne's controversial play, *Look Back in Anger*, and the year of the Suez crisis in which Britain and France tried to impose their will upon Colonel Nasser of Egypt by military invasion. A humiliating withdrawal was forced upon Britain by American disapproval of gunboat diplomacy and their refusal to support the pound. This incident made it crystal clear that Britain was now a much weaker power than the United States, that in politics it had to follow America's lead and that the imperial days of the British Empire were finally over.

British visitors to the Tate in 1956 and 1959 found the work of the Abstract Expressionists strongly marked by its national identity even though the artists themselves were not typical representatives of the majority of Americans. During their years of poverty and struggle in New York they had felt themselves a small, isolated caste of urban intellectuals whose values were at odds with American mass culture and the materialistic consumer society that was developing around them. Greenberg had ended his 1947 *Horizon* article with the gloomy remark: 'What can fifty do against a hundred and forty million?' (Quite a lot as it turned out.) During the 1930s the AEs had been associated with realist styles and with socialist ideals and movements, but by the 1940s and 1950s they had lost faith in such styles and ideologies. Yet, as we shall see later, this did not prevent political use being made of their art.

British painters could not help but contrast the large size of the paintings with the much smaller ones they generally produced. This seemed to be a natural consequence of the greater size of the United States compared to the British Isles. American cars and freeways were bigger than British ones, so why not their paintings? The Americans had not experienced the shortages of materials – such as canvas – that British artists initially faced after the Second World War. British paintings were also smaller because they were produced in small studios or even bedsits, not large lofts, and they were intended for display in smaller homes. They also appeared fussy and fiddly in comparison because they generally consisted of various elements arranged in a hierarchical, parts-to-whole relationship, whereas Pollock's were 'all-over' or 'decentred' in terms of their compositions and the colour-fields of Still's and Newman's canvases stretched from edge to edge. According to William Scott, the impact of the 1956 Tate show was to expand the scale of painting in England. Hilton thought Scott's earlier descriptions of the achievements of the Americans had been too favourable and misleading because, in his view, they were 'stainers' rather than 'painters'.

The fact that the new movement in painting was American in origin and character was also stressed by American critics and curators. (Indeed, since most of the AEs lived and worked in New York – de Kooning once remarked, 'It's not so much that I'm an American: I'm a New Yorker' – a more limited geographical designation was given by certain writers: 'The New York School'. This name was clearly intended to rival 'The School of Paris'.) Yet Pollock, in a statement written in 1944, appeared to deny that art has a national character:

> The idea of an isolated American painting, so popular during the 'thirties, seems absurd to me just as the idea of creating a purely American mathematics or physics would seem absurd ...

But then he added:

> An American is an American and his painting would naturally be qualified by that fact, whether he wills it or not. But the basic problems of contemporary painting are independent of any country.[15]

Pollock seems to be trying to have it both ways: AE was both national and international. Leading British critics such as Alloway, Bowness and Read held that Modernism was an international phenomenon, that it had a 'mainstream' which used – before 1945 – to run through Paris but which now ran through New York.[16]

However, as Rasheed Araeen (b. 1935), a Pakistani artist who emigrated to Britain in 1964, has explained:

> The usage of the term 'international'... does not imply the participation of all peoples, or the cross-fertilisation between the different cultures of the world, but merely the evolution of art styles in the West and their imposition on the rest of the world. It is in the global context of domination that we see the actual role of 'international' art.[17]

In other words, the terms 'international' and 'global' are often disguised signs of economic and cultural hegemony exercised by a powerful state or a multinational corporation. Araeen added:

> The boot of British Imperialism is still there and on its own foot; but there is one difference now. There is a bigger boot of Uncle Sam on the top.

As a result of the ideology of individualism so pervasive in the West and the influence of Cold War politics, great stress was placed on the freedom enjoyed by the individual painters within AE. But a theoretical difficulty follows: how can one reconcile the autonomy and difference of the individuals and at the same time claim that they belong to a stylistic movement, or a national, metropolitan or international school?

In 1955 Greenberg published an essay in *Partisan Review* in which he discussed and praised AE and compared it to European art.[18] The latter was found wanting – even though the Americans had learnt much from European art movements – while the former was judged to be emblematic of its country of origin by being labelled 'American-Type' painting. Risking an accusation of 'chauvinist exaggeration', Greenberg concluded that 'such a galaxy of powerfully talented and original painters ... has not been seen since the days of Cubism'. (British readers had to get used to such extravagant claims.) De Kooning was then singled out for special praise and because of his long life and productive career he subsequently came to be regarded, especially after the death of Picasso in 1973, by himself and his admirers as 'the greatest living painter in the world'.

Patrick Heron, Critic and Painter

For decades now Heron has been one of Britain's leading painters specialising in colourful abstractions. He held his first one-man show at the Redfern Gallery, London, in 1947 but during the 1940s and early 1950s he was perhaps better known as an art critic. From 1945 to 1947 he wrote reviews for *New English Weekly* and from 1947 to 1950 for the weekly *New Statesman and Nation*. Since Heron was an artist, his criticism was informed by first-hand knowledge of painting techniques and awareness of formal issues. An anthology of his art criticism was published as *The Changing Forms of Art* in 1955 in which Pollock was mentioned three times: once in relation to Alexander Calder, once in relation to Davie, and Pollock's painting was praised in an introduction dated October 1954.[19]

Then, for three years – 1955–58 – Heron acted as the London correspondent for the New York magazine *Arts Digest* (later *Arts*) edited by Hilton Kramer. Thus Heron was one of several European critics who fed back to the United States positive evaluations of their art. Initially though, Heron adored French art – especially the paintings of Bonnard, Braque and Matisse – and supported figuration rather than abstraction. A conversion to the latter took place during 1955–56 (after an abortive stab at abstraction in 1952 when influenced by the work of Nicolas de Staël).

Heron became aware of the existence of Pollock and Francis in 1953 as a consequence of the *Opposing Forces* exhibition, but he had no idea that a whole new school of painting had emerged in New York until he was told about it by Scott. During the early 1950s Heron lived in the Holland Park district of London (he moved to Cornwall in April 1956) and it was there that in the summer of 1954 he was visited by Greenberg.[20] The American, it turned out, was familiar with Heron's critical writings and the two men quickly became friends. Heron introduced him to Scott and Hilton and, at his request, showed him the bomb-sites of the East End. However, Heron soon discovered that Greenberg was more interested in promoting the art of his homeland than in learning about British art. Their talk was about Pollock and the other New York artists whose paintings Heron had not yet seen.

When Heron did finally view several examples of AE at the 1956 Tate show, his praise and admiration were unstinting. He informed readers of *Arts* magazine:

> I was instantly elated by the size, energy, originality, economy and inventive daring of many of the paintings. Their creative emptiness represented a radical discovery, I felt, as did their flatness, or rather, their spatial shallowness. I was fascinated by their consistent denial of illusionistic depth...

Despite expressing some reservations concerning the Americans' use of colour and mode of composition, he concluded:

> ... to me and those English painters with whom I associate, your new school comes as the most vigorous movement we have seen since the war.[21]

Even at this early stage Heron distinguished between European and American painting strategies and aligned himself with the former rather than the latter. Two years later Heron began to express doubts about the character of the new American painting. In a review published in *Arts* in May 1958 of an ICA show featuring the work of five Americans: de Kooning, Kline, Pollock, Rothko and Still, Heron continued to praise their paintings – particularly those by Rothko whom he considered 'the best of the living Americans, better than Pollock' – but his positive remarks were hedged around with reservations.[22] For example, he judged de Kooning's paintings to be 'retrogressive' because they still relied upon figuration. (De Kooning's *Woman* series caused a problem for artists who advocated total abstraction and for critics who claimed that the Americans had transcended iconography.) This contradicted what Heron considered to be the main achievement of AE, namely, treating the total painting as the image (rather than a painting which contained an image). 'Meaning', according to Heron, was to be derived from the 'independent, autonomous object' itself, not from references to some external reality. Heron also criticised the supposed 'spontaneity' and 'speed' of Action painting and, in the interests of 'good painting', he called for more deliberation and a more varied tempo.

In order to concentrate on his own abstract painting, Heron took 'a vow of silence' in 1958 and did not write any more articles until 1966. As we shall discover later, during the 1960s Heron was to rue his earlier endorsement of American art.

The impact of American painting on Heron's own art is a matter of dispute. In his published statements Heron is naturally inclined to stress his independent achievements and the differences between British and American abstraction, but also what, in 1974, he termed 'Anglo-American entanglement ... the positive interdependence of British and American painting from the late fifties to the present moment'.[23] Some Heron scholars detect the influence of Francis and Heron himself told Benedict Read in 1993:

> I have often said that the only influence really that I admit to from the other side of the Atlantic was the Sam Francis ... [24]

Other writers detect the influence of Rothko and the larger scale of the American canvases. Brandon Taylor, in contrast, judges that 'Heron's painting of the next few years [after 1956] bears little evidence of having assimilated these "new developments".'[25] The issue is complicated by the role that the light and landscape of Cornwall, and the

possible influence of French art and the work of such British painters as
Matthew Smith and Ivon Hitchens, are deemed to play in Heron's
post-1956 abstractions.

Nevertheless, it seems reasonable to assume that exposure to AE
in 1956 reinforced Heron's decision to become a non-figurative
painter and encouraged him to take more risks. In an article dated
1966 Heron himself admitted: 'Not only were we [that is, Heron and
his painter friends] in varying degrees influenced by them at that
time ... but we openly proclaimed that this was what was happening
... we British openly availed ourselves of the American discoveries,
making them to some extent our own new point of departure [in
order to] advance far beyond the American positions of 1950.'[26]

Heron soon became a total formalist interested only in colour and
space detached from any cultural or socio-political signification. One
of the striking differences between his art and the 'Abstract Sublime'
paintings of Newman and Rothko was the Americans' stress on
'tragic and timeless' subject matter. This gave their paintings an
additional dimension of disguised, spiritual meaning which Heron's
canvases lacked. Heron, the critic-painter, was never interested in
meaning and interpretation or the political potential of art, whereas
Newman once stated that if his paintings were read correctly 'it
would mean an end of all state capitalism and totalitarianism'.[27]

Realism versus Abstraction

No foreign importation enters a situation equivalent to a clean slate,
consequently its impact varies according the state of play of forces
inside the receiving nation. AE entered Britain at a time when there
was a debate raging between the supporters of realism in art and the
supporters of abstraction. During the mid-1950s the neo-Marxist critic
John Berger was promoting the paintings of the so-called Kitchen Sink
School which he regarded as social realist. In 1956 British realists were
represented in force at the 28th Venice Biennale and Jack Smith's
painting, *Creation and Crucifixion*, won first prize at the John Moores'
Liverpool exhibition. Although Smith (b. 1928) rejected the social
realist label, his success in Liverpool and Venice may be regarded as the
high point of realism.

Berger was also an admirer of Renato Guttuso (1911–87), an
Italian communist painter who was widely regarded as Europe's

leading figurative artist. Guttuso visited London in March 1955 and took part in a public debate with Heron on the issue of realism versus abstraction, held at the Italian Institute, Belgrave Square.[28]

As one might expect from Berger's aesthetic preferences and political convictions, he did not welcome AE. In an article written at the time of the 1956 Tate show, he complained about 'the kind of pathological self-deception which claims that the "action" paintings included in the American exhibition at the Tate Gallery have anything to do with art'. [29]

From the debates which took place in the 1950s and again in the 1980s, it is now clear that the choice between realism and abstraction was not simply an aesthetic or formal one, it was also political. To choose realism was to support the left-wing critique of capitalism; to choose abstraction was to become apolitical. Realism was viewed as local and particular, concerned with the world at large, whereas abstraction was perceived as general and universal, or concerned with the inner world (Pollock stated that the source of his work was 'the unconscious') or with the illusory space enclosed by the edges of a canvas. Realism was a depiction of existing reality, whereas abstracts resulting from a process of construction were new additions to reality. At the same time, realism was associated with the past and with parochialism, while abstraction had connotations of the present and future. Juliet Steyn, a British historian of realism, comments:

> Realism came to represent everything that was uncreative, inhibiting to artistic freedom, provincial, ideological. In sum, realism became identified with repression. A space was cleared for an American version of Modernism. By 1959 Berger could write with conviction: 'Abstract Expressionism and New Dadaism are sweeping the field. Nowhere in Western Europe is there a realist stronghold left.' [30]

Even Jack Smith moved towards total abstraction during the period 1957–59. However, it should not be assumed that abstraction displaced figuration altogether, because some British realists continued to paint scenes from everyday life and the British Pop artists of the late 1950s and early 1960s produced representational pictures.

Three Critics Respond: Read, Melville and Alloway

A decade after his first encounter with a Pollock in New York, Read admired Francis's paintings enough to write articles and catalogue introductions about them. In *A Concise History of Modern Painting* (1959), Read did make an effort to assimilate the other members of AE to his linear survey, while simultaneously stressing the European origins of many 'American' artists and the influence of Surrealism on Gorky and Pollock. Read agreed with Pollock that modern painting was an international rather than a national phenomenon, therefore AE was a movement which could not be confined to America. In his view, it did not originate there either. In the 1960 edition of *Art Now: An Introduction to the Theory of Modern Painting and Sculpture,* he also tried to explain American art in terms of Freud's theory of the unconscious and the evolution from scribbling to symbol formation typical of child art.

Melville's reactions to AE were mixed. In some articles he praised the movement but in others he made judgements of this kind: 'The very act of painting has become a violent, mindless exercise, and the pictures that result from this activity are formless demonstrations of a yearning to besmirch and deface.'[31] He also thought the public performances by the French Tachist Georges Mathieu were much more interesting than the paintings that resulted from them.[32] In a talk entitled 'Mythology and Psychology' given at the ICA in February 1954, Melville had applied Jungian concepts to an analysis of AE. In his review of the 1956 Tate show, Melville claimed that AE was 'a mural style' and that the 'matter-of-fact acceptance of paint as a covering for a flat surface' was an example of 'American pragmatism in action'. He also thought that the Americans had 'liquidated iconographical problems'.[33] Melville's review of the 1959 Tate show was more favourable but it still conveys the impression that he was underwhelmed by AE.[34]

Alloway, of course, responded enthusiastically to the contemporary fine art of America as well as to its mass culture. From 1953 to 1957 he served as the British correspondent for *Art News.* Since he had written a book about British abstract artists – *Nine Abstract Artists* (1954) – which discussed Constructivist-type figures such as Anthony Hill, Kenneth and Mary Martin, Victor Pasmore, etc., he was well placed to make a comparison between recent tendencies in British and American abstract art. (The other main strand in British abstraction was associated with St Ives in Cornwall, that is, a more organic, informal style making indirect references to landscape.) Besides *Art News*, Alloway also wrote reviews for the British periodicals *Architectural Design*, *Art News and Review*, the *Listener* and the RCA student magazine *ARK*, therefore a stream of articles about the new American painting appeared.

Like Melville, Alloway was interested in the question of iconography. He raised it in his review of the 1956 Tate exhibition published in *Architectural Design*. In the case of Pollock and de Kooning – who 'found' figurative images during the course of painting – for example, he thought the creative challenge was to establish an iconography capable of withstanding 'the violence of their technique, a tough image that can survive the battering it gets in the act of painting'.[35]

In his article Alloway sought to introduce his readers to Rosenberg's theory of Action painting. He cited Rosenberg's characterisation of Action painters as 'frontiersmen' who fought their battles by improvising according to the specific situation and materials at hand. However, Alloway claimed this 'Davy Crockett phase' was short-lived. He went on to complain about the way other British critics had rejected Action painting and caused confusion by lumping together American and European painters, such as Pollock and Soulages, whom he thought were significantly different. He accused these critics of turning 'action into connoisseurship' by 'making a fetish of quality'.

In November 1956 Alloway chaired an ICA discussion about Pollock. The following month the art historian Frank John Ross was invited to give a talk about contemporary American Painting. During 1957 Alloway organised further lectures and discussions about the same subject. At this time he became friendly with Munsing of the American Embassy. Inside the embassy there was a well-stocked library which enabled Alloway to obtain the books, magazines and records that he needed for his research. There was also a gallery maintained by the United States Information Service. Munsing and the USIS organised exhibitions of new American art which travelled to the provincial English city of York.[36]

Art Student Responses to the 1956 Tate Show

In art schools there are normally some students who welcome new, radical developments in art because they themselves are hoping to contribute to these or to the next wave. Such students often embrace new trends as a way of opposing the tastes and values of the older generation represented by their tutors.

It was relatively easy for art students attending London colleges in the mid-1950s to see the 1956 Tate show with its room of AEs. However, this exhibition also included examples of realist art by Ben Shahn and others who influenced Peter Blake while he was a student at the RCA and Patrick Caulfield while he was a student at Chelsea School of Art.

A number of students were so impressed by the 1956 show that they decided they had to visit the United States. One of them, Malcolm Morley, an RCA student, resolved to emigrate there.

The contrasting reactions of different generations can be illustrated by reference to the clash between certain students and staff at the RCA. Robyn Denny, Richard Smith and William Green were there during the mid-1950s and were strongly influenced by American (and European) abstract, gestural painting. Smith (b. 1931) attended the RCA from 1954 to 1956. His early paintings were abstracts in which the loose, painterly brushwork was indebted to such American gestural artists as Francis, Guston and Tworkov, whose canvases were featured in the 1956 Tate show. In addition, Smith saw examples of Francis's work while visiting Paris in the same year. However, Smith was also interested in mass culture and communications, and his art underwent a change of emphasis especially after contact with erstwhile members of the IG and visits to New York (of which more later).

Denny (b. 1930) had been in Paris in 1950 with the American Neil Noland (brother of the painter Kenneth), where they had made pictorial experiments comparable to Action painting. By 1956 Denny was making blotchy, coagulated, dripped paintings and using fire to scorch their black and gold surfaces. At that time he liked to paint to the sounds of rock'n'roll records. With the benefit of hindsight, he later remarked:

> It's always assumed that Abstract Expressionism at the Tate in 1956 changed the world. Well of course we were influenced by this exhibition, but it was an event waiting to happen. British painting had been very provincial again after the War. It had to bust out again ... [37]

These remarks point to a repression that was in fact characteristic of 1950s' society as a whole, not just of the realm of painting. But this repression was increasingly being challenged by a restive, younger generation impatient with rules, regulations and the culture of conformity (witness the 'Angry Young Men' syndrome). The example of American art thus encouraged a latent tendency.

While most of Green's (b. 1934) output was non-figurative – paintings executed with bitumen on hardboard sheets placed on the floor and via surface-altering methods involving acid, fire and riding bicycles – he did create some photostatic, negative images of Elvis Presley. And when Green held one-man exhibitions he was quite willing to reference American mass culture for publicity purposes; for example, he used the names and photographs of film stars such as Errol Flynn and Susan Hayward.

Even the RCA tutor John Minton (1917–57), a Neo-Romantic figurative and landscape painter and illustrator, was not averse to tackling American themes: in the last year of his life he painted a large, unfinished canvas entitled *Composition, Death of James Dean*. Dean (1931–55), the charismatic star of *East of Eden* and *Rebel without a Cause*, had a tremendous impact on British cinema-goers and his premature death in a car crash came as a shock to them. Tony Messenger was another British painter who also responded to Dean's death two years after it occurred.

9. Tony Messenger with his painting, *30th September 1955*, 1957
[oil on panel, 122 x 244 cm. London: private collection]
in the Young Contemporaries exhibition, RBA galleries, London,
February 1958. Photo: courtesy of Tony and Helen Messenger.

His 1957 picture, *30th September 1955*, produced while he was a student at the RCA, was based on a photograph of the shattered Porsche in which Dean perished.

Earlier, in December 1956, Minton had made a now notorious criticism of Smith's and Denny's work at a meeting of the RCA Painting School's Sketch Club. Minton objected – among other things – to the lack of significant subject matter in abstracts. In a letter of reply (the targets of the attack had not been present), Denny, Smith and Roddy Maude-Roxby denied that they were 'Angry Young Men' of the Colin Wilson and John Osborne variety. Their heroes were, instead, Americans such as Floyd Patterson (world heavyweight boxing champion) and Colonel Peter Everest (a pilot who broke the sound barrier). Presumably they cited Americans outside the realm of art in order to wrongfoot Minton.

Three years later there was still opposition from RCA staff towards informal abstraction: when RCA students invited Alloway to lecture on Action painting (a poster for the lecture, dated 19 February 1959, was designed by Robyn Denny) he, del Renzio and Melville (who took part in the discussion) had to be smuggled into the wartime hut that served as a student common room via a back route.[38]

Abstract Impressionism

Between the two major appearances of American art at the Tate in 1956 and 1959, the Arts Council circulated an exhibition around Britain entitled *Abstract Impressionism*.[39] It was organised by the painter Harold Cohen (b. 1928), who was then teaching in the Fine Art Department of Nottingham University, and the London critic Alloway. Munsing of the American Embassy also assisted in the shipping of paintings across the Atlantic. The catalogue was designed by Richard Smith with a cover by Cohen plus an introduction written by Alloway. The term 'Abstract Impressionism' was American in origin: it had been coined by Elaine de Kooning in 1951 to describe paintings with a uniform pattern of brushstrokes, which retained the optical effects of Impressionism while dispensing with its representational content. In 1956 Louis Finkelstein had also applied the label to Guston's paintings in order to distinguish them from those of the more violent Action painters.

The exhibition toured Britain during 1958, the year in which American Thor missiles were deployed. It brought together works by artists from the United States – Rosemarie Beck, Norman Bluhm, Lawrence Calcagno, Sam Francis, Joan Mitchell, Stephen Pace, Walter Plate and Miriam Schapiro – from Britain – Bernard and Harold Cohen, Barry Daniels, Heron, Ivon Hitchins, Peter Kinley, Peter Lanyon, Richard Smith – and from Europe – Nicolas de Staël, Angelo Ippololito, André Masson, Jean-Paul Riopelle and Pierre Tal Coat. Some of these artists still painted directly from nature (or from memories of nature) but some did not. In his catalogue text Alloway stressed their common interest in painterliness and 'the evocation of light and atmosphere, world of space'.

Clearly, this mixed, thematic exhibition provided an opportunity for British viewers to compare and contrast the new painting of America and Europe (most of the exhibits dated from 1957). There was surely also a subtext, that is a demonstration that here was an international tendency to which British artists were contributing their fair share and holding their own against foreign competition. In the event, the label and exhibition did not succeed in replacing AE. The American character of the latter imposed itself again with the large-scale Tate show held in the following year.

Alloway in America

In July 1958 Alloway lectured at the ICA on 'Art in America Today'. By then he had obtained a United States government grant to study American art and architecture *in situ*. Once in New York he taxed the critic Rosenberg about the usefulness of the term 'Action painting' and learnt more about Pollock's methods from his widow Lee Krasner. He met Newman and paid visits to the studios of Rothko and Still, and the Neo-Dadaists Jasper Johns and Robert Rauschenberg. On his return to Britain Alloway gave a BBC radio talk entitled 'Art in New York Today' which was then published in the *Listener*. He described close encounters with huge canvases, for example, in Still's studio:

> surrounded on three sides by wall-covering pictures, with their sharp, wandering-edge forms, I felt I was in a crevasse. I could not step back for a view that would reduce the whole picture to a simple pattern ... In Rothko's present studio you stand surrounded by big canvases. When I was there his new paintings were in the sombre earth colours that have replaced his earlier luminous reds and yellows. And such was their presence that, although I preserved freedom to move round, I felt buried alive.[40]

**10. Installation shot of the *Jackson Pollock 1912–1956*
Whitechapel exhibition, 1958.**
Photo: courtesy of the Whitechapel Art Gallery archive.

Alloway reported that de Kooning was 'the big man' in New York, not Pollock, Rothko or Still. Bolstered by his first-hand research, Alloway berated 'armchair' British critics for their ignorance of AE and argued that, far from being an art of chance, it was an art of aesthetic order and control.

On his first night in New York Alloway had visited the Artists' Club on Eighth Street where he had recognised a number of younger American artists. He thought they mixed and were accessible to a much greater extent than their counterparts in London:

> Thanks to the crowded art world, where everyone is a knowing witness, there is no faking of intensity, no ready-made standard of finish, no marking time between good works ... Compare this with the situation in London where the artists settle into small colonies and pat each other on the back ... [British] artists get away with mediocre, low temperature works for years in London because not enough people notice or care.

In addition to the *Listener* piece, Alloway wrote a more specialist essay about black and white Action paintings.[41] Even after he emigrated to the United States, Alloway continued to write about AE for British journals – see, for instance, his article 'The American Sublime' published in 1963 in the second issue of the ICA magazine *Living Arts*.

Jackson Pollock 1912–1956

Two years after Pollock's death a large-scale retrospective was organised as a memorial by the International Council of the Museum of Modern Art, New York. It was their first one-person exhibition to circulate in Europe. Twenty-nine paintings and twenty-nine drawings and watercolours were assembled and a commentary for the catalogue was supplied by the American critic Sam Hunter.

In November 1958 the exhibition reached the Whitechapel Art Gallery in London. The important role played by the Whitechapel in the promotion of American art – which continued throughout the 1960s – was due to its curator's enthusiasm for recent American art. Bryan Robertson (b. 1925) organised exhibitions at the Whitechapel from 1952 to 1968. In 1956 he visited the United States on a grant provided by the American Embassy in London and he also wrote a monograph on Pollock which was published in 1960. He later lived in America and from 1970 to 1975 served as director of the Museum of the State University of New York.

The Pollock show aroused considerable public interest. Robertson recalls that the police had to be called to control crowds queuing to get in and when he gave a lecture on Pollock at the Arts Council hundreds were turned away. An art student at the time, I went to see the exhibition and jotted down my reactions in the catalogue: I was impressed by the fanatical extremism of the paintings, their vibrant, violent, unnerving sense of movement. Pollock struck me as a sincere and vital genius although I thought that his emphasis on line militated against the role of colour – the tangled character of his compositions reminded me of barbed wire.

Allen Jones was a student at Hornsey College of Art when he visited the Whitechapel show. He described it as 'breathtaking. It represented a world of possibility and a painting language totally foreign to the tuition I was getting at art school. It showed that the persistence of figurative reference was compatible with abstract formal preoccupations.'[42] In later years he came to share Pollock's interest in Jungian psychology and he also became fascinated by Pollock's 1943 painting *Guardians of the Secret* (the latter was pertinent to his 1970s' paintings known as the 'stage' series).

A number of critics found Pollock's work decorative rather than violent. Neville Wallis, art critic of the *Observer*, acknowledged the 'self-sufficient beauty and invigorating drive of Pollock's best decorations' but he also stressed the limitations of his method.[43] John Berger, the erstwhile supporter of social realism, admitted that the American had talent and was 'a most fastidious, sensitive and "charming" craftsman'.[44] However, in Berger's view, his drip pictures lacked content, any relation to the world outside the artist's studio and therefore were 'meaningless' except as symptoms of cultural decline. Berger believed that the 1950s in the West were a time of 'cultural disintegration' and 'decadence' and that Pollock's limitations testified to this state of affairs.

The New American Painting

After a tour of eight European cities, *The New American Painting* exhibition arrived at the Tate Gallery in February 1959. It was the biggest display of AE paintings to reach London: 81 paintings by 17 artists. It was organised by the International Program of the Museum of Modern Art, New York, in collaboration with the USIS and the Arts Council of Great Britain, and its catalogue essay was written by Alfred H. Barr, a MoMA curator. As Alloway pointed out, the show was unusual in that it was both avant-garde and official.

Much of the press criticism was either lukewarm or negative but many British art students responded positively to the Tate show. Clive Barker, a student at Luton, was influenced by Clyfford Still's work for a time. Patrick Caulfield, who became known as a Pop artist during the 1960s, was in his third year at Chelsea; this time it was the abstraction of Guston that impressed him rather than the realism of Shahn. For a short while Caulfield produced almost completely abstract paintings inspired by Guston. However, he soon became unhappy with the subjective, autographic character of Abstract Expressionist brushwork and changed to an objective, impersonal manner of painting. Later on, he was to admire the work of the American painters Stuart Davis and Jasper Johns.

While at Bradford College of Art, David Hockney had painted urban landscapes influenced by the Euston Road and Kitchen Sink Schools.

11. Installation shot of *The New American Painting* exhibition at the Tate Gallery, 1959, with paintings by James Brooks (left and right) and Theodoros Stamos and Sam Francis (centre) visible.
Photo: courtesy of the Arts Council Archive, Hayward Gallery Library.

However, when he became a postgraduate student at the RCA in 1959, he flirted with abstraction. Years later he recalled:

> American Abstract Expressionism was the great influence. So I tried my hand at it, I did a few pictures, about twenty ... that were based on a kind of mixture of Alan Davie cum Jackson Pollock cum Roger Hilton. And I did them for a while, and then I couldn't. It was too barren for me.[45]

Peter Phillips, another RCA student who was to contribute to Pop during the 1960s, remembers:

> De Kooning was the biggest influence at that time because he was at least more Europeanised than the other Americans, so you had perhaps a little more contact with it. Everybody was trying to imitate de Kooning. You had your book of de Kooning open and you were painting your pictures.[46]

Barker, Caulfield, Hockney and Phillips can serve as examples of the power of major exhibitions and movements to alter the natural inclination of a student's work, if only for a short time. In the case of John Hoyland the impact of American art was more indelible: as an art student during the early 1950s he had produced gloomy townscapes of his native Sheffield but exposure to the colour-field paintings of Rothko at the Tate while he was a student at the Royal Academy Schools (1959–60) resulted in a permanent conversion to abstraction.

Art students located in the North found it more difficult to see London exhibitions, even though some made strenuous efforts to do so. During the late 1950s I was studying fine art at the Department of Art, Kings College, Newcastle-upon-Tyne, which was then part of Durham University. Determined to see *The New American Painting* show, I and a friend hitchhiked to London during a snowstorm. The next day we made straight for the Tate – the show was overwhelming in its impact.

At Newcastle the principal tutors were Victor Pasmore (1908–98) and Richard Hamilton. First year students were exposed to what was then the most advanced type of art education – the Basic Course/ Design – a series of exercises derived from the Bauhaus and Paul Klee designed to introduce students to the fundamental elements of visual art and design: colour, shape, line, form, structure, materials, techniques, etc. At that time Pasmore was probably Britain's leading abstract painter and Constructivist, while Hamilton was just beginning to make the Pop paintings for which he was later to become famous.

Constructivism, an international tendency which had its origins in the new art of revolutionary Russia, had its American exponents, for example, Charles Biederman, the maker of brightly coloured, abstract reliefs and author of the self-published text, *Art as the Evolution of Visual Knowledge* (Red Wing, Minnesota, 1948). Pasmore was impressed by Biederman's work and his personal interpretation of the history of art and urged students to read the book.

Although several Newcastle students were initially influenced by Pasmore, the advent of Pollock *et al.* upstaged him. To us it seemed that AE was fresher, bigger, more dynamic and organic, less geometric than Constructivism. Pasmore employed a craftsman to make thick wooden frames to enclose his reliefs. In comparison, the American paintings seemed vast, endless and semi-finished (therefore open-ended). The viewer was intended to stand close to their surfaces so that the all-over patterns of marks or fields of saturated hues engulfed his or her vision. Some had a quality of the sublime that European paintings lacked. The American artists' comments on art had a seriousness and profundity which was in marked contrast to the more prosaic remarks and dry theory emanating from British artists. The English critic David Sylvester interviewed several of the Americans and recordings were broadcast on BBC radio in the autumn of 1960. Statements by the artists also appeared in catalogues and magazines.

One puzzling aspect of Rothko's and Newman's remarks was their stress on the importance of subject matter. They argued that good painting could not be made about nothing and that the crucial subject matter was 'tragic and timeless', yet their colour-field paintings had been purged of figures, objects and narratives. One was left with a sense of enigma. The paintings seemed highly meaningful and yet it was hard to pin down any specific meanings in words. After a period of imitating the Americans it became clear to us that their styles could not simply be adopted in a slavish fashion. What the Americans had arrived at after decades of development could not be copied by British art students without a loss of integrity and authenticity. Our preoccupation then became: 'What comes after Action painting?'

12. John A. Walker, *Installation shot of paintings influenced by American art, final year show,* **1961, Art Department, Kings College (Durham University), Newcastle-upon-Tyne.**
Photo: John A. Walker.

During the 1950s it did not strike anyone as odd that the American painters were deliberately ignoring the industrial, urban, commercial dimensions of American society. Apart from the mass media-derived images of women in de Kooning's work – for instance, his 1954 painting *Marilyn Monroe*[47] – everything kitsch and vulgar was excluded. However, as we saw in Chapters 1 and 2, a small number of British artists and thinkers were collecting and looking at precisely this material in the late 1940s and early 1950s. What the AEs were leaving out became obvious when the various manifestations of British and American Pop art made their appearance in the late 1950s and early 1960s.

Nor did the overwhelmingly masculine nature of the art movement strike anyone as peculiar or unbalanced. Feminism, of course, had not yet happened. Grace Hartigan (b. 1922) was the only female painter included in the 1959 Tate show. For a time she had signed her pictures 'George Hartigan'. The fact that all the artists were white did not appear strange to anyone either. Again this was before the Civil Rights movement, which began in the 1950s, developed a high profile. Art historians have since noted that there were black artists close to the AEs – Norman Lewis for example – and a number of African-American painters had moved to Paris because there was less racial prejudice there.[48]

The Political Use of AE

Writing in retrospect, for a 1984 catalogue about 1950s' realism, Berger claimed that he had been right 'in believing that the hard sell of contemporary American art was politically motivated, and was one of the many chains of American cultural imperialism'.[49] As an art student I was ignorant of the link between art and politics, indeed I foolishly thought there was no connection between the two realms. In 1959 it never occurred to me or my friends that *The New American Painting* exhibition was a vehicle of Cold War propaganda. It was, of course, all the more effective for that very reason. Most British viewers did not think of it as overt propaganda for the system which, by implication, was preferable to the Soviet system. Even if we had known, it would not have made any difference because by that time we admired America and enjoyed its mass culture and subscribed to virtually the same set of values: individualism, freedom of expression, the free market in art, etc. In so far as we knew anything about art in the Soviet Union – and that was precious little – it seemed a dull, reactionary form of narrative figuration where there was no heroic risk-taking such as that associated with Action painting. (We did not even bother to visit the show of Russian and Soviet art held at the Royal Academy in 1959.)

The political machinations behind shows such as *The New American Painting* were only fully revealed in the 1970s as a result of research undertaken by Max Kozloff and Eva Cockcroft.[50] The argument of influential Americans such as Nelson Rockefeller, Porter A. McCray and Thomas Braden was that culture could be more effective than straight politics and that, for example, a privately-sponsored European tour by an American symphony orchestra would be far more successful in winning hearts and minds than a hundred speeches by the president. Consequently, the rich individuals who sat on the boards of museums or who funded CIA front organisations were willing to organise and finance travelling exhibitions of new American art. What was especially effective about such exhibitions was their inclusion of ex-left-wingers such as Pollock, of artists who could be regarded as critics of American society. The underlying rationale was: 'Look, in America, artists are independent beings who are free to do and say what they like, they are even free to be dissidents. That freedom gives rise to original, high quality art, whereas this is not possible in closed, regimented, communist societies. Consequently if you value art and culture then you must agree that the American, capitalist, liberal democratic, open society system is superior.' The reality of life for many black and poor Americans, and for communists during the McCarthyite years, did not of course correspond to the propagandist's image. This is one reason why abstract paintings were useful: they ignored harsh, social realities.

These kinds of propaganda activities were routed via private individuals and institutions because if they had been supported by official government organisations they would have been attacked by the rabid anti-communists in Congress. Right-wing congressmen such as George Dondero regarded abstract art – even when made by Americans – as 'Red art'! An earlier exhibition of American paintings – *Advancing American Art* (1946) – intended for travel abroad and funded by the State Department was recalled from Prague as a result of criticism from the media, conservative politicians and President Truman.[51] However, with the advent of Munsing and the USIS at the American Embassy in London, private propaganda initiatives began to be supplemented by State Department ones.

As David and Cecile Shapiro have pointed out, it was ironic 'that an apolitical art that arose in part as a reaction to didactic art, as an "art-for-art's sake" antidote to "art-as-a-weapon", should have become a prime political weapon'.[52] Of course, the artists concerned were also unaware of the uses to which their art was being put. Artists exercise power during the production process, but they have much less control over how their work is presented, distributed, contextualised, used and interpreted once it has left their studios.

Conclusion

There is no doubt that AE had a significant – some would say liberating and energising – impact upon the British art scene, and influenced many young painters (for example, Gillian Ayres, Trevor Bell, Magda Cordell, Robyn Denny, William Green, D. Hamilton-Fraser, John Hoyland, Albert Irwin, William Mills, Henry Mundy, Richard Smith, Aubrey Williams and Bryan Wynter). It also opened the way for the influx of American art movements that were to follow.

At the same time, it was not the kind of art that had much of an appeal outside the modernist fraction of the art world – only 14,000 people visited the 1959 Tate show. (The organisers of American art exhibitions for export fully realised that their target viewers were educated and cultivated Europeans, that working and lower middle-class Europeans would be content with American mass culture.) Most Britons did not like or appreciate abstract art – they still don't. However, some were willing to accept it when presented via textile and wallpaper designs. Harold Cohen, for example, designed a furnishing fabric for Heals in 1959 entitled *Vineyard* that was clearly indebted to Action painting and Tachisme. Lesley Jackson, in *The New Look: Design in the Fifties* (1991), identifies several more examples of the influence of Pollock and Francis on the decorative arts of Britain.[53]

The kind of painting which did have a wide appeal to the British was Pietro Annigoni's 1955 portrait of the young Queen Elizabeth II. (When displayed at the 1955 Royal Academy Summer Exhibition it was seen by 250,000 visitors.) Despite the fact that Annigoni was Italian, his royal portrait satisfied the conservative taste of the public. The main popular cultural event of the early 1950s was the 1953 coronation of Elizabeth II. The nation was optimistically informed this marked the beginning of 'a new Elizabethan age'. Annigoni's portrait was highly illusionistic, skilfully executed and provided excellent propaganda for the monarchy but it also exemplified the existence of a sycophantic, debased Renaissance tradition of art which was completely anti- or non-modernist and non-critical.

There was little or no market for a young British artist who decided to paint abstractions in the late 1950s. The fact that serious, established artists such as Pasmore and Hamilton had to teach to earn a living (the former until 1961, the latter until 1966), indicated the shortage of British patrons of contemporary art.

Furthermore, by the time AE was seen in its full glory in London (1959), it had passed its peak in New York and was being outmoded by the Neo-Dada/Assemblage works of Johns and Rauschenberg, the Happenings of Allan Kaprow, Jim Dine and others, and by Hard-Edge painting and Post-Painterly Abstraction. The relation of some of these movements to British art will require separate treatment.

Moreover, by 1960, the generation of RCA students consisting of Hockney, Derek Boshier, Pauline Boty, Allen Jones and Peter Phillips had ceased to flirt with abstraction and had committed themselves to representation. These students were to become famous as the Pop artists of the early 1960s. However, in certain instances initial pictorial mannerisms remained indebted to gestural painting and some of their iconography was derived from America.

During the mid-1960s two articles were published in Britain which summed up the impact of AE on British artists.[54] The first, Norbert Lynton's 'British Art and the New American Painting', was published in Cambridge Opinion in 1964. In it Lynton argued that the qualities of American painting which impressed British artists (he did not name individuals) were vigour, size, unorthodox techniques, plus certain qualities of colour, form, gesture and image. The second article, Alan Bowness's 'The American Invasion and the British Response', appeared in Studio International in 1967. Bowness followed Heron by distinguishing between three generations of British artists who, due to their different age profiles, had differential responses to AE: (1) The Older Painters (those over 45 in 1956: Bacon, Pasmore, etc.) who were little influenced because they were set in their ways; (2) The Middle Generation (those aged between 30 and 45 in 1956: Davie, Frost, Heron, Hilton, Wynter, etc.) who were influenced to some degree; and (3) Younger Painters (those under 30 in 1956: Denny, Smith, Green, Hoyland, etc.) who were influenced the most. Although this three-level model is rather pat, it remains a plausible account of what happened. By 1960, Bowness concluded, 'The British assimilation of the New American painting may be said to have been completed, and the turning away from Paris towards New York irrevocably accomplished.'

4 Abstraction and Pop in Britain During the 1960s

As the affluence of the United States and Britain increased during the 1960s, so the art worlds of both countries expanded: more galleries were opened and more exhibitions were mounted and dispatched across the Atlantic. The relation between British and American art became more fluid and complicated due to the increasing number of visits British and American artists paid to each other's countries and because the flow of information increased in volume. Furthermore, London became – during its mid-1960s' 'swinging' phase – an exciting cultural centre that began to rival New York. British culture – mainly in the popular sphere of rock music – also began to impact upon the United States and so, arguably, a more equal relationship developed in the 1960s than had pertained during the previous decade.

Throughout the 1960s exhibitions took place in London which were devoted to individual Abstract Expressionists: Rothko (Whitechapel, 1961), Tobey (Whitechapel, 1962), Guston (Whitechapel, 1963), Kline (Whitechapel, 1964), Gorky (Tate Gallery, 1965) and Motherwell (Whitechapel, 1966). These shows enabled British viewers who had seen the 1959 Tate survey to deepen their knowledge of some of its leading participants. However, they had to wait until a Tate show of 1972 to learn more about the art of Barnett Newman.

As already indicated, once the impact of Abstract Expressionism had been absorbed by British artists during the second half of the 1950s, the problem – for those who believed in a linear, progressive model of modern art – became 'What next?' Abstract Impressionism was one possibility floated by Alloway and Harold Cohen in 1958 but it had proved to be a dead end. For some young abstract painters on both sides of the Atlantic the answer seemed to be: keep the large scale and saturated colours but reduce the gestural characteristics of Action painting in order to make the colour-fields flatter and the shapes more geometric and hard-edge.

Some young British artists wished to distance themselves from the pastoral tradition of British painting – which they thought still lingered on in St Ives – in order to stress urban and environmental aspects. Richard Smith, speaking in New York in 1965, criticised his elders as follows:

> Somehow every generation has to make a clean sweep of the criteria of the generation before and this they [Davie, Frost, Heron, Hilton, Lanyon, and Scott] failed to do. For my time Abstract Expressionism was a clean sweep, but the generation over forty in England was still painting Cornish landscapes or pseudo-Braques ... Then they were swept up by the Abstract Expressionist revolution ... They were now painting freely painted paintings and imitating, rather weakly, as it were, the Americans.[1]

No doubt Heron would contest the accuracy of these remarks and accuse Smith of mouthing American propaganda, but Smith's remarks do reveal the state of mind of certain young artists in the late 1950s.

Place and *Situation*

Place was the title of an exhibition of paintings by Smith, Robyn Denny and Ralph Rumney which was held at the ICA in September 1959, seven months after the major Tate show of new American painting. The catalogue's text was written by Roger Coleman, a painter as well as a writer. The paintings displayed were large – 7' x 4', 7' x 6' – and abstract with simple shapes with firm edges, and areas of colour – red/green, black/white – rendered in a even manner. Unusually, the contributing artists collaborated closely on the conception, planning and overall design of the exhibit: individual paintings were produced according to certain common rules and then linked together in a free-standing, diagonal structure resembling a small maze. *Place* added to a short British tradition for collaborative exhibits. Previous examples were: *This is Tomorrow* (Whitechapel Gallery, 1956) and *An Exhibit I* and *II* (London and Newcastle-upon-Tyne, 1957–59), designed by Pasmore and Hamilton.

The basic idea of *Place* was to provide an 'environment' which would foster a new, game-like relationship between the paintings resting on the floor and the perambulating viewer. The latter was forced by the maze into a more intimate relationship with the paintings. The enveloping space typical of 'big canvas' Abstract Expressionist paintings was a specific point of departure. However, in a monograph on Denny published in 1971 David Thompson played down the American connection: 'The exhibition appeared to many people at the time to be American-inspired, although in fact it was about specifically British preoccupations (American painting was in no sense concerned to be communal) ...'[2]

The mass media were another point of departure even though no mass culture imagery was actually quoted; the media were cited as part of the mental and physical context within which contemporary artists lived. For instance, several British artists and critics were fascinated by the expanded spatial and aural experiences provided by American CinemaScope, Cinerama and 3-D movies plus stereophonic sound. These developments in cinematic technology – which Hamilton had lectured on in 1959 – were introduced by Hollywood studios in order to combat the increasing popularity of television. Hollywood hit back by offering viewers intense sensory experiences they could not find at home in front of 'the goggle box'.

Place was an ambitious project but in reality it supplied a rather tame aesthetic experience. Most reviews were unsympathetic. However, the show is historically significant for the intention of three British abstractionists to assert an urban-inspired as against a rural-inspired form of art, to push beyond the pictorial conventions of Abstract Expressionism and to move away from studio art towards a more public art that increased spectator participation.

Denny and Smith later contributed to two other London shows of contemporary abstract art: *Situation* (RBA Galleries, September 1960) and *New London Situation* (Marlborough New London Gallery, August 1961). The word 'situation' had been given currency by the French existentialist philosopher Sartre and it was also adopted in the late 1950s by the European, avant-garde, political radicals who called themselves 'Situationists'. The British painter Rumney and the British art historian T.J. Clark were Situationists for a time.

The first of these shows was, like *Place*, a self-help affair: it was organised by a committee consisting of six artists plus the critics Alloway and Coleman. The latter wrote the catalogue's introduction. Two of the requirements for inclusion were: (1) total abstraction achieved by direct execution (that is not worked up from sketches); (2) large size, (that is each work had to be no less than 30 square ft). As Coleman explained, since illusionistic depth was forbidden by the rule of flatness, pictorial space had to be extended horizontally and vertically in order to compensate. Further 'values' were listed and Coleman acknowledged that they

13. Robert Freeman, *Photo of Lawrence Alloway with Portrait*
of 'The Situation Group' (1961) painted by Sylvia Sleigh, **1961.**
Photo: reproduced courtesy of Robert Freeman and Sylvia Sleigh.
© ARS, New York and DACS, London 1998.

had been 'an outcome of the influence of the Americans', but he also
denied that the British artists were 'mere satellites of the Americans'.[3] In
Alloway's view, 'Freedom and confidence' had 'followed, grown out of, a
period of American dependence'.

Alloway was closely associated with the Situation 'group' although,
in fact, he denied there was a group as such. However, his wife Sylvia
Sleigh painted a group portrait of the 1961 artists in a traditional,
figurative manner. Much to Heron's disgust, Alloway was determined
to exclude any semi-abstract artists from St Ives because of their
lingering references to nature.

Many of the Situation artists had been dismayed by what they
regarded as the entrenched amateurism of the British art scene.[4]
Turnbull had visited New York in 1957 and had been impressed by the
tough professionalism of American artists who, for the most part,

rejected a bohemian lifestyle – some male artists even aped business-men by dressing in suits and ties. It was time for British artists to take their destiny into their own hands by means of collaboration and self-organisation instead of waiting for dealers or the arts establish-ment to recognise them.

The strategy worked because part two of Situation – *New London Situation* – was presented by a commercial, private gallery. Besides Denny, other participants included the painters Gillian Ayres, Bernard and Harold Cohen, Gordon House, John Hoyland, Henry Mundy, Peter Stroud, Turnbull and the sculptor Anthony Caro. Some of the painters still favoured a gestural style while others preferred a more geometric look with an anonymous finish.

A third show entitled *Situation* was mounted by the Arts Council and it toured Britain during 1962–63.

The work displayed in the three Situation shows was the British equivalent of what in America Greenberg called 'Post-Painterly Ab-straction', by which he meant mainly the canvases of Frankenthaler, Louis, Noland and Olitski. 'Modernist painting/sculpture' were other terms which were derived from Greenberg's important theoretical essay 'Modernist Painting' first published in 1960. Greenberg's reductive interpretation of the trajectory of modern art was to influence the thinking of many British artists during the 1960s but it provoked critical reactions too.

British viewers had the chance to see examples of Post-Painterly Abstraction early in the decade via the following shows: *Morris Louis* (ICA, May 1960); *New New York Scene* (Marlborough, New London Gallery, October 1961) which included works by Frankenthaler, Noland and Louis; *Kenneth Noland* (Kasmin, April 1963); *Jules Olitski* (Kasmin, April 1964); and *Helen Frankenthaler* (Kasmin, May 1964).

Greenberg was also in London during September 1963 dispensing advice to any British artists prepared to listen. He was in Britain again in November 1965 to chair the jury for the John Moores Liverpool Exhibition. The two other members of the jury were Heron and the critic John Russell. The top prizewinner that year was Michael Tyzack (b. 1933), with a painting called *Alesso 'B'*, an abstract in red, blue and green with a centralised, symmetrical, wedge-shaped form with wavy edges. The second and third prizes were also awarded to abstract painters. Given the composition of the jury, it was hardly surprising that formalist abstraction swept the board.

Hard-Edge Painting and Op Art

In the aftermath of Abstract Expressionism, some young American painters developed a cooler, more controlled type of abstraction. This became clear when examples of American Hard-Edge painting were seen in London via the shows: *West Coast Hard-Edge: Four Abstract Classicists* (ICA, March–April 1960) featuring works by Karl Benjamin, Lorser Feitelson, Frederick Hammersley and John McLaughlin; and *American Abstract Painters* (Tooth & Sons, January–February 1961) featuring Ellsworth Kelly, Alexander Liberman, Agnes Martin, Ad Reinhardt, Leon Smith and Sidney Wolfson. The catalogue introduction for the latter exhibition was written by Alloway.

Kelly (b. 1923), who had been producing this kind of abstract art for some time, and who had lived in Paris from 1948 to 1954, was given a one-man show in London by Tooth & Sons in May 1962. Denny had previously seen a huge Kelly entitled *New York No 1* (1957, Buffalo, Albright-Knox Gallery collection) at an American Embassy exhibition held in November 1958. Kelly's painting consisted of an abstracted version of the two capital letters 'N' and 'Y'. Denny too had been using interchangeable elements based on letters but seeing the Kelly encouraged him to be bolder – witness his *Austin Reed Mural* of 1959.[5]

Hard-Edge painting had stylistic affinities with the older, European tradition of geometric abstraction exemplified by such figures as Josef Albers, Max Bill, Robert and Sonia Delaunay, Piet Mondrian, and with the 'optical' art of Victor Vasarély (1908–97) which dated back to the 1930s and was designed to play havoc with the viewer's retinas. When Hard-Edge painters juxtaposed two areas of intense, complementary colours such as red and green, optical flicker would occur at the border between them. Thus there was an overlap between Hard-Edge and Op art.

Many Op art painters used black lines and patterns on white grounds to generate after-images and shimmering moiré effects. They also produced ambiguous spacial experiences via optical illusions borrowed from diagrams in psychology of perception textbooks. Vasarely held a one-man show at the Hanover Gallery, London, in October 1961, but his work also became known to British art students via well-illustrated books about him stocked by art school libraries. As explained in Chapter 2, an anticipation of 1960s' Op art was the 'perception' section of the 'Fun House' exhibit of the 1956 *This is Tomorrow* exhibition. Op art became fashionable around 1964 and

1965 both in Britain and the United States. Like Pop, it was a fine art phenomenon which appealed to people outside the art world and the style was taken up by fashion and graphic designers. Bridget Riley, Britain's best known practitioner, owed little to American art even though she had seen the 1956 Tate exhibition with its final room of Abstract Expressionists and she had once compared her conception of pictorial space to that of Pollock's. Furthermore, her 1961 painting *Kiss* was very similar to Kelly's Hard-Edge work of the late 1950s (compare *Kiss* to Kelly's 1959 *Rebound*). Riley's Op art will be discussed further in Chapter 7 in relation to its reception in America.

Anthony Caro, Greenberg, Noland and David Smith

British sculpture had achieved an international reputation during the period 1930–60 owing to the achievements of Moore, Hepworth, Reg Butler, Lynn Chadwick and others but, in the view of some younger sculptors, this kind of sculpture was limited by being rooted in humanist or figurative and British landscape traditions. A considera-tion of Caro's career will enable us to see how American abstract art facilitated a new beginning.

During the 1960s Caro (b. 1924) became established as the leading abstract, modernist sculptor in Britain. In the previous decade he had made rather lumpy, single figures modelled in clay and plaster for casting in bronze. He had also worked for a time as an assistant to Moore – an essential experience and career move for ambitious young British sculptors. However, to make his mark Caro needed to escape from being under the shadow of Moore and to break with representa-tion and conventional techniques. He did this by adopting the method of bolting and welding together ready-made pieces of metal – steel or aluminium – in order to produce open (rather than solid) abstract constructions. They were placed directly on the floor in order to eliminate the plinth or pedestal typical of traditional sculptures. To unify them he adopted the habit of painting them with a single colour. This dramatic change of direction was encouraged by Greenberg – who called it a 'breakthrough' – and by a trip Caro made to the United States.

During the 1950s Greenberg and Rosenberg had been the two most influential critical supporters of Abstract Expressionism. So powerful a critic did Greenberg become that several artists were willing to follow the advice he gave as to the future direction of their art. He was even prepared to make changes to an artist's work after his or her death when he thought he could improve it! (This happened in the case of the American sculptor David Smith.)

Greenberg came to Britain in July 1959, and after spending several days with Heron in Cornwall, he visited Caro's London studio. In 1978 Caro recalled:

> Greenberg was totally involved. He more or less told me my art wasn't up to the mark ... He spent all day with me talking about art and at the end of the day he had said a lot of things that I had not heard before. I had wanted him to see my work because I had never had a really good criticism of it, a really clear eye looking at it. A lot of what he said hit home, but he also left me with a great deal of hope. I had come to the end of a certain way of working; I didn't know where to go. He offered some sort of pointer.[6]

Greenberg's recollection of the meeting was as follows:

> I saw his stuff the first time in '59: it was quasi-expressionist, smallish figures, not monolithic figures. I said, is it good enough? And I *didn't* do some missionary work, but I said come over and look at David Smith. And when he came over he met Smith and he met Noland, and went back and *switched*. The first thing he did was *24 Hours*. He gave it to me and I sold it to the Tate [in 1975]. From then on he was on his own. He didn't need to come back here to look at Smith or anybody else.[7]

It was in November 1959 that Caro visited the United States and Mexico for three months with the financial help of a Ford/English-Speaking-Union travel grant. He met and talked with a number of American artists and critics including Smith, Noland, Olitski and, of course, Greenberg. Surprisingly, it was the painter Noland who impressed Caro most:

> Noland was my age. I saw one of his first target shows in New York and thought very highly of it. I liked him as a human being. I talked to him about art and life one night till six in the morning when his train left for Washington. Noland was an ordinary guy: his clothes, the way he talked, were not extravagant in any way, and yet he was also a very good artist ... Noland reaffirmed for me that you put your poetry or your feeling into your work, not into your lifestyle.[8]

The bright colours Caro experienced in the stained canvases of Noland and Louis surely influenced his decision to paint his sculptures with similar shades. The effect of colouration was to reduce the sculptures' tangibility and tactility, and to increase their opticality; in other words to bring sculpture closer to the condition of painting.

Alloway interviewed Caro in 1961 and asked him: 'Did your visit to America in autumn 1959 affect your style change?' Caro replied:

> Before I went to America my work was changing ... America was certainly the catalyst in the change. For one thing I realised that I had nothing to lose by throwing out History – here we were all steeped in it anyway. There's a fine art quality about European art even when it's made of junk. America made me see there are no barriers and no regulations – they simply aren't bound to traditional or conventional solutions in their art ... There's a tremendous freedom in knowing that your only limitations in a sculpture or painting (are) whether it carries its intention or not, not whether it's Art.[9]

14. Anthony Caro, *24 Hours*, 1960.
Steel painted brown and black, 137.2 x 223.5 x 83.8 cm.
London: Tate Gallery collection. Photo: John Goldblatt.

24 Hours, Caro's first abstract sculpture made from steel sheets with the aid of a gas cutter and welder, was bolted together in his garage in Hampstead in March 1960. The cramped space meant that he had to construct the sculpture close to, a manner of working similar to Noland's. The sculpture consists of three different shapes arranged in parallel to one another. The second shape, a disc with a ring at its centre, clearly evokes Noland's target paintings. When finished, the sculpture was coated with dark oak and black household paints. Like so much American art of the period, *24 Hours* is characterised by flatness, frontality and simplicity.[10]

David Smith, the sculptor championed by Greenberg, made constructions from welded metal which he also coated with strong colours. Caro knew his work from photographs and saw a few pieces in New York but he claims it was not until October 1963, when he visited Smith's mountain retreat and workshop – Bolton Landing farm in the Adirondacks, upstate New York – and saw about 80 works standing in a field that he was particularly taken by the sculpture's 'character, personal expressiveness, delicacy of touch ... immense sculptural intelligence!'[11]

From October 1963 until July 1964 Caro taught – with his fellow Englishman and painter Peter Stroud – for two semesters at Bennington College, Vermont. (After Alloway's teaching stint at Bennington, the college became a haven for British artists.) Olitski was also on the staff and Noland was living nearby. In 1964 Caro held his first one-man exhibition in New York at the André Emmerich Gallery. The following year he taught again at Bennington from March to June. In 1965 Smith was killed at the age of 59 in a truck crash close to Noland's house. According to Richard Whelan, Caro subsequently acquired 'a sizable portion of Smith's stockpile of steel forms'.[12]

Regarding the relationship between Caro and Smith, Greenberg wrote in 1965:

> He [Caro] is the only new sculptor whose sustained quality can bear comparison with Smith's ... Caro is also the first sculptor to digest Smith's ideas instead of merely borrowing them. Precisely by deriving from Smith he has been the better able to establish his own individuality.[13]

Caro was later to state that his sculpture had not been influenced by Smith in the early 1960s because he had, in fact, been trying to do something different. Nevertheless, it is clear from Greenberg's remarks that he regarded Caro as Smith's artistic heir, as the artist who would continue and develop Smith's type of constructed, metal sculpture.

In 1963 a survey of Caro's work was mounted by the Whitechapel. The show's catalogue essay was written by Michael Fried, a young American critic who was one of Greenberg's disciples. Fried duly paid homage to his mentor in the essay and gave a summary of Greenberg's Modernist painting theory.

Peter Fuller, the trenchant British art critic writing about this show over two decades later observed caustically: 'Caro's work was nothing if not of its time: it reflected the superficial, synthetic, urban commercial, American values which dominated the 1960s.'[14] On another occasion he declared that Caro's sculptures were merely illustrations of Greenberg's ideas.

During the early 1960s Caro taught part time at St Martin's School of Art in London and therefore his work and ideas inspired a number of British art students, especially those exhibiting in *The New Generation* sculpture show held at the Whitechapel in 1965. Five of the nine participants had been taught by, or had taught with, Caro at St Martin's. This exhibition was sponsored by an arts foundation established by the Peter Stuyvesant company, a Dutch cigarette manufacturer, which also supplied travel bursaries to enable selected artists to visit the United States.

Earlier, in September 1963, Greenberg had been invited to London by the St Martin's' sculptors Annesley, Bolus, King, Scott, Wall and Tucker who wanted to benefit from his critical expertise. The critic's airfare had been raised by each of the artists contributing a share.[15]

While in London Greenberg was the guest of Sheridan Blackwood, the fifth Marquess of Dufferin and Ava, who was the business partner of John Kasmin, the art dealer. Kasmin had opened a gallery at 118 New Bond Street devoted to new, avant-garde British and American art in April 1963 with a show of the target-motif, stain-paintings of Kenneth Noland, the American artist Caro respected so much. Through Kasmin, Greenberg also visited the painter brothers, Bernard and Harold Cohen. The importance of such art world networks is self-evident.

Caro's mid-1960s international reputation was due in considerable measure to the sense of new possibilities and freedom he had gained from his exposure to America and contemporary American art, as well as the critical endorsement of the American writers Greenberg and Fried and the backing of the New York dealer Emmerich.

Not all of Greenberg's relationships with British artists were as harmonious and productive as the one between him and Caro. For example, Heron refused to follow Greenberg's advice and, as we shall see in Chapter 7, the relationship between Greenberg and John Latham was to prove abrasive.

British Pop in the 1960s

Although Situation-style abstractions and Modernist sculptures were purchased by a few private and corporate collectors and museums, and received some critical acclaim, these forms of art were not exactly popular outside the art world. Pop art was more accessible and had a wider appeal because it was representational, anecdotal and contained mass culture iconography familiar to millions. Art historians identify three different generations of British Pop artists: (1) Blake, Hamilton and Paolozzi; (2) Richard Smith and Joe Tilson; and (3), Boshier, Hockney, *et al.*

While Pop was emerging in Britain, in the United States the Neo-Dada art of Johns and Rauschenberg, with its use of mass culture icons and media imagery, was being produced. During the late 1950s, Neo-Dada was known in Britain through illustrations in books and magazines rather than in terms of exhibitions.[16] American Pop art only became visible in New York's galleries in 1962, the year which is generally deemed to mark the end of the influence of Abstract Expressionism. British Pop had developed before and independently of American Pop, thus it was already in existence when exhibitions of the latter began to arrive in Britain.[17] In the main, British Pop artists learnt about their American counterparts when they paid visits to New York and Los Angeles, and when they met American Pop artists in London.

This Chapter examines works of art depicting American subjects produced during the 1960s by two senior British Pop artists – Hamilton and Blake – and by four younger Pop painters – Boshier, Boty, Hockney and Phillips – who had trained at the RCA, as well as certain Pop sculptures by Clive Barker. Richard Smith's work will be considered later.

Hamilton and Blake

Throughout the 1960s American themes obsessed Hamilton: witness his paintings *Pin-Up* and *Glorious Technicultura* (1961), *AAH!* (1962), the series *Towards a Definitive Statement on the Coming Trends in Men's Wear and Accessories* (1962–63), *Portrait of Hugh Gaitskell as a Famous Monster of Filmland* (1964), *Interior 1* (1964), *My Marilyn* (1965) and *I'm Dreaming of a White Christmas* (1967). Thus Hamilton's American iconography included car styling, a jukebox, the New York cityscape, horror films, *Playboy*-type pin-ups, American menswear, football and space helmets, Charlton Heston, President Kennedy, Marilyn Monroe, Bing Crosby and film-still interiors from several Hollywood movies.

When Americans like Munsing first saw Hamilton's early Pop paintings, they thought he was mocking America, but the artist denied this was his intention. His first, deliberately satirical work was the 1964 'portrait' of the British Labour Party leader Hugh Gaitskell, whose policies Hamilton, a Party member, disagreed with. In this instance American movie horror imagery – primarily Claude Rains made-up for his role in *Phantom of the Opera* (USA, 1943) – was applied to a British politician as an act of criticism.

For many years Hamilton habitually wore American-style clothing. Like Peter Blake, he favoured light blue jeans and a jacket of the same material, with a pair of sneakers. His desire to identify with American sports stars and astronauts was demonstrated by a magazine cover he produced with the help of the photographer Robert Freeman and the

15. Richard Hamilton (art director), *Cover of Living Arts (2),* **1963.**
Photo: Robert Freeman, reproduced courtesy of R. Hamilton.

stylist Betsy Schermer which, in effect, contended that people can live out their fantasies with the help of appropriate clothes and accessories. In 1963 the ICA's magazine *Living Arts* published its second issue, which contained Hamilton's 'Urbane Image' article. On the magazine's cover was an oblong, colour photograph taken by Freeman from a high vantage point. It was a 'wraparound' in the sense that it filled both front and back covers.

Hamilton wore an American football uniform and helmet borrowed from the Pan Pacific Company and the American High School (even though his physique was that of a thin, puny Englishman) while straddling the bonnet of an open-topped 1963 Ford Thunderbird. Across the extended boot of the car was draped a female model – Jenny Freeth – dressed only in lingerie supplied by Silhouette Corsets. Scattered on a pink sheet around the car were various props and products: a NASA Mercury space capsule borrowed from the Shepperton Film Studio set of a James Bond movie, a refrigerator crammed with food, a typewriter, a telephone, a toaster, a Hoover Constellation vacuum cleaner and a combined record player and radio called 'The Wondergram' which, one gathers from a record sleeve, is playing a Gene Vincent hit. Hamilton holds up a football in one hand as if in triumph.

Clearly, this staged photo was a sustained attempt to emulate the type of American advertising that Hamilton had been admiring and using for years. It was a valiant effort but, in my view, it does not finally convince. The British cultural historian David Mellor has noted Hamilton's 'Americanophilia' and has characterised the scene captured in Freeman's photo as 'a comic tableau', an elegant 'burlesque'.[18]

Hamilton's 'Urbane Image' article discussed and illustrated several of his Pop paintings, including the series on forthcoming trends in menswear. In places Hamilton's writing matched the extravagant prose typical of advertising copy in fashion magazines:

> We live in an era in which the epic is realised. Dream is compounded with action. Poetry is lived by an heroic technology. Any one of a whole range of hard, handsome, mature heroes like Glenn, Titov, Kennedy, Cary Grant, can match the deeds of Theseus and look as good, menswearwise.

This statement could serve as a programme for the *Living Arts* cover photo.

In contrast to Hamilton, Blake's approach to popular culture was non-intellectual and was developed apart from the Independent Group.

Blake tended to paint people – wrestlers, tattooed women, film and Pop music stars – who gave him personal pleasure. He was attracted to such examples of English folk culture as the circus, commercial lettering, funfair heraldry, music and boxing halls, toy shop windows and female pin-ups rather than to the sophisticated advertising produced by Madison Avenue agencies.

Blake was born in Dartford, Kent, in 1932 and he studied graphic design at Gravesend before attending the RCA Painting School from 1953 to 1956. His friends at the RCA included Smith and Tilson. During the 1950s Blake's iconography was predominantly British in origin. When, in 1954, he painted comics, it was the wholesome British children's weekly the *Eagle* that he depicted, not an American comic book aimed at teenagers and adults. However, in *Litter* (1955) there is part of a *Captain Marvel* comic book and in *On the Balcony* (1955–57) a copy of *Life* magazine appears.

Since the vast majority of Blake's paintings were figurative, Abstract Expressionism had no appeal for him. However, he did respect and was influenced by certain American realists, such as, Bernard Perlin (the Tate Gallery possessed one of his pictures), Ben Shahn, Honore Sharrer and Andrew Wyeth. Paintings by the latter three were featured in the 1956 Tate show of modern American art which Blake had visited.

Much of Blake's work has a graphic or illustrational look and is an uneasy blend of academic and modern characteristics. It relies upon detailed, precise drawing and a painstaking technique of painting – at first in oils and then in acrylic – colouring in and building up the image in thin layers. Nevertheless, there are some signs of modernism: leaving certain passages unfinished; copying photographs or collaging them on to the surface; painting people and things head on so that they parallel the picture plane; combining representational images with abstract, heraldic-type designs. When Blake used mass culture imagery he did not simulate their graphic style as Roy Lichtenstein was to do later. Either he presented material such as photographs unchanged or he rendered them in his 'realist' manner.

When, in the late 1950s, Blake began to attach photographs of film and Pop music stars directly to hardboard sheets and wooden doors, this new development was due to the influence of the 'combine' constructions of Johns and Rauschenberg. At first, Blake only knew their work through reproductions. His 1961 collage *The First Real Target?*, which features an archery target, was clearly a belated, humorous riposte to Johns's target paintings of 1955. Similarly, his diagonal stripes in alternating colours were derived from a 1958 catalogue illustration of a sculpture by the American artist H.C. Westermann.[19]

American subjects became pre-eminent in Blake's oeuvre between 1959 and 1964. They included: the Hollywood movie stars Jean Harlow, Kim Novak and Tuesday Weld; the singers Elvis Presley, Sammy Davis Junior, Ricky Nelson and Frank Sinatra; the black performers Bo Diddley and La Vern Baker; the Pop music groups the Beach Boys and the Lettermen; and the duo, the Everly Brothers. (In the 1960s Blake actually met and became friends with the Everly Brothers and later made family visits to Don Everly's home in Nashville.) Blake greeted the arrival of American rock'n'roll in Britain during the mid-1950s with enthusiasm and bought Chuck Berry records in Portobello Road market. Blake would often borrow his images of rock performers directly from record sleeve photographs – witness *The Lettermen* (1963) and *Bo Diddley* (1963) – and he would shortly be designing record covers.

Blake had populist ambitions: by painting such mass media icons as the Beatles he hoped to appeal to the same audiences that they reached. While his paintings could not really achieve this aim because of their expense, restricted number and mode of distribution, his design for the

16. Peter Blake, *The Lettermen*, 1963.
Oil on hardboard, 124.5 x 185.4 cm. Kingston-upon-Hull: Ferens Art Gallery collection. Photo: courtesy of Hull City Museums, Art Gallery and Archives.
© Peter Blake 1998. All rights reserved DACS.

Beatles' *Sergeant Pepper* album (1967), undertaken with his wife Jann Haworth, did.

Girls with their Hero, (1959–62) deals with the cult of Elvis Presley. The word 'Elvis' appears amidst over a dozen different images of him quoted from photographs. Three excited female fans shown in the top, left-hand corner want to capture and possess him but they have to make do with media surrogates and merchandise – records and still photographs – because although Presley was in Europe while serving in the American army stationed in Germany, he never performed live in Britain.

The theme of fandom and collecting is also evident in Blake's prizewinning *Self-Portrait with Badges* (1961) in which he appears in a blue denim outfit (and sneakers) adorned with Elvis badges. Incongruously, Blake stands in a damp English garden holding an Elvis fanzine. The contrast between this static self-portrait rendered in a fussy, academic style and the energy and sexuality of one of Presley's early live performances could not be more striking. In spite of the paintings devoted to Presley, Blake later confessed that he did not really like him.

In the 1960s most Pop artists produced works about Marilyn Monroe. Blake's affection for her has lasted until the 1990s: in 1991 he presented a series of works – including one entitled *Shrine to Marilyn* (a collage of photos and magazines above a mantelpiece with objects) – at the Waddington Gallery stand, International Art Fair, Olympia.

As Ken Russell's imaginative documentary *Pop Goes the Easel* (a black-and-white film made for the BBC television arts strand *Monitor*, transmitted in March 1962) revealed, Blake was friendly with several RCA students younger than himself, such as Boshier, Boty and Phillips, even though he was no longer a student there himself, having left in 1956.

The RCA Pop Painters

Derek Boshier (b. 1937) was a fan of rock'n'roll during the early 1960s, but it entered his work only as a minor theme. In 1962 he made graphite drawings celebrating the music and stardom of Bill Haley and in the same year he painted *I Wonder What My Heroes Think of the Space Race* which featured two Americans who had suffered tragic, violent deaths: President Lincoln and Buddy Holly. The latter, lead singer and guitarist of the Crickets, had been killed in a plane crash in February 1959. This work – executed in a loose, semi-abstract, painterly style – included images of American rocket launches and astronauts in their space suits. Since it also included references to the Soviet space programme, it dramatised the fierce competition between the two superpowers for the mastery of space. While the painting was being created in 1961, Yuri Gagarin of the USSR and Sam Shepherd of the US had orbited the Earth.

In *Rethinking, Re-Entry* (1962) an American Atlas ICBM climbs from North America – which is curiously still a British colony – until it crashes into the Pacific. Its tube-like exhaust trail contains jigsaw puzzle pieces which metamorphose into naked humanoids which are sucked along and then spewed out. The implication is that American, space-age technology is likely to end in disaster. The image of a falling or free-floating man, which appears in many of Boshier's pictures, was derived from one of William Blake's watercolours. For Boshier, the figure was symbolic of Everyman and the idea of liberty.

Boshier was more politically conscious and critical than Peter Blake. He read books by such American writers as Marshall McLuhan (*The Mechanical Bride*, [1951]), Vance Packard (*The Hidden Persuaders* [1957] and *The Status Seekers* [1960]), John Galbraith (*The Affluent Society* [1958]) and Daniel Boorstin (*The Image*, [1962]), which contained critiques of American mass culture and society. Several of Boshier's paintings dealt with Signal toothpaste which had coloured stripes in it – a marketing gimmick of the period – which Boshier made use of as emblematic of the way in which advertising was increasingly conditioning and controlling the behaviour of consumers. *So Ad Men became Depth Men* (1962) refers specifically to Packard's critique of American advertising in his bestseller, *The Hidden Persuaders*.

In the Russell documentary Boshier explained that he used American imagery taken from newspapers, magazines and cornflake packets not because he was in love with them, but because of their 'symbolic meaning', because he had become aware that Americanisation had 'crept into the social life' of Britain. Boshier was thus one of the few British artists who employed the art of painting in order to explore the phenomena of American power and the process of Americanisation. For example, in *Situation in Cuba* the American-backed attempt to invade Cuba in April 1961 was criticised, as was American cultural imperialism in *Pepsi-Culture* (1961) in which the Union Jack flag is cornered by two Pepsi-Cola bottle tops. At the top of *England's Glory* (1961), an English matchbox is being invaded by the Stars and Stripes.

**17. Tony Evans, *Portrait of Derek Boshier with his painting
'England's Glory'* (1961), first published in the Grabowski Gallery
Image in Revolt catalogue of 1962.**
Photo: courtesy of Caroline Edwards and
the Timelapse Library Ltd, Recloses, France.

For a while in the mid-1960s Boshier became a completely abstract artist making brightly coloured, shaped canvases. A strong influence on this change of direction were the 'chevron' paintings by the American Kenneth Noland which Boshier saw in Paris on his way back to Britain after a year-long stay in India. In spite of his reservations about America, he eventually ended up living there.[20]

Pauline Boty (1938–66) came from a middle-class, suburban family background (her father was a Surrey accountant) and she trained as a designer of stained glass at Wimbledon School of Art during the mid-1950s. As a student she enjoyed American pop culture: she wore 501 jeans and jived to Buddy Holly's hit records. In 1959 she moved to the RCA which was then very much a male-dominated institution. It proved difficult, therefore, for Boty to gain recognition as a Pop artist particularly since Pop was 'virile' and included so many representations of women as sex objects.

18. Pauline Boty, *It's a Man's World I*, 1964.
Oil on canvas with collage, 91 x122 cm. Private collection.
Photo: courtesy of John Boty and the Women's Art Library, London.

By 1961 Boty was making Surrealist-style collages and abstract paintings with rainbow-like bands of colour inspired by the patterns and rhythms of 1930s' Hollywood musicals. Two years later her iconography had expanded to include images of Elvis Presley, American bomber aircraft and pilots, the boxer Cassius Clay, the Chicago mobster Big Jim Colosimo, the movie star Marilyn Monroe, as well as the shooting of President Kennedy in Dallas, all transcribed from photographs. Boty often employed a photo-spread mode of composition in which the appropriated American images were juxtaposed against a range of other images derived from Cuba, Europe, history, etc., in order to make feminist (even before the emergence of a feminist discourse about art) and political points; see, for example, *It's A Man's World I* (1963) which includes portraits of the Beatles, Einstein, Lenin and Proust as well as American male heroes. This depiction of patriarchical power and achievement includes a red rose, the conventional symbol of love; Boty, the proto-feminist, still liked men.

Sue Watling, a Boty expert, reports that Boty was a great fan of American movies, especially 1950s' Westerns and that she strongly identified with Monroe, the actress who seemed to have everything but who experienced so much unhappiness in her private life.[21] Boty played Marilyn in RCA reviews, painted her – *The Most Beautiful Blonde in the World* (1964) – and collaged her image. Like so many others, Boty was devastated by Marilyn's death from an overdose of sleeping pills in 1962.

Boty never travelled to the United States, though she did once meet Bob Dylan. Her husband Clive Goodwin, however, visited Cuba and Watling suggests that this may have influenced Boty's reference to that communist thorn in America's side. Boty had a social conscience and a political and environmental awareness: she was concerned about events in America and she worried that the right-wing Senator Barry Goldwater might win the Presidential election of 1964.[22] In *Countdown to Violence* she depicted American police using dogs on civil rights protesters, Vietnam monks burning themselves to death, and the presidential cortege.

Because of her beauty and vivacity, Boty appeared on television chat shows and had opportunities to act on stage and in movies. But due to her tragically early death from leukaemia in 1966 at the age of 28, she was prevented from fulfilling her early promise as an artist, stage designer and actress.

Peter Phillips (b. 1939) hailed from the industrial city of Birmingham and trained initially as a commercial artist. Throughout his career Phillips has manifested a special interest in the materials and techniques of painting, and the methods of image-transfer, used by sign painters and illustrators.

America loomed large from his earliest years: during his childhood an aunt sent him *Superman* and *Captain Marvel* comics and at children's matinees in local cinemas Bowery Boy movies made him curious about the reality of the United States.[23]

While studying at the Birmingham College of Art and Crafts in the mid-1950s Phillips tried his hand at social realism, but when he moved to London and the RCA in 1959 he discovered that abstraction was in

19. Peter Phillips, *Motorpsycho/Tiger*, 1961–62.
Oil on canvas with lacquered wood, 206 x 152.5 cm.
London: private collection. Photo: reproduced courtesy of the artist.

vogue. He flirted with Abstract Expressionism for a brief period but, because he disliked drips and really preferred 'neat, clear-cut' images with smooth surfaces comparable to those of glossy magazines, he soon returned to a highly controlled, impersonal type of representation. Even so, American abstract art left its mark in terms of an increase in the size of canvases and a greater boldness in the presentation of content. Also, abstract designs and patterns – five-pointed stars, stripes, chevrons, diamond shapes – were to be included alongside images borrowed from magazines such as *Hot Rod Yearbook, Life* and *Playboy*.

Phillips composed his pictures according to the deliberate methods of montage or collage rather than the improvisation typical of Action painting. However, the selection and placing of images was to some degree intuitive so the meaning of the juxtapositions was often enigmatic or plural and indeterminate; therefore it is hard to discern what comment, if any, Phillips was making about the admass society.

His Pop paintings certainly reflected his teenage passions for popular culture in the raw which was both American and European: Monroe and Bardot (two mass media portraits which were collaged directly to the support), American Indian chiefs and the Phillips bicycle company emblem, an American football player and the Union Jack, Jackson Pollock and a beautiful woman from a German magazine; targets that simultaneously evoked Johns's 1955 paintings and air rifle ranges found in British funfairs. Johns and Rauschenberg, whose work Phillips knew through reproductions, were an important influence. In 1976 he told Marco Livingstone:

> I had a girlfriend who went to New York, who lived there and who used to get a lot of stuff sent to me, I was incredibly impressed by Johns' and Rauschenberg's ways of working.[24]

In Russell's documentary Phillips is shown enjoying a lift in an American car driven by a black male hipster. Phillips' blonde girlfriend is also filmed playing a pinball machine inside their West London flat. Magazines with illustrations of monsters are shown to indicate the source of one of his picture's imagery.

At first glance Phillips's pictures appear to celebrate popular culture but, as Livingstone has pointed out, many of his paintings are rather menacing. *Motorpsycho/Tiger* (1961–62), for example, features a sinister figure resembling an American football player: his crash-helmeted head is tiny compared to his arms and chest; the latter is emblazoned with a snarling tiger's head; beneath – at the level of his genitals – are the innards of the bike's machinery rendered diagrammatically and below that an abstract, chevron-shaped border painted in a Hard-Edge manner. During the 1950s the male British enthusiasm for riding motorbikes at high speed – the so-called 'ton up boys' – was shared by many Americans, as was evidenced by the 1954 film *The Wild One* starring Marlon Brando as a motorcycle gangleader. (In 1962 Brando was to appear in Phillips's drawing *Star Players*.)

Such images were normally contained within diagrammatic or game-like formats derived from playing cards, board games, slot and pinball machines, jukeboxes and strip club spy holes. As in the case of Allen Jones, Phillips delighted in the heterosexual cult of the pin-up. His 1963 painting *Gravy for the Navy* employed a drawing by Alberto Vargas, the famed American illustrator of erotic female flesh, which had been published in *Esquire* magazine. When Jones visited Los Angeles in 1966 he made a special point of visiting Vargas.

In one of the first books about Pop art, Mario Amaya argued that Phillips, in spite of his American references, 'remained basically European in his sense of space composition. Unlike Americans who open up their canvases, he uses a crowded space, exquisitely organised and carefully manipulated so that it can easily contain the many objects he integrates into a formal pattern.'[25] In fact, the presentation of pictorial content via a series of compartments resembling a pinboard crowded with images, or a comic/magazine/ newspaper layout, was common to all four artists featured in Russell's documentary. R.B. Kitaj, the American studying at the RCA at the same time as the British Pop artists, may well have been an influence in this regard because his early pictures were often compartmentalised. (Rauschenberg and James Rosenquist were two other American artists who employed a similar compositional strategy, although on a much larger scale and in a much bolder fashion.) In Phillips's case there were European sources too: the work of Fernand Léger and even the compartmented Christian pictures by early Renaissance masters such as Cimabue and Giotto.

During the mid-1960s Phillips spent some time in America. The work he produced there will be discussed shortly. Although Phillips moved to Zurich in 1966 (he currently lives in Spain), his late 1960s' and 1970s' paintings – large, oblong pictures featuring a dynamic assembly of airbrushed, *trompe-l'oeil*, overlapping images – continued to mine American sources. There were diagrams from *Scientific*

American, illustrations from John Audubon's *Birds of America* and images of Plymouth automobiles. Elvis Presley also appeared in the photo-realist work *Mosaikbild 6 X 12* (1974), consisting of 72 panels arranged in a grid. Titles which include expressions like 'Select-O-Mat' and 'Art-O-Matic' evoke American consumerism and these paintings are also American in their aggressive, kitsch-like quality.

This text has foregrounded Phillips's interest in America but he has summed up his attitude to the material culture of the United States as follows:

> I've never been analytical about American things. I like American things, but I also like Japanese things, I like French things, I like Swiss things. American cars possibly I liked more, simply because of their greater baroqueness; they just had more interesting things to paint in them than stylised Italian cars.[26]

In 1965 he also played down the national character of painting when he remarked:

> In the final analysis it's not going to matter much whether it's American, English or French ... Good painting is going to triumph over any sort of nationalism.[27]

One of Boshier's friends at the RCA was David Hockney (b. 1937). Hockney grew up in the northern industrial town of Bradford. He later told Melvyn Bragg how important the American movies he saw there were to him.[28] The strong shadows typical of Hollywood films caught his attention and he drew the conclusion that America, unlike Yorkshire, was a land of bright sunshine. After studying at Bradford College of Art, Hockney attended the RCA as a postgraduate from 1959 to 1962. During Hockney's Pop phase at the RCA his iconography mainly derived from his personal life (homosexual desires and love affairs) and British mass culture (Cliff Richard, Typhoo tea packets). His improvisational brushwork and unfinished painting style did owe something to American gestural painting but also to the work of Francis Bacon, Jean Dubuffet and lavatory graffiti. Kitaj, an older American student, gave Hockney valuable advice and encouraged him to paint subjects from his lived experience and personal convictions. Another American artist who was to influence Hockney in the early 1960s was Larry Rivers.

20. *David Hockney with 'Life Painting for a Diploma' 1962.*
Oil on canvas, 122 x 91 cm. Collection of the artist.
This photo first appeared in *Town,* Vol. 3, No. 9 (September 1962).

Apart from the short period when he emulated the Abstract
Expressionists, Hockney's main American references while at the RCA
were: the poems of Walt Whitman (a nineteenth century homosexual
writer), the Cha-Cha dance craze and images from *Physique Pictorial,* a
magazine published in Los Angeles by Bob Mizer featuring naked
young men enjoying an erotic, hedonistic lifestyle. The word 'physique'
appears in Hockney's *Life Painting for a Diploma* (1962) which also
depicts a skeleton and a muscleman. In addition, his painting
Domestic Scene, Los Angeles (1963) – a shower scene showing two
male nudes seen in profile – was inspired by photographs in *Physique
Pictorial.* This work was produced before Hockney had been to LA. (In

this respect Hockney was following a precedent established by Edward Burra.)[29] It was this aspect of America that was to draw Hockney to the West Coast in January 1964. California, it appeared to Hockney, was more relaxed about homosexuality than Britain with its repressed attitude to anyone who deviated from 'normal' sexual behaviour. The laws against the 'crime' of adult homosexuality in Britain were only repealed – following the Wolfenden Report recommendations of 1957–60 – in the late 1960s.

Hockney first paid a visit to New York in 1961 while still a student. This and his other trips to the United States will be described in detail shortly.

Pop Sculpture: the Work of Clive Barker

During the 1960s Barker became noted as a Pop/Surrealist sculptor producing objects covered with black leather or made from shiny metal representing such things as zips, a paintbox, false teeth and van Gogh's chair and sunflowers.[30] A number of Barker's sculptures have been about art or have been acts of homage to the work of other artists.

Barker was born in Luton in 1940 and studied at Luton College of Technology and Art from 1957 to 1959. Finding the sculpture tutor unsympathetic, he concentrated on painting. Tuition was provided by the abstractionist John Plumb.

Barker's father was employed by Vauxhall Motors and after cutting short his art school education Clive himself worked there for a while on the assembly line. It was during this industrial experience that Barker was attracted by the leather upholstery and chrome-plated metal of new cars. Barker moved to London in 1961 and became friends with Alloway, Francis Bacon, Peter Blake and Richard Smith.

Although Barker enjoyed American mass culture and admired the design of American cars, American Pop art was not an influence during the early 1960s. However, as a result of exhibiting at the Robert Fraser Gallery, he came into contact with three American Pop artists: Jim Dine, Jann Haworth and Claes Oldenburg.

Like Warhol and several other American Pop artists, Barker was impressed by the design and form of the Coca-Cola bottle and made several Coke bottle sculptures, some with straws, for example, *Three Cokes* (1969). As a child Barker had watched many American crime movies and Westerns; during the 1960s he was to have lunch in London with Marlon

Brando who had directed and starred in *One Eyed Jacks* (1961). Such Westerns later inspired Barker to produce chrome-plated bronze sculptures of cowboy boots, decorated with fancy leatherwork, and spurs – for instance, *Rio – Homage to Marlon Brando* (1969).

Most of Barker's work stems from his lived experience in Britain and his interest in the work of European artists such as Bacon, Magritte, Morandi, Soutine and van Gogh. Even so, during the 1960s, several sculptures employed American mass culture iconography or were homages to the work of American artists and in 1971 he made a series of drawings that were direct responses to a first-hand experience of the vast expanse of the United States. Barker's gleaming sculptures of common objects can also be regarded as anticipations of the early work of Jeff Koons, the American master of kitsch art; such as, for instance, Koons' stainless steel *Rabbit* of 1986.

Conclusion

Some art historians have used the American terminology 'uptown' and 'downtown' to distinguish between two varieties of Pop. The former refers to the more highbrow Pop art associated with erstwhile members of the Independent Group such as Hamilton, while the latter refers to the more vulgar, lower-class work of the RCA Pop artists. Certainly, it would seem that the RCA group, being younger than the IG members, had a more immediate and immersive relation with mass culture, particularly the one emanating from the United States. Yet, as we have seen, Boshier was conscious of the process of Americanisation and documented it. This matter was also addressed by the British mass media, for example in the *Sunday Times* Colour Section thematic issue of 1962 which asked: 'How American are We?'[31]

Joe Tilson (b. 1928), a student at the RCA from 1952 to 1955, and a minor contributor to the Pop art movement, has stressed the need to distinguish between the art students' fascination with America and the precise way in which that interest inflected their work:

> It's easy to get this period terribly wrong. There are two quite distinct things you have to trace. The first is the interest in Americana and American culture generally. The second is when it's used, and who it's used by. The first thing is easy ... most of us grew up with that culture, it was Peter Blake's, Richard Smith's and Robyn Denny's basic cultural background as it

21. Robert Freeman, cover photo: 'How American are We?'
The *Sunday Times* Colour Section, 8 April 1962.
Photo: reproduced courtesy of the *Sunday Times*/News International
Syndication, London. © DACs 1998.

was mine. We all grew up watching Betty Grable movies and listening to
Benny Goodman and modern jazz. But that's not the same thing as getting
it into your art. Peter Blake managed to introduce it ... but Robyn Denny
never got it into his art and he was one of the principal protagonists of
Americana at the College ... It edges into Dick Smith's work ...[32]

Tilson's remarks about the influence of American mass culture are
virtually a programme for much of this text. But, in addition, what
have also been distinguished and discussed are the influences of
American abstract art and criticism on British artists.

5 The Lure of America: British Artists in the United States

Visits to the United States by Alloway, Caro, Davie, Holroyd, McHale, Paolozzi, Read, Robertson, Scott, Peter Smithson and Stirling have already been described. Progressive graphic designers associated with the RCA also looked to American design for inspiration and visited America. Alex Seago has discussed them in his book, *Burning the Box of Beautiful Things*.[1]

In the immediate post-war years, crossing the Atlantic was difficult for most Britons because of money shortages and visa restrictions. Initially, many trips were made on huge liners but travel became easier and quicker once aircraft started to replace ships and cheap charter flights began to be provided by companies such as Flying Tyger.[2]

When it became clear – by the mid-1950s – that New York had replaced Paris as the world's art capital, increasing numbers of British artists, art students and critics began to go there instead of, or in addition to, Paris. Such visits and longer-term residencies were made possible by the availability of teaching jobs in American universities and art colleges, finance provided by the State Department, scholarships awarded by American universities such as Yale and grants by American philanthropic foundations such as the Bollingen, Commonwealth Fund of New York (Harkness Fellowships), Ford, Graham, and Huntington Hartford.

More and more Britons were thus able to compare the reality of America with the impressions they had gathered from the mass media. It also enabled them to see more American architecture, art, design and mass culture at first hand and to meet American artists and critics on their home turf. This chapter will look at a range of artist visitors and consider the various effects that the United States had on them and their work mainly during the period 1957–70.

Malcolm Morley

Morley, a pugnacious individual and self-confessed clumsy painter and sculptor, spent the first 27 years of his life in Britain and then emigrated to the United States. His mature work was produced in America and his success and reputation as an artist were secured there. Naturally, American subjects have loomed large in his iconography. The large scale, energy, intense colours and productivity of his work indicate that Morley is now more American than British. Risk-taking is a habit associated with American artists which Morley, who has several times drastically changed his artistic direction, shares. However, according to Richard Francis, 'His Englishness as an artist remains: he has assimilated the watercolour tradition, and looks to English masters such as William Coldstream, Victor Pasmore and Francis Bacon as partners.'[3]

Morley was born in Highgate, London, in 1931 and learnt to draw and paint, with the aid of a correspondence course and an art class, during a three-year spell in Wormwood Scrubs prison for housebreaking. After his release he worked in a hotel and painted in St Ives. He later studied at the Camberwell School of Art from 1952 to 1953, and then at the RCA from 1954 to 1957. It seems that Morley was an angry young man who felt ill at ease amongst the cool, sophisticated students at the RCA where his contemporaries included Blake, Denny, Smith and Tilson. His early works were tonal landscapes influenced by Sickert and the Euston Road School. Morley later characterised the English people and their culture as 'tonal' (rather than 'chromatic'). One skill he learnt at this time – using grids to enlarge and transfer drawings to canvas – was to prove useful in America. Morley was not a Pop painter but some of his later 'Super-Realist' works have been featured in surveys of Pop art.

Morley reconnoitred New York City in 1957 and then moved there for good in 1958. There were two reasons for his emigration: first, he had met a young American woman on a London bus and they were married and lived in Brooklyn for a while; second, he had been impressed by the Abstract Expressionist paintings featured in the 1956 Tate exhibition. At first Morley supported himself in New York by working as a salesman in Brentano's bookshop and then by waiting on tables in Longchamps restaurant. Curiously, it was while serving food that he met one of his heroes – Barnett Newman. The latter kindly

visited Morley's studio and gave him encouragement. Morley also
frequented Max's Kansas City club near Union Square in order to mix
with the art crowd. Ivan Karp, a gallery assistant, introduced him to the
Pop artists Oldenburg and Lichtenstein, and to Jill Kornblee who was to
become his first dealer. Richard Artschwager gave him valuable advice
in the mid-1960s and Lichtenstein was instrumental in his obtaining a
teaching post at the State University of Ohio, Columbus, during the
year 1965–66. Later on, Morley taught at the School of Visual Arts,
New York (1967–69) and at the State University of New York, Stony
Brook (1972–74).

Morley exhibited abstract paintings at the Kornblee Gallery in 1964
but he became much better known a few years later for his pioneering
contributions to the Photo-Realist movement, that is highly detailed,
acrylic paintings derived from photographs of reality rather than reality
directly perceived. (In its use of existing images Photo-Realism
resembled Pop art.) Morley employed a grid to divide his source images
into squares; he then turned the images sideways or upside down in
order to negate their content and painstakingly copied the squares.
Klaus Kertess remarked:

> Morley had found a way of merging the traditional skill that he had acquired
> in England with the intentions and ambitions of the New York avant-garde.
> He laid an American grid over his English grid.[4]

Morley generally left wide, white borders around his images in order to
indicate their third-order origin (third-order because they were paintings of reproductions of photographs). Paradoxically, the pictures were
vivid delineations of real things but at the same time representations of
a rival medium of pictorial communication.

Trans-Atlantic liners and cruise ships were favourite subjects
because Morley was seeking an iconography 'untainted by art'. There
were also biographical reasons: as a child he had delighted in making
models of battleships – his first painting had been of a tugboat – and in
his youth he had worked on tugs and barges in the North Sea and the
Atlantic. He had crossed the latter in a liner to go to America and he
could see such vessels moored in New York's harbour from his
eighth-floor, walk-up studio in lower Manhattan. He tried to paint
them from direct observation but they were too large to be seen in
detail so he switched to using photos on postcards, slides and travel
posters.

22. Malcolm Morley, *'United States' with New York Skyline*, 1965.
Acrylic on canvas, 115.5 x 151 cm. Chicago: private collection.
Photo: courtesy of the artist.

In his 1965 painting *'United States' with New York Skyline*, New York's skyscrapers provide a dramatic backdrop to the glamour of ocean travel represented by the *United States* liner heading for the open sea. The *United States*'s maiden voyage had taken place in 1952 and its last was in 1969. Cunard withdrew the *Queen Elizabeth* and the *Queen Mary* from service in 1967. Thus Morley's paintings of liners were virtually memorials to the era of the great passenger liners which, by the late 1960s, had ceased to be financially viable due to the competition from air travel.[5]

Another tribute to the architecture and tourist attractions of New York was the 1973 *New York City Postcard Fold-Out*. This huge work (180 x 870 cm), a free-standing structure made from several sections like a screen and painted on both sides, was based on a set of postcards issued in concertina form. Such paintings suggested that we cannot view tourist magnets like New York except via the pictorial clichés of the travel industry.

Los Angeles is another famous American city depicted by Morley: *Los Angeles Yellow Pages* (1971) represents LA indirectly via its chrome-coloured telephone directory which has a photo of the city's downtown zone on the cover. The surface of the phone book is smeared with pigment because Morley had used the original as a palette and it is also disfigured by a jagged tear running up the centre. Naturally, these additions can be interpreted as meaning that danger and disorder, whether from earthquakes or riots, threaten life in LA. These ideas are carried further in *The Day of the Locust* (1977), a painting based on a poster of *Los Angeles Yellow Pages* together with a smaller reproduction of one of Morley's liner pictures hanging on the wall of his studio. The title derives from Nathanael West's novel about Hollywood and in the foreground there is a battle scene with toy soldiers, a theme drawn from the novel. Although representational, this painting is by no means naturalistic. Its basic imagery is so disrupted by paint marks and superimposed figures, helicopters, ladders, etc. that it conveys a sense of chaos and catastrophe. In a critical review Adrian Lewis argued that both Morley's development as an artist and his paintings' compositions were marked by a 'willed set of discontinuities'.[6]

The fact that Morley has painted such a wide range of ready-made images implies a certain indifference to their subject matter, but some of his works seem to indicate a political consciousness; for example, *Race Track* (1970), a depiction of a South African horse racecourse which has been crossed out in red. However, others seem strangely conformist. For instance, the painting *US Marine Sergeant at Valley Forge* (1968) reproduces a highly patriotic scene: an American soldier holding the Stars and Stripes in front of an arch commemorating the suffering of George Washington's army – the one that fought the British for the independence of the United States – at Valley Forge, Pennsylvania during the harsh winter of 1777–78. Since this was painted while the divisive Vietnam war was raging, it would seem that Morley was endorsing – unless his intention was ironic – rather than criticising his host nation's military adventure in South East Asia. Another painting depicting the suffering of American soldiers, this time set in Vietnam, is *At a First Aid Centre in Vietnam* (1971). It is a grey, brown and blue rendition in emphatically worked pigment of a double page spread featuring a documentary photograph of wounded men, plus a border with a caption, by *Life* magazine's war photographer, Larry Burrows.

During the late 1970s Morley once again changed his materials and style: he reverted to using oil paints and watercolours and began painting in a more instinctual, Neo-Expressionist manner. According to the artist, it was a shift 'from perfection to imperfection', a break with 'the law of constancy'. He also began to paint watercolours from nature and to depict in oils tableaux that he arranged in his studio. One of the latter was based on the famous American television series and movie, *M.A.S.H.*

For 18 months (1977–79) he resided in Tampa, Florida, where he visited the Busch Garden Zoo and Theme Park. Lush green vegetation and parrots made their appearance in several canvases which took water-colours as their starting point. His 1979 canvas, *Christmas Tree – The Lonely Ranger Lost in the Jungle of Erotic Desires*, is a fantasy reminiscent of Henri Rousseau's jungle scene, *The Dream* (1910): plants, trees and cacti fill the whole space. The jungle provides a setting for a motley collection of creatures and objects: multicoloured parrots, a huge snake, a Red Indian figure, a cowboy on horseback, a steam train and the naked legs of three female dancers. By using models and toys Morley was able to generate peculiar variations of scale within his pictures. The meaning of such bravura confections was unclear. Lewis has speculated that Morley was motivated by 'a desire to escape the process of "making sense", partly through increasing erotic sensuality'.[7]

In addition to Florida, the different habitats of Arizona, the Bahamas, Barcelona, Britain, Costa Rica, Crete, Egypt, Greece and Kenya were also reflected in his pictures of the 1980s and 1990s. With good reason Morley has been dubbed 'a traveller artist'.

Morley's childhood in London had been unhappy and in his youth he had been a juvenile delinquent. These experiences seem to have left a legacy of bitterness. In a conversation with Ted Castle in 1981, Morley expressed anger towards his homeland.[8] He attacked the monarchy and the stupidity of the British, and complained about the nation's belated recognition of his artistic achievements (a Whitechapel exhibition was being planned for 1983). He also condemned the Arts Council for being 'a giant octopus' and criticised the British Government's military occupation of its 'colony', Northern Ireland. What particularly incensed him was the British indifference to the suffering and death in Long Kesh prison of the IRA hunger striker Bobby Sands (1954–81). While living in America Morley had retained his British passport but he told Castle that he now felt ashamed of being British and was considering returning it in order to become an American citizen. Morley's righteous anger was somewhat vitiated by his assertion: 'The only reason I would like to become a great painter is to fuck all the women in the world.'

Despite Morley's dislike of Britain, the British art establishment insisted on honouring him: in 1984 he was awarded the first Turner Prize of £10,000. However, not everyone agreed with this judgement: Brian Sewell declared that Morley's paintings were 'deliberately bad' (it is hard to distinguish good 'bad' painting from bad 'bad' painting) and Peter Fuller objected that Morley had lived in the United States for so long that he hardly counted as British any longer and, furthermore, Morley should not have won because he was untalented. America, according to Fuller, had been a negative influence:

> His parasitic relationship to the most transient and anti-aesthetic aspects of North American 'culture' is evident for all to see. Morley represents the negation of all the best qualities of British art ... He is just another empty and synthetic product of the International Art Corporation Inc ... if Morley had kept at it [watercolour painting from nature] – and not been seduced by North American anti-art – he might have developed into a serious painter.[9]

No doubt Morley's commercial and critical success in America cushioned him from such vitriolic attacks printed in small circulation British art magazines.

Richard Smith

As indicated earlier, Smith was an abstract painter influenced for a time by the impastoed canvases of Nicolas de Staël while a student at the RCA in the mid-1950s, despite the fact that he shared a flat with the Pop painter Peter Blake for a year. In fact, Smith was later to span the divide between abstraction and Pop. He saw the 1956 and 1959 Tate shows featuring the new American painting and while his paintings were, as Marco Livingstone has explained, 'indebted to Abstract Expressionism in their vibrancy of colour, compositional simplicity, energetic brushwork and sheer impact of scale', they betrayed 'no signs of the existentialist angst of the older generation' and made 'no metaphysical claims'.[10]

A 1958 painting such as *Salem 1* clearly shows the influence of such painterly, gestural American artists as Francis, Guston and Tworkov. Francis, whose work Smith saw in Paris in 1956, was to have the most significant effect in terms of the relaxed manner oil paint was brushed on to the surface. The drips and dribbles typical of Action paintings executed with fluid pigments were also to be retained. Towards the end of the 1950s, Smith's abstracts became increasingly lyrical: colours, according to the artist, were 'sweet and tender' and a shimmering, translucent effect was achieved via layers of thin pigment and loose, overlapping brush-strokes to produce a hedge-like density. The starting point for his colour schemes was generally soft focus colour photography typical of glossy magazines rather than nature directly perceived.

Although Smith was clearly a committed abstract painter during the mid-1950s, he was simultaneously interested in the collages of Kurt Schwitters and fascinated by the 'presentation' techniques employed in American mass culture. He read McLuhan's 1951 critique of advertising, *The Mechanical Bride: Folklore of Industrial Man*, and made contact with members of the ICA who had constituted the IG. Hamilton was an artist he particularly respected. Smith studied communication theory and reviewed films for the RCA student magazine, *ARK*. In 1959 he collaborated with Denny on a photomontage insert for *ARK* No. 24 entitled *Ev'ry Which Way: A Project for a Film* and made from images of British and American cities and personalities. This was a pictorial proposal for a film about the urban/media environment, which would absorb its spirit and turn it into an art form. The artists' ambition was to reorient British art away from rural landscape towards cityscape. Later on, in 1962, Smith wrote an article – 'New Readers Start Here' – for *ARK* which generously celebrated the RCA Pop painters Boshier, Hockney and Phillips.

Incidentally, many of the student editors of *ARK* had made a point of visiting the United States. In 1961 Brian Haynes (with Hockney and others) took a charter flight to New York and then toured around in Greyhound buses. Haynes was amazed by the huge, three-dimensional billboards; Britain, in contrast to America's advanced stage of economic development, suddenly seemed to him like 'a Third World Country'.[11] He took a camera with him and the result was a photo-essay in *ARK*, No. 32 (Summer 1962). Haynes's images presented quite a critical view of America: they included depictions of the racial segregation in the southern states; a shot of a waste dump piled high with discarded cars illustrated the profligacy of American industrial production and the casual degradation of the environment; a photo of a wall of wanted men posters indicated a high level of crime; a colour photo of a drunk sprawled out on the pavements of the Bowery signified endemic social problems. So, Haynes's coverage did reveal the downside of the American dream. Smith, however, was to evince no concern about such issues.

Given Smith's interest in American art and mass culture, it was highly likely that he would be drawn to the United States should finance become available. There were several reasons why he was primed to leave England: the class-ridden social structure; the stuffy traditional culture exemplified by magazines like *Country Life*; and the fact that there was an arts hierarchy in which painting had a low position after literature, theatre, etc. The award of a Harkness Fellowship enabled him to travel to New York in the autumn of 1959 – aged 28 – where he lived and worked until the summer of 1961, apart from a visit to Canada in 1960.

A second period of residence in the United States occurred from 1963 to 1965. To see more of America Smith made trips outside New York; for instance, in the summer of 1965 he taught at Aspen, Colorado; later, in 1967, he was artist-in-residence at the University of Virginia, Charlottesville, and in 1968 he taught at the Irvine Campus of the University of California.

When Smith first arrived in New York he was greeted by the slightly older British artist Harold Cohen who helped him to settle in. Cohen (b. 1928) was also in the USA on a Harkness Fellowship and he lived in New York from 1959 to 1961. Like so many others, Cohen had been impressed by the Abstract Expressionist paintings he had seen in Britain but what he saw in the galleries and studios of New York prompted a reassessment:

> I realised quite suddenly that what we had bought was an ideal. We had seen too little to be able to distinguish the good from the bad; anything in which the ideal could be seen – the ideal of free, unfettered action – was O.K. But in New York it was painfully clear that Abstract Expressionism was an academy, founded on the work of de Kooning and a very few others.[12]

After months of uncertainty as to his direction as a painter, Cohen embarked on a programme of reduction and simplification which resulted in abstract canvases resembling those of Newman's, an artist whom Cohen knew and greatly admired. The Allan Stone Gallery gave Cohen a one-man show in May 1961. Cohen returned to work and teach in Britain during the 1960s, but eventually the pull of America drew him back: at the time of writing he lives and works in California.

Smith rented studios in the district near the Staten Island ferry and became acquainted with American artists living in Coenties Slip, near the tip of Manhattan. He was delighted by the large working spaces that American artists enjoyed in old industrial buildings. Paint supplies were more generous than in England and since thicker wood was used to provide a 'chassis' for stretching canvas over, his paintings became more object-like.

Smith adjusted to the new environment with ease and soon began to enjoy the ambiance and varied culture of New York. As he recalled in 1992: 'It was exciting and it was hip in a way that was so easy. Hearing jazz at the Five Spot, and you know, eating at Ratner's, and just being around.'[13] He also drank in the famous Cedar Bar, went to the cinema, Happenings and parties. He found a warm welcome in the New York art world and identified himself with an emergent younger generation of American artists such as Al Leslie and Michael Goldberg. Amongst the artists he met were two from Chicago: Ron Slowinski and Robert Natkin. He also encountered Kline and Rothko and became friends with Newman, Jim Dine, Robert Indiana, Ellsworth Kelly, Agnes Martin, James Rosenquist and Jack Youngerman, and, via Greenberg, Kenneth Noland. He was impressed by an exhibition of Noland's target paintings and visited Noland in his home town of Washington DC. Various curators and dealers also dropped by Smith's studio. In the early 1960s American Pop art and Post-Painterly Abstraction were just appearing in galleries and, since Smith's work related to both, one can see why it appealed to New York's art world.

Smith had made allusions to popular culture – 'to show an alliance' – even before he arrived in America. The paintings undertaken between 1959 and 1962 became representational in the sense that they contained simple forms such as hearts, zigzag bands of colour and discs with radiating beams. The latter were based on spinning tops and wheels, spotlights, and moving 'neon signs that go click-click-click'. Boxes floating in space seen at acute angles were also recurrent subjects; they reflected the impact of American advertising and packaging, especially that associated with marketing cigarettes. Smith argued that since virtually all goods were supplied inside boxes, the box constituted the image of the product.

At first sight many of these canvases appeared to be completely abstract but their oblique references to mass culture could be discerned with the aid of titles such as *Special Offer*, *Slot Machine* (a crude simulation of a one-arm bandit displaying a winning combination), *Billboard*, *Product*, *Premiere*, *Panatela* (a cigar band motif), *Chase Manhattan* (a bank's corporate logo), *Revlon* (cosmetics), *MM* (Marilyn Monroe), *McCalls* (a women's magazine), *Kent* (a brand of filter cigarettes), *Trailer* (a film strip), and *Zoom* (a movie camera technique). Smith's tactic of using close-ups to disguise representation was demonstrated by *Flip Top* – a near view of a flip-top carton with cigarettes protruding – and by *Lee 1* and *Lee II* (1961), two square paintings consisting of white wavy and straight lines on blue grounds. If the viewer guessed that the word 'Lee' derived from the brand name Lee Cooper, then the referent suddenly became obvious: the white stitching/back pockets on a pair of blue, denim jeans.

Smith enjoyed listening to jazz and rock'n'roll and so some titles alluded to broadcast sound and music. *WADO*, for example, was the name of a radio station while *Patty-Maxine-Laverne* were the Christian names of the Andrew Sisters, a trio of singers.

When Smith depicted commercial products, unlike other Pop artists, he omitted the lettering and slogans associated with particular brands. This was because he was more interested in the methods and codes of visual communication than in their overt messages. Smith did not provide an economic or political critique of American publicity, but instead celebrated its seductive, optical characteristics in another medium. What intrigued him was not the hard or soft sell but the hard or soft edge.

Evidently, Smith delighted in working in the gap between abstraction and representation, in teasing spectators (will they be able to identify the object/product or not?) and in transforming publicity into paintings, the immersive experience of mass media into objects of aesthetic pleasure. The strategy was primarily formalist in intention, but Smith also hoped to capitalise on the wider accessibility of mass culture. In 1963 he remarked: 'In annexing forms available to the spectator through the mass media there is a shared world of references. Contact can be made on a number of levels.'[14] And in 1992 he observed: 'I wanted to bring that kind of imagery into high art, so that people could respond to the high art in a more direct way.'[15] He also enjoyed the interplay between flat surface and illusionistic depth: some works featured boxes seen in isometric perspective which were visually ambiguous. This kind of painting belonged to the category that critics dubbed 'Abstract Illusionism'.

On his return to Britain in 1961 Smith taught at St Martin's and he made a short, 8 mm colour film with Robert Freeman which revealed some of the sources of his iconography: Philip Morris, Newport and Salem cigarette packs, wristwatch faces, car tyres, slices of cake from Betty Crocker cakemix advertisements, etc. Details of products and ads

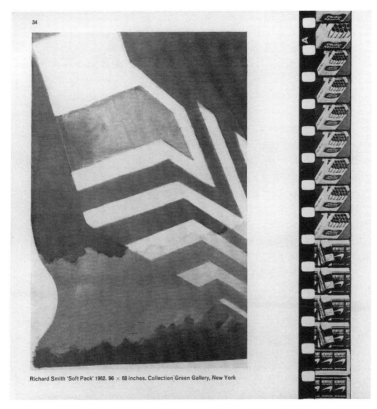

Richard Smith 'Soft Pack' 1962. 96 × 68 inches. Collection Green Gallery, New York

23. Richard Smith, Page from *Living Arts*, No. 1, 1963, showing *Soft Pack*, 1962, and frames from Robert Freeman's 8mm film *Trailer*.
Photo: reproduced courtesy of R. Smith.

were shown via close-ups and then intercut with shots of Smith's paintings to illustrate similarities and differences. The soundtrack featured examples of 1950s' Pop music, most notably numbers by the Shirelles, the black American female vocal group.

Trailer was first screened at the ICA in November 1962 where Smith also gave a talk. The public discussion which followed, chaired by Hamilton, became heated when Roy Ascott, Bernard Cohen and others found fault with Smith because of his refusal to comment upon, or take a moral stance towards, his mass culture sources. According to the diary of Richard Morphet, Smith's critics argued that he was strengthening the success of advertising by taking it as his subject matter and, since he was becoming famous as an artist, he ought to take more responsibility for his behaviour.[16]

Smith also held exhibitions in his Bath Street studio, EC1, (in which there was a hammock with cushions made from the Stars and Stripes) and at the ICA. Swinging London was in the making: Smith's visitors included the Beatles and the fashion designer Ossie Clark. The money from sales of paintings enabled Smith to return to New York.

By 1963 Smith was altering the standard rectangular shape of the support so that it matched the shape of the image, hence the inclusion of Smith's works in *The Shaped Canvas*, a mixed thematic exhibition organised by Alloway at the Guggenheim Museum in 1964. The next logical step was 'constructed canvases', that is, stretching canvas over complicated wooden frameworks so that forms literally thrust outward from the picture plane in a manner comparable to American hoardings with projecting cigarette packs. *Giftwrap* (1963), a large and well known example, was first shown in Kasmin's New Bond Street Gallery. By such means Smith inverted the illusionistic depth of traditional painting and invaded the spectator's space.

The paintings that Smith produced and displayed in the United States attracted the attention of various American collectors, critics and curators such as Richard Bellamy, Henry Geldzahler, Ivan Karp and Peter Selz. Bellamy of The Green Gallery gave Smith three one-man shows (1961, 1963 and 1964). This gallery also showed American Pop artists such as Oldenburg, Rosenquist, Segal and Wesselman. Several paintings were sold from Smith's first and second American shows.

Asked by Bruce Glaser in 1965 to compare the situation in New York and London, Smith declared that 'in the major arts New York has more strength. New York is really more radical than London'.[17] British art, Smith contended (parroting Greenberg), was hampered by good taste and timidity. Furthermore, the British public was conservative and therefore unwilling to respond to radical art, whereas in New York he thought there was an educated public more willing to accept breaks with tradition. British painting tended to be complex in composition compared to American painting. Smith considered that his painting had become simpler due to his exposure to the new art he had encountered in New York. One of the characteristics he retained from Abstract Expressionism was the idea that the whole painting was an image. So, even though his imagery became 'more central and emblematic', he tended to make it overlap the edges in order to ensure that it did not seem like an image within the canvas. Heron was to criticise much American painting because of its reliance upon a central, symmetrical form; this was one convention that Smith avoided.

Smith's close association with the United States prompted Mario Amaya to describe him as 'Anglo-American' and the American critic Brooks Adams to claim that Smith's 'ambiguous, sensuous paintings straddle two cultures'.[18] However, other writers have been at pains to stress Smith's Englishness: he was too reserved to indulge in the extreme romanticism of Abstract Expressionism; there was a residue of the English landscape painting tradition in his abstracts (Smith himself once remarked that he was only interested in Britain's rural landscape at a second remove, that is, as it was filtered through mass media imagery). Writing in 1966, the curator Bryan Robertson claimed that England had done little to encourage or support Smith, that he 'could not have survived economically without prolonged residences in the United States'.[19] Robertson also maintained that America had provided a 'sympathetic mental climate' and he regretted the fact that England lacked a 'sense of radiance' and public art commissions because, had there been any, Smith could have illuminated the British environment.

After his spells in America, Smith settled in Wiltshire for a decade (1968–78). But eventually the career opportunities which became available in America – the chance to mount several exhibitions and a big painting commission for a shopping centre in Dallas – encouraged him to return to New York in 1979.[20] Later on, in 1988, Smith acquired a studio in Telluride, Colorado. He now divides his time between Colorado and New York.

A Figurative and Landscape Painter in America: Keith Vaughan

Vaughan (1912–77) was a self-taught British artist, illustrator and art school tutor whose landscapes and figure paintings were grounded in the practice of drawing from nature and human models. However, his shapes, forms and colours were also strongly influenced by modern and contemporary art: Cézanne, the early Cubism of Picasso, the Neo-Romantic art of Graham Sutherland and the semi-abstract style of Nicolas de Staël.

Because Vaughan was a homosexual, his favourite subject matter was the male nude, represented in a generalised fashion and integrated into an abstracted, landscape setting. As his art developed, brushwork became more evident and expressive. Although predominantly a figurative artist, he did produce some totally abstract easel paintings and public murals.

Vaughan's reputation as an artist of quality was established in the 1940s and 1950s. His first one-man show in America took place at the George Dix Gallery, New York, in 1948. His work was later displayed at the Durlacher Gallery, New York, in 1952, 1955, 1957 and 1966. A reviewer of the 1955 exhibition commented: 'The result is correct, elegant, aloof, measured – and just a little anaemic.'[21]

One American who saw and admired Vaughan's pictures was Byron Burford, a landscape artist and Dean of the Art Department of the University of Iowa. He decided to invite Vaughan to Iowa City as an artist-in-residence. Subsequently, Burford was to extend the same invitation to two artist friends of Vaughan: Hockney in 1964 and Patrick Procktor (whom Vaughan had taught at the Slade) in 1965. Philip Guston – an Abstract Expressionist whose work Vaughan respected – it transpired, had taught Burford and been artist-in-residence at Iowa during the period 1941–45.

At the age of 46 Vaughan travelled to New York from Liverpool on the RMS *Sylvania* in January 1959, so he missed the major show of Abstract Expressionism held at the Tate in February–March of that year. Courtesy of the Americans, he enjoyed the luxury of a first class cabin; the sea voyage took eight days. A detailed account of life on board ship and his fellow passengers was recorded in Vaughan's private journal.[22] Following a rapid tour of the New York galleries and museums – where he was impressed by the work of Winslow Homer – he travelled by train to the Mid-west. During a stopover at Chicago, he visited the collection of the Art Institute to admire its Monets and Cézannes.

The state of Iowa impressed him with the 'clear, white, sharp' quality of its light and there he received a friendly welcome from Burford and other faculty members. Vaughan was required to tutor postgraduate students on a one-to-one basis. His teaching duties were so light – four half-days per week – that he had plenty of time to work in the top-lit studio Burford made available to him. The studio had been purpose-built for visiting artists and was located two or three miles outside of Iowa City. Its spaciousness and lack of windows intimidated Vaughan; he kept the doors open so that he could look out. Later he told Procktor that when inside the studio he felt 'as though he was at the bottom of a fish tank'.[23]

Vaughan was delighted with the munificence of his first paycheque –
$1,250 – and was tempted to buy a Ford Thunderbird, an American car
which had taken his fancy. During his stay – winter and spring –
Vaughan discovered oil pastels and Polymer Latex acrylics, and he
painted a series of small-scale landscapes in oil and in gouache. (Unlike
Hockney a few years later he did not find the terrain of Iowa boring.)
On trips into the countryside and to small towns, Vaughan made many
quick sketches of timber farm buildings. They reminded him of those
in Essex even though the American ones were larger. Malcolm Yorke,
Vaughan's biographer, writes:

> A snow-covered landscape where the whole surface is seemingly reduced to
> one dazzling colour and texture challenged Vaughan to respond to the
> whites with subtle mixtures of lavenders, blues, pinks and yellows, and to
> play these off against the brutal geometry of tree trunks, wooden buildings
> and black square buildings.[24]

Landscape oils such as *Snow at Amana II* did not stress the huge sky
and vast horizons of Iowa. They were squarish pictures composed of a
series of loosely painted, interlocking, rectangular and oval patches of
tone and colour. Some works – for example, the gouache *Hayfields,
Iowa* – could be mistaken for formal abstractions.

Once spring arrived, Vaughan was able to see more of America: by
car and Greyhound buses he visited Minnesota, Mississipi, Nebraska
and Wisconsin. He was struck by the 'extraordinary prevalence of
mortuaries, neon-lit and glittering like cinemas'. After a short holiday
in Mexico City with a young American lover, Vaughan travelled to
New York – where he paid a visit to the Gurlacher Gallery – and then
returned to Britain on the SS *United States*, the liner Morley was to
depict in 1965.

Vaughan had enjoyed his sojourn in the United States and he had
recorded an aspect of the American landscape but, because he was
fully-formed as an artist and set in his ways, his art and personality
were not radically altered by the experience. Even while in Iowa he had
written in his journal: 'America has not changed me (why did I ever
imagine it would).'[25] Later, in New York, during the sweltering heat of
June he wrote: 'I learnt more from the palm of Raul's [a 16-year old
Mexican youth with whom he had an affair] than from all the
complicated network of your [America's] glittering highways and
supermarkets.'[26] Even so, some British reviewers of a London show

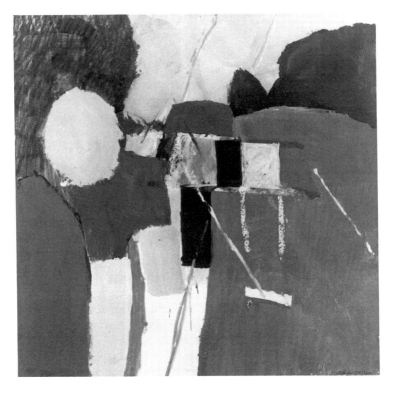

24. Keith Vaughan, *Hayfields, Iowa*, 1959.
Gouache, 45.7 x 47 cm.
Photo: James Mortimer, reproduced courtesy of the Keith Vaughan estate.

held in 1960 thought that Vaughan's American trip had helped to brighten and lighten his palette, loosen his brushwork and boost his confidence.[27]

A retrospective of Vaughan's art was held at the Whitechapel in 1962. He continued to paint, teach and live in London until 1977 when, fearing a lingering, painful death from bowel cancer, he committed suicide at the age of 65.

Three British Abstract Painters in America:
Heron, Frost and Hoyland

Throughout the 1960s examples of Heron's paintings were included in mixed exhibitions shown in the United States. He paid his first visit to New York in April 1960 to attend the opening of his first, American, one-man show held at the Bertha Schaefer Gallery. He was warmly welcomed and the critical reception was favourable: American review-ers praised the richness and subtlety of his colour schemes and contrasted his work with Rothko's.

Heron and his wife Delia met up with Greenberg who took them to see a Louis show that the critic had arranged at French & Co. He also showed Heron some of Noland's target paintings and some abstracts by Olitski. It was the first time Heron had seen any works by these three American painters. Ad Reinhardt was another important abstract painter Heron discovered during this trip.

At a Rauschenberg exhibition held at Castelli's the Herons encoun-tered, by chance, Barnett and Annalee Newman. The latter were friendly and hospitable: they took the British couple out for a long, merry lunch at a Brooklyn seafood restaurant and during the cab journey Barnett showed them the districts where he had grown up. Their lunchtime conversation ranged over many topics and Heron recalls that Barnett advocated that artists should write about their work and not leave this task to critics.[28]

A second one-man exhibition of Heron's paintings was mounted by the Schaefer Gallery in April 1962. The Big Apple was bitterly cold and this time Heron found that there was an 'unmistakable but unmen-tioned' atmosphere of 'cultural chauvinism' on the part of the Americans. He returned from the United States with an attack of hepatitis which took ten weeks to cure. The Schaefer Gallery gave Heron a third one-man show in 1965.

In the spring of 1978, after a successful retrospective exhibition at the Art Museum in Austin and a lecture programme at the University of Texas, Heron returned from America once again in a state of collapse from a lung infection (he has been an asthma sufferer all his life). Visiting America, it would seem, was becoming a stressful experience for him. He was unlikely to have been influenced by American art during these trips because he had firmly established his own direction by the end of the 1950s.

Terry Frost (b. 1915), a friend of Heron's and a fellow resident of Cornwall, was an art school tutor and an intuitive, gestural, abstract painter whose work was often inspired by visual experiences of the land and sea. During the 1950s Frost had seen the exhibitions of Abstract Expressionism in Britain and he had warmed to the paintings of Motherwell and Tomlin in particular. But he had also visited Paris in 1957 and been exposed to the abstract works of Robert and Sonia Delaunay, Herbin, Kupka and Soulages. In 1960 Frost was, like Heron, given a one-man show by Bertha Schaefer. He spent three weeks in New York staying with Larry Rivers. Years later he told David Lewis:

> In New York they all came to my exhibition, de Kooning, Rothko, Kline ... Newman and Motherwell took me to their studios. I accepted it all as normal and they accepted me. They were all painters struggling to get somewhere like I was. They worked hard; they would sleep until noon, do eight or nine hours in the studio, and then starting at eleven at night proceeded to drink me under the table! Then we'd go at four in the morning and have breakfast at a Chinese restaurant.[29]

Via Greenberg, Frost also met Noland and Olitski.

When, in 1981, Peter Davies asked Frost, 'What were the main consequences of this American trip?', he replied:

> The influence was simply to have met these artists. Most people say that '60–'62 was my best period after I'd been to New York; because they were great, they treated me with respect. A little bit of success is a very good thing and I don't begrudge it for anyone. In this country it was demoralising.[30]

A second exhibition at the Schaefer Gallery followed in 1962 and two years later Frost had a one-man show in San Franciso. According to Michael Tooby, Frost made a polemical speech at the opening in which he attacked:

> 'the Marshall Plan, and the concomitant of strategy and marketing of Abstract Expressionism, for denying Europe and other regions of America access to the East Coast gallery and museum network. The British ambassador is reported to have walked out.' [31]

During the summer of 1964 Frost taught at the nearby University of

California, San Jose. He was gratified by the well-equipped studio that came with the appointment. Lewis reports:

> For the first time he was introduced to water-based acrylics, a medium which, because of its bright matt quality, accentuated what he was already referring to as the 'heraldic' character of his paintings of that period. But even more telling were the hot dry colours of Southern California and the vastness of American space. He was driven into the desert and was amazed to find not the barrenness he had expected from seeing Wild West movies but an incredible richness and variety of colours and textures ... and vast differentiations of scale, from mountains to petals.[32]

Frost was a mature painter by the time he visited America and therefore it was unlikely that the fundamentals of his art would change as a result. Nevertheless, as Lewis's remarks imply, the landscape of the West did have some impact upon his palette.

John Hoyland (b. 1934) is another British abstract painter who, like Heron, adores intense colours. With the aid of a Peter Stuyvesant Foundation bursary, Hoyland paid his first visit to New York in 1964. He and Paul Huxley (who also had a Stuyvesant travel grant) were given a conducted tour of the Emmerich and Kootz galleries by Greenberg to view paintings by Louis, Noland and Hans Hofmann. Hoyland expressed doubts about the quality of the Nolands and was instructed by Greenberg to 'look again'. However, the British artist was very taken with Hofmann, an artist he had never heard of before. Hofmann (1880–1966), a German-American artist, educator and theorist, had emigrated to the United States in the 1930s. He had been associated with the Abstract Expressionist movement but had been respected more as a teacher than as a painter, consequently his work was omitted from the major 1956 and 1959 exhibitions shown in London. Hoyland quickly became a devotee of Hofmann's abstractions, so much so that he eventually curated a show of his late work at the Tate in 1988. In his catalogue appreciation of Hofmann, Hoyland recalled:

> During those years, the early sixties, we were regularly bombarded by American Art and we awaited each new instalment like food parcels to a half-starved community. I had been fortunate to meet Motherwell, Rothko, Reinhardt, Frankenthaler, Noland and Olitski both here and in the USA;

and was very much in awe of them, particularly the older generation. They were my Gods and seemed remote and unreachable, with the exception of 'Barney' (Newman).[33]

Hoyland believed that Rothko and Newman had 'led painting towards Conceptual art' but this was not a direction he wished to follow. One reason why Hofmann appealed to Hoyland was that he offered a way forward, 'a new exuberant openness with strongly visible European roots'. Paradoxically, it was an artist in New York who prompted Hoyland to feel that he could reconnect with the European artists he had admired as a student, especially those artists who had tried to be 'abstract and figurative at the same time'. Since Hoyland subsequently worked on a large scale and used pouring, splattering and staining techniques of applying acrylic pigments to produce bold, energetic, chromatic abstractions, many observers would categorise him as an 'American-Type' painter. Reviewing a London show of Hoyland's in 1969, Charles Harrison remarked: 'Hoyland has most successfully assimilated major influences from the American painters without compromising his own identity.'[34]

There is much evidence to suggest that Hoyland had his admirers in the American art world: he was given one-man shows by American galleries in 1967, 1969, 1972 and 1979. He also spent time working in New York in 1967 and again in 1969, 1972 and 1978. (Huxley too spent two years – 1965–67 – working in New York on a Harkness Fellowship.) Clearly, Hoyland found the United States a congenial environment in which to paint and exhibit.

John Latham and Assemblage

In 1961 New York's Museum of Modern Art mounted a major exhibition on the theme of Assemblage/junk sculpture or three-dimensional collage. (It later travelled to Dallas and San Franciso.) William C. Seitz, its curator, had earlier been to Europe to select work for the show. Assemblage was a historical and international tendency, consequently it was not identified as exclusively American. Its origins were deemed to be Cubist, Futurist, Dada and Surrealist collages, found objects and mixed-media constructions. The immediate inspiration for the survey was the resurgence in assemblage or collage techniques associated with Europe's Nouveau Réalisme and America's Neo-Dada.

Among the American artists included in *The Art of Assemblage* were Lee Bontecou, John Chamberlain, Bruce Conner, Joseph Cornell, Robert Indiana, Jasper Johns, Ed Kienholz, Louise Nevelson, Robert Rauschenberg, Simon Rodia and Richard Stankiewicz. Contemporary European artists included French and Italian representatives of Nouveau Réalisme and Affiches Lacérées. In this exhibition, therefore, American and European artists were treated as equals. Works by several British artists were displayed, the principal example being Latham's *Shem* (1958), a dark relief the support of which was an old door. This sculpture was subsequently purchased by MoMA.

During the late 1950s Latham (b. 1921), whom some critics believe to be the most radical avant-garde artist that Britain has produced since the 1940s, was making reliefs from scorched and mutilated second-hand books, wire, spray-paint and other materials.[35] The appearance of *Shem* in the MoMA show prompted Latham to cross the Atlantic for the first time. He spent three months in New York in the autumn of 1961. Kasmin, his British dealer, rented a suite at the famous Chelsea Hotel where an informal exhibition was held. During his stay Latham produced a considerable body of work but, unfortunately, many pieces subsequently went missing. He met other Assemblage artists such as Johns and Rauschenberg; he also encountered de Kooning of the older generation of Abstract Expressionists and Warhol of the new generation of Pop artists. A fellow resident at the hotel with whom Latham became acquainted was Kenneth Noland who introduced him to the critic Greenberg. This brief contact was to become highly significant later in the decade.

Seitz's catalogue essay for *The Art of Assemblage* did not mention Greenberg and the latter's Modernist painting theory, but his exhibition can now be seen as positing an alternative to Greenberg's purist aesthetic because Assemblage was, by definition, hybrid and impure. This was one of the reasons why Latham came to oppose Greenberg's ideas.

Although Seitz's exhibition did not travel outside the United States, its accompanying, well-illustrated book/catalogue was widely read by European artists and art students.[36] One part of the text discussed what Seitz called 'the collage environment': the urban clutter of signs and advertisements, the tons of junk and waste materials which some artists find inspiring and from which they make art. To an extent, therefore, Pop art was implicit in Assemblage.

In his book Seitz also described and illustrated Happenings by the American artist Jim Dine and self-destroying machine spectacles by the

Swiss artist Jean Tinguely; thus again the contention was that this was an international tendency. In Lucy Lippard's view, Assemblage was 'a secondary phenomenon' which 'served to blur the distinctions between a wide-ranging group of divergent manifestations'. It was, she argued, 'received as the beginning of a trend when in fact it was the end. By presenting an exhaustive survey of the additive tradition, the exhibition virtually killed Assemblage and prepared the way for a new art [that is, Pop art]'.[37] Nevertheless, since 1961 many artists have continued to employ assemblage as a method of making art, therefore Seitz's exhibition remains a significant milestone.

Just before his American trip, Latham had been experimenting with abstract films involving the stop-motion animation technique to record coloured paper discs. He called the unedited reel of film *Talk* and took it with him to New York. At Alloway's suggestion it was screened to a small but enthusiastic audience which included the dealer Betty Parsons and the painters Newman and Lee Krasner Pollock.

While in the United States Latham travelled by Greyhound bus to Washington DC where he spent a few days. The purpose of his visit was to repair *Observer II*, which an American collector had lent to the Gallery of Modern Art. At that time considerable critical attention was being paid to the so-called Washington Colour School, that is mainly the paintings of Louis and Noland. The British artist took a particular interest in the stained canvases of Louis because they were residues of making-processes (flooding fluid acrylic paint on to unprimed canvas or running stripes of liquid pigment down a canvas). For some years Latham had been preoccupied with the dimension of time and the conception of art as the trace of an event.

Latham made a second trip to New York in 1962. In November of that year works by Latham and several other European artists were included in *The New Realists* exhibition organised by the Sidney Janis Gallery. Examples of Assemblage and Le Nouveau Réalisme were displayed alongside examples of the new American Pop art. However, participation in this show did not enhance the reputations of the European artists because American reviewers thought their work inferior and outmoded in comparison to that by the younger American Pop artists.

Like so many other visitors to New York, Latham was stimulated by its fast pace and round the clock energy, but his family and interests in England eventually caused him to return. In any case, without long-term financial backing from an American dealer, he could not afford to remain. Latham was a strong-willed individual who had confidence in his own art and his evolving theories of time and the nature of the cosmos, so exposure to the United States and American art did not alter the direction of his art to nearly the same extent as it did other British artists who made the Atlantic crossing during the 1960s. However, one can detect the influence of American stain-painting on unprimed canvas in certain paintings of the mid-1960s executed with spray guns.

Since the 1960s Latham has exhibited in, and travelled to, New York, Pittsburgh and Los Angeles.

Colin Self

During the 1960s Self became noted as a skilful draughtsman, printmaker and sculptor. Although he has often been associated with British Pop art, his perspectival style of drawing was more naturalistic than Pop and, while the content of his work was often drawn from mass culture, particularly the found photographs which he collected so assiduously, it was too critical and pessimistic to be considered a celebration of consumer society. However, what Self did respect about Pop art was its use of everyday subject matter – which made it, unlike abstract art, accessible to ordinary people – and the fact that the origins of most British Pop artists were, like his own, working class.

Self, the eldest of nine children, was born in Norwich, Norfolk, in 1941. His father was a sign-painter and Self has been an advocate of 'people's art' throughout his adult life. At school he showed aptitude in technical drawing and metalwork. Later he studied at the Norwich School of Art and the Slade, London, from 1961 to 1963. At Norwich the only tutor he found helpful was the painter Michael Andrews. Once at the Slade he reacted against the vogue for large abstract painting because he thought it elitist and pretentious. Instead he made small drawings of banal objects such as armchairs and sofas (sometimes with figures) set against an empty white background. Wanting exact reproduction rather than expressiveness, he used pencil or ballpoint to draw the furniture in a deliberately impersonal manner. The 'beautiful technique' which Self strove to perfect was intended, he explained, as a pictorial form of 'sarcasm'.

While in London he met Blake and Hockney. They purchased some of his works and encouraged him to follow his own direction. In 1959 Self was impressed by an American film entitled *The Savage Eye* (directed by Ben Maddow and others). This movie – an exposé of social degeneration – influenced the content and style of drawings of cinema interiors he was to make during the mid-1960s. In 1962 he hitchhiked 8,000 miles across the United States. Altogether he spent three months there, six weeks of which in Los Angeles. Self recalls that exposure to the reality of America and ordinary Americans helped to dispel the glamorous images and myths that he had imbibed during his youth via mass media representations. America, he discovered, was not the land of freedom promised by the *Statue of Liberty* in New York harbour.

A second visit to the States took place in 1965. This time Self worked for a while in New York where he was struck by the odd behaviour of the street people and he noticed signs for fallout shelters. The latter supplied him with the name for a set of drawings. In the same year Self employed a quotation from a Bob Dylan song for the title of one of his drawings of a stripper and a public shelter. Self then spent several weeks with Hockney in Boulder, Colorado. Subsequently Self, Hockney, Patrick Procktor, Norman Stevens and two American students drove to California in Hockney's Oldsmobile Starfire. They stayed overnight in motels and, in San Franciso, at the YMCA. On the way the British artists paused to view San Francisco's Golden Gate Bridge and to visit Disneyland.

Among the American subjects Self tackled were automobiles, New York street vistas, junk food, fashion models, Disney cartoon characters, and cinema screens and interiors. *New York Street and Woman* (1965), a typical example, is a pencil drawing of two American cars, seen from road level, rendered with tone and mass; on the extreme right is a dark close-up of a woman's head and shoulders. In the background are rectangular skyscrapers rendered in line only. The contrast between the several distinct elements of his drawings with their different scales and degrees of completion – which do not add up to a fully consistent spatial composition – gives these images a surreal, dislocated feel.

As a teenager Self had been disturbed by warnings given by the philosopher Bertrand Russell that humanity faced annihilation unless it renounced nuclear weapons. Self is one of the few British artists whose work explicitly acknowledged the fear prompted during the Cold War period of the 1950s and 1960s by the proliferation of evermore powerful nuclear weapons. In drawings, sculptures and dioramas, Self depicted missiles, Lockheed SR-71s, Handley Page Victor bombers, fallout shelter

25. Colin Self, *Fall Out Shelter Series: Public Shelter No. 110*, 1965.
Pencil, coloured crayon and collage, 55.75 x 38 cm.
London: James Kirkman collection.
Photo: Prudence Cuming Associates.
© Colin Self 1998. All rights reserved DACS.

signs, the mushroom-shaped clouds of thermonuclear explosions and the victims of atomic bombs. His best known and most horrific work is a sculpture made from fibreglass, hair and polyurethane of a blackened and mutilated female corpse called *H-Bomb Victim* or *Beach Girl: Nuclear Victim* (1966). In certain works – for example an oil painting of 1963 – there were piquant juxtapositions: a B-52 nuclear bomber plane and two women wearing expensive fashionable clothes. Such montages were designed to generate a sense of unease and impending doom.

In his 1965 drawing *Fall Out Shelter Series: Public Shelter No. 110*, Self depicted in profile an overweight American woman who is about to guzzle a hot dog. She seems oblivious to the only other element in the composition: the shelter sign. The woman sits on a gleaming bar stool whose mushroom-like shape subliminally evokes that of an atom bomb's cloud. As far as Self was concerned, the American hot dog was as significant a modern, technological invention as the rocket. Sometimes he was willing to conflate the two. For example, in his chromium-plated copper sculpture *Hot Dog* (1965), a gleaming, phallic frankfurter nestling inside a split roll metal container evokes a missile in its silo or launcher.

Joan Ruddock, veteran CND activist, reports that:

> The establishment of US bases in Britain began with the Spaatz-Tedder agreement of 1946. By 1950 Lakenheath, Mildenhall, Scrampton and Marham had become B-29 bomber bases. Subsequently, under a new 'Ambassador's Agreement', four additional airfields were given to the USAF – Greenham Common, Upper Heyford, Fairford and Brize Norton.[38]

She also noted that, a few years later:

> Following the launch of the Russian Sputnik in October 1957, the USA perceived a 'missile gap'. As a consequence, Britain agreed to take American intermediate-range Thor missiles. Bases in East Anglia were rapidly prepared for their deployment.[39]

In response, civil disobedience action was taken; for example, an attempt was made in 1959 to blockade a construction site at Swaffham. The nuclear bomber and missile bases at Lakenheath and Swaffham were both in Norfolk. Self once spent a weekend on an ancient farm located next to such a base. Years later he recalled:

> By day one could see a solitary, massive white nuclear missile poised vertically and still. By night the howling of guard dogs chilled the air and imagination. Animal and technological threat were united in one fearful ground.[40]

During 1965 such memories prompted several pencil drawings, for example, *Guard Dog on a Missile Base, No. 1*, which depicts the head and mouth of a snarling dog next to a row of 'Bloodhound' missiles pointing diagonally towards the sky. The making of this drawing spanned the Atlantic: Self began it in Niagara Falls in the summer of 1965 and completed it in Norwich in the autumn. Earlier he had made 'hybrid', mixed-media sculptures of aircraft and submarines from shiny metal and the skins of carnivores: for instance, the 1963 work, *Nuclear Bomber*. His aim was to make the metaphorical connection between human technology and animal killing instincts even stronger. According to Christopher Finch, Self's art was a paradoxical mixture of 'terror and pleasure'.[41]

One, non-military American product that particularly impressed Self was a customised car created by Joe Ballion, a noted Californian customiser of the 1950s. According to Self, it embodied 'all the abstract qualities of what the world was like at the time ... it's explosive; it's elephantine; it's really sinister'.[42] No American sculpture that Self had seen impressed him as much. In 1968 he made an etching from a photo of Ballion's bulbous monster. It was part of a series of prints entitled *Power and Beauty* issued by Editions Alecto, London, in an edition of 75.

Self's analyses of contemporary society and material culture led him to conclude that displacement and escapism were occurring: sexual and aggressive urges were expressed indirectly via the design and look of manufactured products such as cars, furniture, fur coats, interior decor and machine parts. Entertainments such as cinema going and television viewing were 'tranquillizers' which reduced the mental stress caused by fear of nuclear war. He commented: 'The new culture incorporates the crisis into its new behaviour patterns.'[43]

26. Colin Self, *Guard Dog on a Missile Base, No. 1*, 1965.
Crayon, 86.4 x 106.6 cm. London: Tate Gallery collection.

Artists, Self considered, were economically dependent on the powers that be, nevertheless, they could act as witnesses and make social and political comments. Self has referred to himself as an 'anarchist'.

There is no doubt that the work Self produced in the 1960s was heavily indebted to his lived experience of the United States and its mass culture. However, Self retained a European scepticism and brought to his representations a critical, moral consciousness that distinguishes his art from that of other young British artists who also spent time in the USA during the 1960s. Self did not have a one-man show in an American private gallery during the 1960s but his work was featured in a show entitled *British Drawings: New Generation* held at MoMA, New York, in 1967.

In 1986 Self held an exhibition at the ICA in London.[44] It was his first solo show for many years. The catalogue contained a series of disjointed statements in which Self complained about neglect by art institutions, the financial exploitation and destruction of his works, and 'unfair dismissal' from a teaching post at Norwich School of Art which resulted in his registering as unemployed in 1981.

Self asserted that he had never been a real Pop artist because his 1960s' work had refused to celebrate material wealth. He also claimed that he and other British artists had not been influenced by the American Pop artists. Indeed, the boot had been on the other foot: 'Thought to have been influenced by them, when Dine, Ruscha, Oldenburg were over here, consciously being influenced by us.'[45] (Like Dine and Oldenburg, Self exhibited at the Robert Fraser Gallery in 1966.) The American sculptor David Smith, however, was praised for being a 'Zen Nature Poet'.

Self's works on display at the ICA were more traditional than those he made in the 1960s and very diverse in content, media and style: there were ink and charcoal drawings, romantic landscape paintings, mixed-media collages, and sculpted heads made from concrete. In his catalogue statements Self identified himself strongly with the watercolourist John Chrome and the peasant poet John Clare whom he dubbed 'the real nineteenth century *Europeans*'.[46] He also identified himself with nature and rural England, in particular the flat expanse of his native Norfolk which, paradoxically, was not conceived parochially but in pan-European terms:

> I'm a Greater European, who comes from the country of Norfolk. Its massive boundaries stretch from the Urals to Portugal in the west, from Lapland and Iceland down south to Sicily, Crete and Turkey.[47]

Thus it would seem that, two decades after his American experiences, Self had become even more conscious and proud of his local region and his European identity.

David Hockney

For some British-born artists the appeal of America was so strong that they uprooted themselves and went to live there. Hockney is the best known example.[48] His first visit to the United States took place during July–August 1961 while he was still an RCA student. He stayed in Long Beach and also in Brooklyn with the family of Mark Berger, an older, gay American student he had met at the RCA. An advert on American television for Lady Clairol, a hair-colouring agent, prompted Hockney to dye his hair blond because 'blondes have more fun'. When Hockney left the RCA with a gold medal for distinction in 1962, the attention he paid to his self-image and dress – large, round, black spectacles, a crew cut, a gold-lamé jacket with matching carrier bag, white shoes, small cigars – was surely influenced by American fashions and promotional/marketing methods. The fact that Hockney was media-friendly and photogenic was demonstrated by his appearance in the new colour supplements that British quality newspapers brought out in the early 1960s: in May 1963 he was photographed by Lord Snowdon for a *Sunday Times* Magazine feature on new British painting.

While in New York Hockney made many sketches, visited museums and gay bars and met Oldenburg. He even managed to sell some of his prints. The 24-hour nature of New York impressed him: 'The life of the city was stimulating, the gay bars ... it was a marvellously lively society. I was utterly thrilled by it ... the fact that one could watch television at three in the morning, and go out and the bars would still be open ...'[49] In Britain at that time television transmissions ceased before midnight and daytime and late-night drinking was restricted by licensing laws which many Britons and foreign tourists found absurd.

A series of 16 etchings entitled *A Rake's Progress*, which Hockney began in September 1961 on his return from America and completed in 1963, depicted episodes from his Hogarthian sojourn in New York. From the prints we learn that he observed male athletes training in Central Park, viewed presidential monuments in Washington, heard the gospel singer Mahalia Jackson in Madison Square Garden, and noticed New Yorkers listening to the WABC radio station via transistor

**27. David Hockney, *A Rake's Progress London/New York 1961–62*
Plate No. 3: *The Start of the Spending Spree and
the Door Opening for a Blonde*, 1961–63.**
Etching and acquatint, 50.8 x 61.6 cm.
Published by Editions Alecto, London, in an edition of 50.
© David Hockney.

radios. At first he mistook the radios for hearing aids; indeed, he was shocked by the seeming prevalence of deafness among young people!

A light-hearted, erotic painting – *I'm in the Mood for Love* (1961) – was also generated from sketches made in New York. Peter Webb describes it as follows:

[it] shows Hockney as a horned devil in glasses, sandwiched between two very phallic skyscrapers, one of which he is clasping. There is graffiti from the subway: 'To Queens Uptown'; 'No smoking'; 'BMT', and also the date 'July 9th', his birthday. The letter 'P' appears in the sky, and a badge from New York bearing the title of the painting used to be attached to the canvas until it was stolen.[50]

Following a successful one-man show at the Kasmin Gallery, Hockney was able to afford a second visit to New York in December 1963. This time he met Henry Geldzahler, a homosexual museum curator, Warhol and the film-star Dennis Hopper. Then, in January 1964, he flew to Los Angeles. It was not the local art scene which attracted him to California but the prospect of sunlight and handsome young men. At first he stayed in Santa Monica (18 miles from the centre of LA) and acquired a bicycle to explore the city and then a Ford Falcon car to drive to Las Vegas. One of the first places he visited in LA was the studio of *Physique Pictorial.* He remained in the United States for almost a year. When Hockney lived in LA he normally rented dwellings and studios or was a guest in friends' apartments. It was not until 1982 that he bought the house in Montcalm Ave, Hollywood Hills, that he had rented since 1979.

Asked about his first impressions of the West Coast, Hockney told Mark Glazebrook:

> Well, California did affect me very strongly. When I first went there ... with the intention of staying for six months to paint there I didn't know a soul. Somehow I instinctively knew I was going to like it. And as I flew over San Bernardino and looked down – and saw the swimming pools and the houses and everything and the sun, I was more thrilled than I've ever been arriving at any other city, including New York, and when I was there those first six months I thought it was really terrific, I really enjoyed it, and physically the place did have an effect on me. For the first time I began to paint the physical look of the place.[51]

Hockney was also to compare his home town of Bradford unfavourably with LA:

> I think visually it's [Los Angeles] a stunning city. Wherever you drive it's interesting ... It's the exact opposite of Bradford. There it's always dark, it's always raining, the buildings are black, the climate is cold. So when you come to Los Angeles, by comparison it looks like a sunny paradise ... People are more physical here because in the sun you're more aware of your own body. You wear less clothing ... Human beings are more joyful in the sun. [52]

Just before he travelled to the United States, Hockney characterised his home town as 'boring' to a reporter from the *Evening Standard* even though his Yorkshire accent and Northern, working-class roots

contributed to his popularity in swinging London and charmed the
Americans.[53] Some British readers will feel that Hockney's denigration
of Bradford was unfair; after all the sun does shine there in the summer
months. Nor does he mention the negative aspects of LA: air pollution,
crime, the abject poverty and gang violence in the black and Latino
ghettos. Virtually the only negative remark Hockney has made about
America concerns travel and the homogenisation brought about by its
nationwide, fast food outlets: 'Every time you pull into a restaurant you
know what the menu's going to be. Gets you down a bit.'[54]

One might assume that Hockney perceived LA with the fresh eye of
an outsider but, as Webb notes,

> His mental picture of Los Angeles was strongly coloured by the writings of
> John Rechy whose novel *City of Night* he had read in London. Rechy had
> written with real sexual passion about the sleazy underworld of gay bars and
> cruising parks around Pershing Square.[55]

When Hockney visited the square one evening he found that the reality
was different from the fiction: the square was bleak and deserted
because the gay bars and clubs had closed. Nevertheless, it became a
subject for a painting entitled *Building, Pershing Square, Los Angeles*
(1964). Andrew Causey has pointed out that, 'Emptiness rather than
the life of the bars attracted Hockney as he started to paint a city which
he was never to show as bustling or populous but only as buildings
fronts and street signs.'[56]

Hockney is now famous for his colourful, acrylic paintings of California's sun-drenched houses and gardens, office blocks, interiors, shower
rooms, palm trees, the water and splashes of swimming pools, portraits of
homosexual couples and other residents. When such paintings were first
seen in Britain by people who had not been to LA, they communicated a
convincing impression of the place, but the question arises: 'How complete and accurate a picture does Hockney give?' Most strangers to LA
notice its dependence on the automobile and its many freeways but
Hockney seems to have ignored these features. (A much later painting –
1980 – does depict a winding road familiar to him as a car driver, that is,
Mulholland Drive.) Hockney's representations of LA are in fact partial,
selective and, aside from their frankness about homosexuality, sanitised:
mostly they focus on the private property and lifestyles of the rich, not the
living conditions of the poor. The fact that LA is an industrial as well as a
residential city and tourist attraction is not evident from Hockney's

28. David Hockney, *Portrait of Nick Wilder*, 1966.
Acrylic on canvas, 183 x 183 cm.
New York: Harry N. Abrams family collection. © David Hockney.

images. Of course, the British artist did not think of himself as a social realist with a responsibility to address political events and issues.

In an illuminating critique of Arcadian-type representations of LA, Paul Melia observed:

> In August 1965 – the year Hockney painted two naked boys in a sun-drenched pool and titled his picture so as to serve as a synecdoche for the region – racial hostility turned an incident into a riot which lasted for six days. In the Watts rebellion – as it became known – 34 people were killed, and another 1,032 were wounded or injured. White-owned businesses over an area of eleven square miles were burnt, causing property damage of more than $40 million.[57]

A comment by Andrew Causey seeks to undermine the usual, utopian conception of Hockney's Californian images and to suggest that there are signs of alienation within them:

> The vision of Hockney as the north European artist who finds in California a new equivalent for the relaxed Latin culture of the Mediterranean, to which Northerners have traditionally been drawn, is a seductive half-truth. Hockney is a natural radical coming to Los Angeles to enjoy the leisure and ease of an open, prejudice-free city. His painting, nonetheless, is full of lonely and disturbing images.[58]

Causey also characterises Hockney's California pictures by such adjectives as distant, inert, untouchable and timeless. Other writers accuse him of voyeurism because he treated the male body as merely a sex object.

While many of Hockney's paintings and drawings relied on direct observation, others were dependent on specially taken photographs or ready-made ones bought from the Athletic Model Guild or found in magazines and real estate brochures. For example, the bedroom in the 1967 painting *The Room, Tarzana* was derived from a photo in a Macy's mail order catalogue. Even the sinuous lines and diagrammatic patterns used to represent the surface of water in swimming pools were indebted to existing imagery, such as the 'spaghetti-style', abstract paintings of Bernard Cohen.

Throughout the mid- and late-1960s Hockney spent long periods in the United States working and teaching at various university art departments in California, Colorado and Iowa. His 1964 painting, *Arizona*, which predictably depicts a desert landscape with the head of a native American Indian wearing a feather headdress, was actually painted in Iowa City. Another work executed in the same year in the same state – *Iowa* – emphasises the sky rather than the farmland. This was because, according to Hockney, excitement in Iowa was confined to 'the clouds coming up over the landscape' (the state is noted for its violent thunderstorms).

Rocky Mountains and Tired Indians, a highly contrived, stylised and tongue-in-cheek composition, was painted in the summer of 1965 while Hockney was teaching in Boulder at the University of Colorado. The contents – a cross-section of mountains, a wooden totem in the shape of a bird, two Indians, and a modern chair, all represented in profile – were derived from a geological textbook and photos rather

29. David Hockney, *Rocky Mountains and Tired Indians*, 1965.
Acrylic on canvas, 170 x 235 cm.
Edinburgh: Scottish National Gallery of Modern Art collection.
© David Hockney.

than drawn from life. While the Rockies were near Boulder, Hockney
could not see them from his studio because it had no windows. Real
native Americans were not available as models because the nearest
lived 300 miles away.

In his 'scenic style' paintings of America Hockney sometimes
reflects upon the experience of being a traveller and tourist and upon
the issue of pictorial representation itself. According to Causey, the
clichéd imagery in such paintings as *Rocky Mountain and Tired
Indians,*

> comment upon the desensitising of the average person's experience of the
> foreign or unfamiliar. Instead of looking for a new experience the tourist
> looks to a guide book to discover the approved reaction. The Indians and the
> wooden bird are emblems of foreign travel and substitutes for actual
> experience. The process of change from the personal to the cliché parallels a
> shift in the modern world in general from travel to tourism. Paradoxically,
> however, Hockney the traveller does not, on account of his love of cliché,
> become Hockney the tourist. While the distinction between travel as
> original, and tourism as recycled, experience appears to place Hockney, with

his interest in appropriated imagery, in the second category, his teasing, ironical approach raises him above supposed attachment to either the original or the second-hand. His paintings are comments on a changing way of seeing rather than being themselves part of the change.[59]

To reach Colorado from Britain Hockney had flown to New York in May 1965 in the company of his friend and fellow painter Patrick Procktor who had been invited to teach in Iowa. Procktor had left-wing sympathies and resented having to sign an oath of allegiance to obtain a visa to gain entry to the United States. He spoke Russian and he had acted as an interpreter for parties of peace-loving Americans visiting the USSR. He had found them politically naive and unsophisticated and very unused to being abroad. While at the Slade he had disliked having de Kooning and the rest of the New York School stuffed down his throat by Alloway and Andrew Forge. At ICA meetings there were people who, in Procktor's view, had 'completely sold out to the Yanks'. [60]

Procktor also blamed Hollywood for conveying false impressions to the British about the realities of life in the United States. Before visiting the United States, Procktor had produced a painting of the book depository in Dallas from which President Kennedy was presumed to have been shot. He thought of it as a prefiguration and entitled it *AmeriKa* after a book by Kafka because Kafka too had imagined America without having been there.

The two British artists spent four days on a whirlwind tour of New York. The city shocked Procktor who found it 'hideously ugly and hard and rude'. He also thought American art was 'repulsive'. He enjoyed the Metropolitan Museum but not the Guggenheim. What impressed him most about New York were its restaurants. Despite his negative first impressions of America, Procktor was to produce quite a lot of work there and he was later to acknowledge a certain debt to the United States:

> The idea of Americans and the success they enjoyed was attractive to me, because I was always trying to look for the key to success. My perceptions had been sharpened and enlarged by my experience of America, and the large pictures of 1966 and 1967 had shown the impact of American scale ... [61]

In New York Hockney bought a car for the cross-country trip. It was an Oldsmobile convertible coloured plum and cream with polychrome, metallic-plum unholstery. Its exotic appearance caused a negative, racial reaction in the rural Mid-west. In his autobiography Procktor recalls this question being asked: 'Why are you driving that flash nigra car?'[62] The Oldsmobile was later used to transport Hockney and three other British artists to California.

While in the USA Hockney painted portraits of such Americans as the curator Geldzahler, the art dealer Nick Wilder and the collectors Betty Freeman, Fred and Marcia Weisman. His 1968 painting of the Weismans depicted the two patrons standing outside their modernist dwelling in California alongside sculptures by the British artists Moore and Turnbull. (When the Weismans bought the painting they gained a picture of part of their collection while at the same time expanding it.) During his years in America Hockney naturally made friends with many Americans, but he also enjoyed the company of many artists from Britain, such as Barrie Bates, Blake, Boshier, Lancaster, Procktor, Self, Smith and Norman Stevens.

Hockney's first one-man show in America was held at the Charles Alan Gallery, New York, in 1964. It received positive reviews and sold out. Acclaim and money were thus two additional reasons why America appealed to Hockney. As he became increasingly successful, his lifestyle became that of the international jet set.

At the time of writing, Hockney has probably lived longer in the United States than he has in Britain. And given his documentation of Californian life and architecture, he is virtually an American scene painter. (He is an admirer of the landscape and urban paintings of the American realist Edward Hopper.) While Hockney has retained some British, linear and graphic skills and has been influenced by such European masters as Matisse and Picasso, there could not be a clearer example of the power that America has exerted over British art.

Two Pop Artists in America: Richard Hamilton and Peter Blake

Although Hamilton had spent the 1950s analysing and quoting images of America, he had no direct experience of the country until 1963. His first visit there occurred when he was invited to attend a Duchamp retrospective at the Pasadena Museum, California. Hamilton had long been an admirer of Duchamp and had collaborated (1957–60) with George Heard Hamilton on the production of a typographic version of 'The Green Box', Duchamp's collection of notes and drawings for his major work, *The Bride Stripped Bare by Her Bachelors Even.*

30. Richard Hamilton, *The Solomon R. Guggenheim (Gold)*, 1965–66.
Relief made from fibreglass, cellulose and gold leaf, 122 x 122 x 18 cm.
Humlebaek, Denmark: Louisiana Museum of Modern Art collection.
Photo: John Webb. © Richard Hamilton 1998. All rights reserved DACS.

Hamilton's interest in the ideas and work of the French Dadaist
showed that his artistic and intellectual concerns extended beyond
American mass culture. However, Duchamp had lived in New York so
long that he was virtually an honorary American. Furthermore, irony
was something which Hamilton felt that Duchamp and much American mass culture had in common.

In October 1963 Hamilton lectured on *The Bride* ... at the
Guggenheim Museum, New York. The museum's building is an
eccentric, inverted spiral-shaped structure which had been designed
during the period 1943–46 by America's most famous modern architect – Frank Lloyd Wright – and built between 1956–59. Hamilton
must have been impressed by it because on his return to Britain he
produced – during 1965–66 – a series of six reliefs made from fibreglass
and cellulose showing the exterior of the building with its concentric
bands of concrete. The reliefs were then sprayed in different colours:
black and white, all black, all gold, Spectrum (rainbow hued), Metal-

flake and Neopolitan. The reliefs gleamed because they had a high gloss finish. Seeing them displayed in the Robert Fraser Gallery in October 1966, one was reminded of the choice of flavours and colours available in an ice cream parlour.

Compared to Hamilton's complex pictorial compositions of the period 1957–63, the Guggenheim reliefs were simple, bold and kitsch-like. In other words, they were closer in design and impact to American Pop than to British Pop. (Hamilton told Michael Craig-Martin in a conversation held at the ICA that seeing American Pop had made him regret his penchant for lyrical painting passages in his own work. He was also impressed by the 'throw-away' attitude of the American Pop artists.) And since the Guggenheim is a landmark building, they were also emblematic of New York. Three of the series were acquired – somewhat incestuously – by the Guggenheim Museum itself.

Hamilton also lectured on *The Bride ...* at Yale University and in Boston, and then travelled with Mr and Mrs Duchamp from New York to California. In Los Angeles he encountered Warhol and Oldenburg who were showing there. He also met West Coast artists such as Larry Bell, Billy Al Bengston and Robert Irwin. An outing was organised to see the famous illuminated signs of the gambling mecca, Las Vegas.

On a visit to a joke shop in Pacific Ocean Park (POP!), Venice, Los Angeles, Hamilton bought a lapel button bearing the enigmatic message 'Slip it to me'. Its 'audacity and wit' appealed to him, plus the uncertainty of its meaning, although it did have a strong sexual connotation. On his return to Britain he made, in 1964, a large, wooden version of this badge and painted it orange and blue. (The optical flicker caused by the complementary colour contrast recalled Duchamp's 1936 *Fluttering Hearts*.) The object combined Hamilton's interest in Pop and Op art, American culture and the work of Duchamp (the badge was a found object/ready-made). Again this work – entitled *Epiphany* – was direct, flat and centralised in composition compared to Hamilton's earlier works. *Epiphany* was later (1987–89) made into a multiple – an edition of twelve on aluminium bases.

Hamilton's most explicit homage to American Pop art was a 1964 screenprint entitled *A Little Bit of Roy Lichtenstein for ...* (name of recipient to be inserted). This was an enlarged detail of a Lichtenstein painting illustrated on a poster for a Castelli Gallery, New York, show held in September 1963. A field of red dots – derived from the 'benday' printing process – covers most of the print

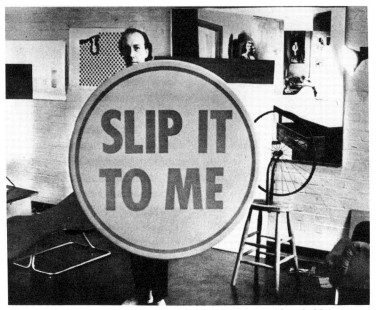

31. Richard Hamilton, *Interior shot showing Hamilton holding
'Epiphany'*, 1964. Behind Hamiltons's head to the left is
the screenprint *A Little Bit of Roy Lichtenstein for ...*, (1964).
Photo: © Richard Hamilton 1998. All rights reserved DACS.

while strange black marks intrude upon them from the edges. In this
example of meta-art, Hamilton subjected Lichtenstein to the same
process that he inflicted upon American comics. The effect of the
enlargement was to emphasise still further Lichtenstein's printed
matter sources and to transform his figurative image into an abstract
one. The two-colour prints were inexpensive to produce so Hamilton
gave them to friends.

It would seem from the Guggenheim reliefs and *Epiphany* that
Hamilton did learn to be bolder and simpler from his exposure to
the reality of the United States and American Pop art even if that
influence was to prove short-lived. American film stars such as
Marilyn Monroe and Bing Crosby appeared in his collages and
paintings after his journey across the United States and he wrote a
substantial essay on the work of Lichtenstein for *Studio International*
in 1968 but, by the end of the 1960s, Hamilton's fascination with
all things American faded. He then turned his attention to English,
Irish and European subjects.

In November 1963 Peter Blake was commissioned by the *Sunday Times* to travel to Hollywood to produce a portfolio of images to be reproduced in the newspaper's colour supplement.[63] The feature was to be the first of a series in which artists were dispatched to exotic, foreign places with which they had some affinity. It was Blake's first trip to the United States. His 22-year-old bride, Jann, daughter of the Hollywood art director Ted Haworth, accompanied him. For her, of course, it was

32. Peter Blake, *Big Do-Nut Drive In*, 1963.
Coloured pencils, 30.5 x 25.4 cm.
Private collection. © Peter Blake 1998. All rights reserved DACS.

an opportunity to visit her home town. Blake made a series of drawings in pencil (some coloured) with bodycolour (gouache) added. One image, based on a tourist polaroid photograph, showed Peter and Jann in the street next to Grauman's Chinese Theater crouching behind a pavement imprint of Roy Rogers' hands and his horse Trigger's hooves.

A poster-like drawing depicted the movie capital's skyline at night with palm trees and the beams of searchlights which were switched on for major movie premieres. This image was based on a window-sticker transfer. Another drawing depicted a tiger alongside Mabel Stark, an 80-year-old animal trainer, taken from a picture postcard of Jungleland, Hollywood's zoo. The subject harked back to Blake's earlier use of English circus motifs. On Twentieth Century Fox Corporation headed notepaper Blake drew props made for the 1963 blockbuster, *Cleopatra*.

Two drawings done 'on location' focused on the local landscape and architecture: one showed the Pacific Ocean (amusement) Park in Santa Monica which was frequented by teenage surfers and the other the Big Do-Nut Drive In, a roadside café in the San Fernando Valley with a

33. Peter Blake, *'The Meeting' or 'Have a Nice Day, Mr Hockney'*, 1981–83.
Oil on canvas, 99 x 124.5 cm. London: Tate Gallery collection.

cartoon-like cut-out of a fat boy and a doughnut-shaped sign on its roof. This kind of crude, figurative, Pop architecture pleased some visitors from Britain, for instance, the art critic Alloway and the architectural critics Banham and Charles Jencks (who was originally American).

Blake's images were clearly magazine illustrations rather than major, independent works of art. As usual some of them derived from existing imagery rather than from direct observation. They demonstrated an affectionate response to a place only previously imagined. In the main, Blake's style of representation remained English in character – it did not change in response to the experience of Californian light and design.

While in Los Angeles Blake took the opportunity to see the towers in the black ghetto of Watts constructed by the 'outsider' artist Simon Rodia, an illiterate labourer from Italy. The towers were made from steel and mortar columns and then decorated with 70,000 fragments of glass, pottery, shells and tiles. They took Rodia over three decades (1921–54) to build. Two years later, in 1965 (the year Rodia died),

34. **Gustave Courbet,** *The Meeting or Bonjour Monsieur Courbet,* **1854.**
Oil on canvas, 129 x 149 cm.
Montpellier: Musée Fabre. Photo: courtesy of Musée Fabre.

Blake painted a head and shoulders portrait of Rodia, based on a magazine picture, as a tribute to him and his remarkable monument.

Given the fact that many American private and public galleries gave one-man shows to British artists during the 1960s, one might have expected Blake to have had his share. However, Blake's attitude to the American art world has been antagonistic and uncooperative because, as he explained in 1983:

> I have never accepted the opportunity to have a one-man show in the United States. The reason for this is that when I was represented in group shows there, during the 1960s, the critical reaction was of the kind which implied here was a fifth-rate English Pop artist copying the work of American Pop artists. This was so far from the truth that I decided there and then that this was a game I wanted no part in, and I would not show in America, and I have never done so.[64]

In October 1979 Blake again travelled to LA – in the company of fellow painter Howard Hodgkin – to view an exhibition of British art. They stayed with Hockney in his Montcalm Ave home which had, of course, the obligatory swimming pool. On their return to England, Blake and Hodgkin each agreed to paint three pictures memorialising their American trip. One of Blake's was a figures-in-a-landscape painting, the composition of which derived from a famous nineteenth century source, namely, Courbet's *The Meeting or Bonjour Monsieur Courbet* (1854). In Blake's version – *The Meeting or Have a Nice Day, Mr Hockney*, (1981–83) – Hockney plays the role of Courbet, Blake the part of the patron Bruyas and Hodgkin that of the servant. Given Blake's history of using popular imagery, it was ironic that Courbet's composition had itself been borrowed from a popular source: a print of the Wandering Jew. In this strange conjunction of past and present, Blake attempted to synthesise European art traditions with the rather nondescript modern Californian landscape – the beach promenade at Venice – peopled by displaced Englishmen and American roller skaters.

Peter Phillips and Gerald Laing

Peter Phillips's childhood curiosity about the United States was eventually satisfied when he journeyed to New York on a Harkness Scholarship in September 1964. Other British artists were also in New

York: in November he, Allen Jones and Laing were photographed sitting in the Feigen Gallery. The image appeared in the *New York Times* with the caption: 'We're here because the excitement is here.' Earlier that same year the Beatles had toured America, their records had topped the American charts and they had been greeted with mass hysteria. Young, 'mod' British artists were thus assured a warm welcome in the United States.[65] Phillips remained in New York for two years but in 1965 he also travelled around the country by car with Jones. In California they visited Hockney and Vargas. During the period 1965–66 Phillips also undertook an artistic collaboration with Laing (see below).

Shortly after his arrival, the American Pop artist Robert Indiana paid a visit to Phillips's studio and the latter soon became acquainted with another major contributor to the movement, James Rosenquist. In Phillips's view the difference between American and British Pop was that the former focused on a single image or theme while the latter favoured more complicated compositions involving images taken from a variety of sources.

Phillips anticipated 'culture shock' and so went prepared so that he could start work straight away: he took with him to America drawings and slide-images for a number of 'Custom paintings', named after the largely American habit of customising cars and motorcycles by their owners or by specialist coachwork companies such as Starbird. The mass production methods of modern industry had resulted in highly uniform goods (the opposite to a mass-produced model is a 'custom-built' car), hence the desire to alter them by adding painted decoration or accessories in order to tailor them to the tastes of individual customers. In southern California the customising of vehicles began in the late 1940s. Its originator was Van Dutch Holland. The so-called 'kustom car cult' involved the total fabrication of unique vehicles from new parts or from a mixture of old and new parts.

As Marco Livingstone has noted, Phillips's Custom paintings feature cars and car parts combined with 'unrelated elements: labyrinths, diagrams of nuclear power stations ... heraldic patterns from Battersea Funfair, pin-ups and an array of dazzling abstract patterns and geometric devices'.[66] The paintings were exhibited at the Kornblee Gallery when Phillips held a one-man show there in November 1965.

While in New York Phillips invested in some airbrush painting equipment and experimented with its use. He had long admired the commercial illustrator's skill with this instrument. Obviously it enabled him to achieve an impersonal and unifying effect when recycling images taken from diverse sources. During the 1970s, when Photo-Realism was in vogue, Phillips visited the studios of two American practitioners, Chuck Close and Ben Schonzeit, in order to see how they used airbrush tools to achieve their results. Phillips reported feeling like an amateur in comparison to the skill of the Americans and was compelled to 'update everything'.

What did Phillips learn from his encounter with America? Speaking to Livingstone in 1976, he explained it was total commitment, taking things to extremes, being even more aggressive and banal. He told another interviewer that in America both the artists and the public took art more seriously than in Britain where there was still a 'gentlemanly, polite' attitude.[67]

Gerald Laing (b. 1936), a painter and sculptor from Northumberland who contributed to British Pop art during the 1960s, trained at St Martin's from 1960 to 1964 after spending five years as a professional soldier. Richard Smith was teaching at St Martin's and was a positive influence. In 1963 Laing produced *Souvenir of the Cuba Missile Crisis*, the subject of which was an incident which occurred in October 1962 when the world held its breath as the leaders of the two superpowers confronted one another and all-out nuclear war seemed imminent. *Souvenir* was an oil painting on narrow, vertical lengths of wood which had two facets so that one image – Khrushchev with the Hammer and Sickle emblem – was visible from one viewpoint and a second image – Kennedy with the Stars and Stripes – was visible from another. Looked at head on, there was a chaos of marks and colours. The political perspectives associated with each of the three viewpoints are obvious.

Laing first visited America in the summer of 1963 where he shared a studio at Coenties Slip, New York, with Indiana. The following year Laing returned to New York and this time he stayed until 1969. The dealer Richard Feigen had invited him and subsequently the Feigen Galleries in New York, Chicago and Los Angeles gave him eight one-man shows between 1964 and 1970. Thus his art became better known in America than in Britain. During 1966 Laing was for a time artist-in-residence at the Aspen Institute for Humanistic Studies, Colorado, and six years later he was artist-in-residence at the Aspen Center for the Visual Arts. He also taught at the University of New Mexico, Albuquerque, from 1976–77 and at Columbia University, New York, from 1986–87.

Like Hamilton, Laing was beguiled by newspaper and magazine images of people – astronauts, beach girls, dragster and racing car drivers, sky divers, American starlets and French film stars such as Anna Karina and Brigitte Bardot – who had been 'formalised and rendered, in a sense, heroic by their accoutrements'.[68] The mass media bring such people to our attention but they also keep us at a distance: we know them only as two-dimensional images. Laing was determined to remind us of this fact by foregrounding the means of representation used by the medium of newsprint. For example, his paintings emphasised the small black dots of ink from which half-tone, screened photos in newspapers are composed. Zones of hand-painted dots were usually set against organic patterns which were flatly rendered in vivid blues, reds and yellows. The results, emblematic and decorative, were similar to the paintings of the Americans Allan D'Arcangelo and Indiana.

Male figures dressed in helmets and other protective clothing, risking their lives and experiencing stress in machines, often populated Laing's early canvases (some of which were shaped). American racing cars appealed to him so much that he had himself photographed in one before travelling to New York. Drag racers were so extraordinary in their design they reminded him of sculptures. He considered them to be 'extreme examples of both specialisation and fantasy'. Their conspicuous extravagance was to him 'a foil to the grim utilitarianism of the post-war Britain' of his youth.[69]

In the autumn of 1964 Laing mounted a show of dragster paintings at the Feigen Gallery in New York. Banham was later to claim that British viewers were more open to such popular subjects than American art lovers because of the 'European habit of treating all American periodicals as equal and reading them all indiscriminately'.[70] Banham argued that, due to specialisation and social snobbery, American art lovers were unlikely to study magazines such as Movie Monsters and Hot Rod. He did, however, pay tribute to the pioneering writings of Tom Wolfe on such topics as Kustom Kar shows and Las Vegas.

In 1966 Laing provided illustrations for an article Banham wrote for Art in America about 'the hand-crafted colouring, for decorative and informative purposes' of American racing cars. Banham declared:

> ... these applications of color and symbolism ... can be demonstrated to follow strongly ritualized patterns, and since they deal with problems of identity, luck and honor under conditions that are commonly compared to

those of battle, they may be confidently classified as a branch of heraldry, adapted to the facts and mythology of mechanical motion.[71]

Hence his description: 'mobile heraldry'. This article was a deliberate attempt to bring to the American art world's attention the kind of affectionate, informed analyses of American popular culture which had taken place at Independent Group meetings during the early 1950s.
    Alistair Mackintosh has observed:

> Laing's subjects are symbols of the American scene, metaphors of the speed and brilliance which American popular culture seems to epitomise for this side of the Atlantic.[72]

However, the darker side of the American dream was manifested in Laing's 1964 painting *Lincoln Convertible*, the subject of which was the assassination of Kennedy in November 1963. 'In the early 1960s,' Laing later recalled, 'there was a general feeling of optimism fuelled by our emergence from the post-war period ... coupled with a belief in the ability of technology to solve our temporal and perhaps even our

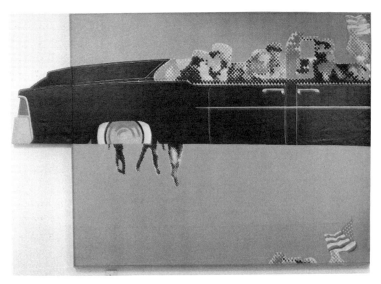

35. Gerald Laing, *Lincoln Convertible*, 1964.
Oil on canvas, 185.4 x 282 cm. Photo: courtesy of the artist.

spiritual problems' but later in the decade this was followed 'by the hubris of radical politics, sexual freedom, drugs and moral relativism, and the nemesis of dislocation and disease'.[73]

From 1965 to 1969 Laing concentrated on making painted sculptures which were predominantly flat silhouettes playing illusionistic games. They emerged as a result of pruning away the painted backgrounds of his pictures so that the remaining forms – for example, the billowing folds of a parachute – could interact directly with the gallery space. From sheets of aluminium, steel and reflective, chromium-plated brass he cut out abstract, hard-edged shapes resembling axes, pins, waves, smoke, ripples, cones and phalluses which he then complemented or disrupted by adding colours and curvilinear patterns. Technically speaking, these meticulously engineered and finished objects were indebted to the custom car phenomenon of America.

One of Laing's house guests during April 1966 was the British sculptor Clive Barker who had crossed the Atlantic in order to satisfy his curiosity about America. As explained earlier, Barker admired American design and mass culture and some of his chrome-plated sculptures were American in subject matter. New York seemed familiar to him because he had seen it so many times in movies and been told about it by Richard Smith. One thing that did impress him was the care and expense lavished on the display and packaging of consumer goods. During this trip Barker saw American painting rather than sculpture. He visited Lichtenstein's studio, met Larry Bell and Tom Wesselmann. He also encountered Warhol at the opening of the latter's exhibition at the Leo Castelli Gallery. Warhol showed *Cow Wallpaper* and *Silver Clouds*, that is, helium-filled, floating pillows. Warhol too was fond of reflective surfaces – they were a key element in the aesthetic of the 1960s. Shiny surfaces attracted the gaze but then confounded it by providing distorted images of the object's surroundings.

According to Barker, the short experience of New York and contacts with American Pop artists did not have any impact on his work but they did make him feel less isolated because he realised that there were other artists working in a similar vein. Later on, in 1971, he made a long journey across America that encompassed 22 states. The artistic result was a series of drawings executed on envelopes, one for each state that he visited.

The American dealer, Jill Kornblee, took an interest in Barker's sculptures and included examples in some mixed shows but, at the time of writing, Barker has not had a one-man show in the United States. However, he estimates that about a third of his oeuvre is in American collections.

According to Mackintosh, Laing eventually realised that 'the artistic climate of New York did not suit him. Each work produced at that time seems to have been an attempt to astonish more than the last, a fact surely dependent upon the pressure of living in New York, an artistic forcing house where the artist develops his ideas under the public gaze'.[74] Laing even concluded that the freedom enjoyed by artists during the 1960s had resulted 'in an orgy of self-indulgence and the collapse of skill'.[75]

He returned to Britain – northern Scotland – in 1969 where he spent a year restoring an old castle. (However, he later married an American and began to divide his time between Kinkell Castle, Ross and Cromarty, and Manhattan.) For a period he made abstract, three-dimensional sculptures in response to the prehistoric standing stones of the Scottish Highlands. Some of these sculptures were placed in landscape settings. But then, during the year 1976–77 he taught at the Department of Art, University of New Mexico, Albuquerque. Inspired by the etched glass technique which he saw used on the windows of a customised van, he made abstracted portraits of his fellow Englishman Malcolm Morley in etched glass and lithography. They were issued in small editions. Laing and Morley had shared an exhibition at the Max Hutchinson Gallery, New York, in 1976.

In the late 1970s and 1980s, Laing's sculptures became much more figurative and traditional in character: portrait heads and whole figures modelled in clay and then cast in bronze. (One half-length female nude was entitled *An American Girl* [1978]; Andy Warhol and Patti Smith also served as subjects for bronze portraits.) Laing's stylistic volte-face was nearly disastrous for his career because the Americans who had valued his Pop art considered that he had reneged on his past achievements and become an old-fashioned, academic artist.

Hybrid Enterprises

Laing and Phillips had met briefly in London. As we have seen, they shared an interest in American automobiles and customising. Finding themselves in New York during 1964–65 they joined forces to form a company called 'Hybrid Enterprises', the aim of which was

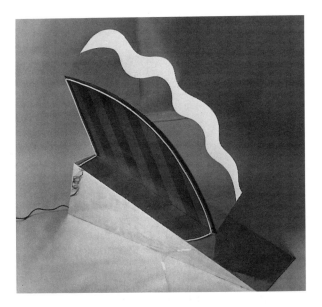

36. Hybrid Enterprises (Gerald Laing and Peter Phillips), *Hybrid,* **1965.**
Aluminium, plexiglass, plastic, brass, fluorescent tube,
132.5 x 175.2 x 43.8 cm. Photo: courtesy of G. Laing.

to devise an ideal art object by using the consumer research methods
associated with the American automobile industry.[76] (It should be
noted that even in America such methods – which involve an
averaging of tastes – did not always yield a successful product: the
1958 Ford Edsel car failed to sell despite all the market research
which had contributed to its styling.) The idea was prompted by the
blatant way art was treated as a commodity in America. Initially,
Laing found such commercialism stimulating but later on he became
disturbed by 'the growing sickness of the art scene'. As far as he was
concerned, Hybrid was 'a satirical attack on business methods,
market research and the hard sell'. Phillips viewed it as an amusing
gesture that tried to capture the culture and time of New York in
1965.

Phillips and Laing set out to discover what art-literate consumers
such as critics, collectors and dealers really desired and then to supply
it. Two immaculate boxes containing samples of materials, colour

wheels, shapes, textures, optical patterns, fluorescent light, and questionnaires were created and then the artists, wearing snappy clothes plus blue and white HYBRID buttons, interviewed 137 people in Chicago, London, Los Angeles and New York over a three-month period. Once the data had been collected an attempt was made to process it via Bell Telephones' computers. Finally, a three-dimensional object called *Hybrid* was constructed in accordance with the preferences revealed by the survey. Phillips and Laing stated that, 'having produced an object for mass consumption, we will market "customising kits" for HYBRID – thus selling the *illusion* of individuality or "personalisation" for HYBRID'.[77]

Marco Livingstone has described the *Hybrid* sculpture as follows:

> ... aluminium, plexiglass and a fluorescent tube with a wedge shape, the striped pattern at the side producing a chevron image with the aid of the reflective metal surface. Its composition, as Laing acknowledges, was 'an assemblage of trendy '60s notions', as well as an anticipation of the renewed popularity which sculpture was to enjoy in New York in the form of Minimal art.[78]

Hybrid's appearance reminded some critics of British, New Generation sculpture.

Two, full-size *Hybrids* and 25 desk models or 'conversation pieces' were exhibited, along with the research kit, at the Kornblee Gallery, New York, in April 1966 and a number were sold. Writing in 1974, Laing recalled that 'the art establishment was deeply offended and chose to ignore the event. But the media had a ball. [The exhibition was reviewed by several art periodicals, newspapers, and the project even made the pages of *Life* magazine.] [79] So I suppose that HYBRID, THE PEOPLE'S CHOICE, was a democratic art event.'[80]

Allen Jones and Frank Bowling

Jones is notorious for his erotic – feminists would say sexist – paintings, prints and sculptures; their imagery derives from soft-core pornography, lingerie and fetish-wear imagery. His earlier motifs consisted of aircraft, the Battle of Hastings, parachutists, red London buses, self-portraits and 'marriages' of male and female figures. However, intense fields of colour, abstract patterns and the objecthood of shaped canvases strongly appealed to him and he has repeatedly claimed – somewhat strangely – that form is more important to him than content. Certainly, his work is a curious amalgam of abstraction and figuration, intellectual control and intuitive painterliness.

Born in Southampton in 1937, Jones grew up in London and then studied at Hornsey College of Art from 1955 to 1959 and the RCA from 1959 to 1960. The work of two American painters impressed him: Pollock (seen at the Whitechapel in 1958) and Kitaj, a fellow student.

In 1961 Jones made a print entitled *Space Race* which referred to the technological battle then taking place between the USA and the USSR, but its style was primitivistic – influenced by Dubuffet, rather than by popular culture. Around this time Jones came to the conclusion that the London art scene was a second-hand reflection of what was happening in New York, that 'the European way of working was a soft option – somehow not tough enough', so he felt compelled to experience America for himself.[81] The prospect of a one-man show in November 1964 at the Feigen Gallery spurred him to cross the Atlantic. In New York Jones soon became convinced that people looked at paintings much harder than they did in London. Jones and his first wife Janet spent 1964–65 in Manhattan living in the Chelsea Hotel and then travelled by car across America. The following year, having obtained a Tamarind Lithography Fellowship, he visited Los Angeles. Subsequently Jones taught at the Universities of Florida (1969), Los Angeles at Irvine (1973) and California at Los Angeles (1977).

During his first period in the United States Jones's interest in sexual subjects, especially women's legs wearing 1940s' stiletto-heeled shoes and black stockings with suspender belts, became more overt. He later told Peter Webb: 'I wanted to paint a picture free from the ideas about picture-making that had become almost a dogma whilst I was living in New York in 1964. I wanted to paint a pictorial affront.'[82] The ideas referred to were probably those of Greenberg and Post-Painterly Abstraction, a dominant tendency in art at the time.

While in New York Jones produced *Curious Woman* (1964–65) – a companion piece to *Curious Man* (1964) which he had taken to America – a semi-abstract study of a lascivious blonde painted on a board with large areas of wood grain left exposed. The woman's breasts, thrusting out a low-cut, green and red polka dot dress, are rendered as relief elements. (Hamilton's *Pin-Up* of 1961 was a precedent.) The epoxy-filled, plastic falsies were the fruit of shopping trips to trick-game stores on Broadway.

37. Allen Jones, *Curious Woman*, 1964–65.
Oil on wood with epoxy-filled plastic falsies, 122 x 102 cm.
Aspen, Colorado: John and Kimiko Powers collection.
Photo: courtesy of the artist.

He also made a print entitled *Woman* (1965) based on a photograph by Bert Stern of the film star Elizabeth Taylor dressed for her role in *Cleopatra* (1963). Jones substituted a red diamond shape – a quadrangular mandala symbolising 'conscious realisation of wholeness' – containing a sperm-like form and two green mouths for Taylor's head but he retained her shoulders and cleavage. (The full photo of Taylor appears in his 1974 print, *One Way Traffic*.) *Woman*, according to Marco Livingstone, 'reveals the impact of his encounter with contemporary American art – both Pop and Abstract – in its brazen frontality and centralised image, high-pitched colour, stripped-down form and uncompromising hard edges'.[83] Brigitte Bardot and Carroll Baker were two other female movie stars whose visages found their way into Jones's early prints.

An archetypal American pin-up was featured in the offset lithograph entitled *Miss America* (1965), the source of which was a kitsch postcard depicting Miss America, dressed in a cowboy outfit, standing in a Western desert landscape next to a huge cactus. The image is repeated three times as if tumbling down the surface of the print. This work was part of a portfolio entitled *Eleven Pop Artists* (Vol. 1) which was sponsored by the cigarette company Philip Morris.

In 1964 Jones met Hockney in New York. The latter pointed out that Jones's hermaphrodite figures were very similar to reproductions in fetish magazines and mail order catalogues. As a result, Jones began to collect this kind of material along with the tamer *Playboy*. What Jones admired about drawings in fetish magazines was their directness of communication and their sublimated sexual energy.

Like Laing, Jones had one-man shows at the Feigen Galleries in Chicago, Los Angeles and New York during 1965. He was also interviewed by John Coplans for the prestigious art magazine *Artforum*. [84]

Since Jones is a skilled and innovative printmaker, he naturally welcomed the opportunity to spend time at the Tamarind Lithography Workshop in Los Angeles during the summer of 1966. Tamarind was a famous and influential American print workshop founded by June Wayne in 1960. The aim of Tamarind, a non-profit-making organisation funded largely by the Ford Foundation, was to promote the art and craft of lithography by training the printers of the future and by bringing fine artists and master printers together. Among Jones's lithographs printed there were: *Man Woman* (1965, also known as *Tamarind 1*); *A Fleet of Buses* (1966, a portfolio of five prints); and *A New Perspective on Floors* (1966, a second portfolio showing women's legs encased in sheer stockings and wearing high-heeled shoes, standing on chequered tiled floors and stairs). It seems that Jones tore and folded the paper his lithographs were printed on in order to subvert Tamarind's 'fine print' ethos.

Unlike Hockney, Jones ignored the physical environment of the United States. However, there was one exception. During 1968–69, while he was a guest professor in the Department of Painting at the University of South Florida at Tampa, he asked the campus photographer to take a number of colour snaps of the locality. Jones planned to turn these into a series of four, three-colour screenprints – to be entitled *Florida Suite* – at the university's print workshop, but due to technical problems they were not published as an edition until 1971 (in fact, they were printed in London at the RCA). To avoid tourist-type

38. Allen Jones, *Flats*, from the *Florida Suite* (1968), 1971.
One of four, three-colour photographic offset lithographs, 63.5 x 45 cm.
Edition of 25.
Printed at the Royal College of Art, published by Marlborough Fine Art.
Photo: courtesy of the artist.

depictions of Florida, the scenes that Jones selected were extremely
nondescript: a car outside a carwash; a view of some white, flat-roofed
apartments; a chair in a garden; and a view of a road with flower beds
and palm trees. All were familiar to Jones from his daily routine but
three of the images had a desolate quality because of the absence of
people. Ed Ruscha's books of photographs of the tacky urban landscape
of Los Angeles were a comparable project by an American Pop artist.

Jones must have benefited from his first trip to the United States
otherwise he would not have returned. In a 1968 interview he
acknowledged that America had influenced him but he only realised
this after he had returned home: 'I learned something from the heraldic
use of colour used by American Pop artists.'[85] Compared to British Pop
art, Jones once explained to Kasmin, American Pop was flat and had a
graphic, heraldic quality. British Pop painters, he thought, retained
'spatial, aerial illusionism'.[86]

On another occasion he recalled that exposure to the high pressure New York art world was not without risks for young British artists:

> Max Kozloff wrote an article called something like 'English Go Home' and in it he mentioned Boshier and me. He was talking about the New York art scene and how if a young artist came to town and wanted to make it within the establishment of the time he had to conform to certain conditions ... you had to use hard edges and flat colours and no brushmarks and it all had to be related to the edge ... He was talking about the depersonalisation of certain younger artists he had liked, of which I was one. He thought New York wasn't being very good to us and his best advice to us was to go back home. I thought about this and at the time I wanted to come home anyway. When I got home I had a feeling of liberation ... [87]

From these and other remarks it would seem that the time Jones spent in America served to clarify the differences between British and American Pop art and to strengthen his sense of British identity.

Frank Bowling was born in 1936 in the tropical country of Guyana (then a British colony) situated on the north-eastern edge of South America and came to England in 1950 to finish his schooling. In 1953 he spent time in Paris, Germany and Holland. Seeing European masterpieces in museums aroused an interest in visual art. Later, he did his National Service in the RAF and then worked as an artist's model. From 1955 to 1962 he studied at the City and Guilds School, Chelsea School of Art, the Slade and the RCA. He attended the RCA at the same time as Kitaj and the Pop generation of Boshier, Boty, Hockney and Phillips but, although his painting was figurative – images of suffering, women giving birth, self-portraits, etc. – and was often based on photos and news cuttings, the style was expressionist rather than Pop. (Francis Bacon and Goya were strong influences.) Even so, he did share an exhibition, entitled *Image in Revolt*, with Boshier at the Grabowski Gallery in 1962.

In London during the early 1960s he met the American painter Larry Rivers and they became friends. Rivers introduced him to the technique of using an epidiascope to transfer images to canvas.

In 1961 Bowling went to the United States for the first time in the company of Barrie Bates (later known as Billy Apple) and Hockney. The following year he was awarded a travel scholarship by the RCA which he used to return to Guyana. He then visited the United States again in

1964 and 1965. This time he was excited by American architecture and abstract painting. He then began to work on a larger scale and to tackle socio-political subjects such as beggars and the execution of an African post-colonial leader.

After leaving art school Bowling had some success in terms of grants, exhibitions, prizes and critical acclaim. In 1966 he exhibited *Mirror* (1964–66) – a semi-abstract, interior scene with figures descending a spiral staircase – at the Royal Academy where it was dubbed 'painting of the year'. Nevertheless, having been left out of the Whitechapel's *New Generation* show, he concluded that the British art world was neglecting him because of endemic racism and because his iconography was political rather than Pop. Seeing no future for himself in Britain he decided in 1966 to settle in the United States.[88] The American critic Frank O'Hara also advised him to do so. Bowling was to live in New York for a decade.

He arrived in America in the year that Guyana became independent and the battle for civil rights in the southern states was escalating. In April 1966 Bowling was awarded a Grand Prize at the first World Festival of Negro Arts held in Senegal. From 1967 to 1971 he struggled with the issues raised by black consciousness, but in the end he concluded that making 'good' art was more important to him than making 'black' art (most of which was bad in his view). In any case, if the latter existed – and this he doubted – it 'had nothing to do with his real self'. He also decided that Modernism was his creed and declared himself to be 'a formalist' but, at the same time, someone whose lived experience was that of a black artist. (No doubt there are some black artists and theorists who would accuse Bowling of denial and capitulating to a dominant, white, American conception of art.)

In London Bowling had known John Latham and, initially, he was, like Latham, anti-Greenberg. When Bowling and Greenberg first met there was antagonism but after a visit to Bowling's studio Greenberg relented. Bowling read Greenberg's writings and found that he agreed with the critic's theory of Modernist painting. He also began to be influenced by the stain-painting of the American Post-Painterly Abstractionists. Like Pollock he laid the canvas on the floor and, like Frankenthaler, Louis and Olitski, he poured acrylic paint on to it. What resulted were highly decorative, improvisational, semi-abstract compositions. For example, *Who's Afraid of Barney Newman* (1969) was a stain-painter's homage to Newman's vertical 'zip' motif. However, Bowling's zip traverses a crude map of South America, thus evoking autobiographical meanings.

Bowling's paintings became completely abstract in 1971 following a one-man show at the Whitney Museum, New York. Since then he has made large paintings with thick, densely textured surfaces enlivened by marks and incisions. One of Bowling's sources of income in the United States was the art criticism he wrote for *Arts Magazine*. He began to live and work again in London during the mid-1970s.

Given the fact that Bowling has lived in Britain and the United States for considerable periods and has learnt from the art of both nations, he can be categorised as an Anglo-American artist rather than a purely British or purely American one. His South American colonial experience, consciousness of race and the value of the tribal art of Africa add a third layer of complexity to his cultural identity. Curiously, Bowling has credited Greenberg with enabling him to see that Modernism – the modern, international ideological framework for making art – belonged to him as much as to white artists born in Europe or North America.[89]

Mark Lancaster, Andy Warhol and Bryan Ferry

During the 1960s Warhol (1930–87) emerged as the most infamous American, camp, Pop artist, underground film-maker and media celebrity. His silver-hued New York studio – known as 'The Factory' – became a magnet for visitors from all over the world.[90] It was a site of extraordinary creativity and a meeting place for people ranging from transvestites and museum curators to pop music stars. British visitors included Mick Jagger of the Rolling Stones and the painters Hockney and Mark Lancaster.

Lancaster (b. 1938) became noted during the 1960s as a Post-Painterly Abstractionist employing Minimalist devices such as grids and the repetition of basic units. He studied fine art under Hamilton in Newcastle-upon-Tyne from 1961 to 1965. An early painting, *Postcard* (1962–63), was figurative and Pop in subject matter if not in style: its iconography was derived from postcard photos of two American movie stars, Brando and Dean, whose faces were then combined. Besides Hamilton's work, Lancaster admired that of Jasper Johns, Richard Smith and Frank Stella.

From July to September 1964 Lancaster visited New York. Warhol's studio was his first stop. Hamilton, who had met Warhol in Los Angeles, advised Lancaster to phone him when he arrived in New York.

Lancaster did so and was invited round. At the entrance he was greeted by Baby Jane Holzer, one of Warhol's 'superstars'. Warhol and Jack Smith, the American independent film-maker, were shooting *Batman Dracula*, a homoerotic vampire, silent movie which was never completed. Since Lancaster was a handsome young man, he was invited to strip to his underpants, which were then covered in silver foil, and assigned a walk-on part as one of Dracula's victims. Later he also appeared in the quasi-pornographic *Couch*, named after the battered Factory couch upon which all the action took place.

According to Fred Lawrence Guiles, Lancaster became one of Warhol's entourage:

> Andy escorted Mark around town. He sent him over to Henry Geldzahler, who introduced the young artist to Jim Rosenquist, Robert Indiana, Roy Lichtenstein, Frank Stella and Marisol ... When pop artist Ray Johnson was ill with hepatitis in Bellvue hospital, Andy sent Lancaster there as a 'get-well present'.[91]

At a weekend party in Provincetown, Lancaster was greeted by Norman Mailer with a punch in the stomach. This assault by America's most famous macho, heterosexual author was apparently prompted by the pink coat Lancaster was wearing. The British artist was lucky in the sense that Mailer only used his fist – earlier, in 1960, Mailer had been arrested for stabbing his wife Adele with a penknife at a party celebrating his candidacy for mayor of New York.

During his many visits to the Factory, Lancaster assisted Warhol in the production of various paintings. Lancaster later recalled:

> I was very impressed by the way Andy worked – not at all in the way he presented himself as working. I helped out that summer when a number of Marilyns, Lizes, Jackies, and the first Flowers were made. I also put onto stretchers the Most Wanted Men paintings, the images of which had been rejected and painted over at the New York World's Fair, which had just opened.[92]

He also informed Richard Morphet: 'One was simply creating so much beauty so easily and with so little effort and so little concern: I found Andy's fantastically passive attitude to life very beautiful.'[93] Printing images via silk screens was a technique Lancaster himself was later to adopt.

Lancaster's own paintings were influenced by those by Stella dating from 1962 to 1964. At first sight there might seem to be no common ground between Stella's and Lancaster's abstractions and Warhol's Pop paintings but flatness, impersonality, repetition and simplicity were shared characteristics. Furthermore, as in the case of Smith, there were disguised references to American mass media and culture in some of Lancaster's paintings. For example, Morphet reports:

> Lancaster's first paintings after his return from the States in 1964 centred round the imagery of the Howard Johnson Company ... whose urban restaurants and highway Motor Lodges are immediately recognisable by their vivid house style ... and two distinctively contrasting colours, sharp turquoise and pungent orange. *Place* 1964, four five-foot square canvases composed a ten-foot square enlargement – almost literal, but disembodied – of a Howard Johnson table napkin with an undulating garland motif.[94]

A pair of paintings entitled *Zapruder* (1967) employed arrays of green-coloured rectangles – with some variation of colour from

39. Mark Lancaster, *Zapruder*, 1967.
Liquitext on canvas, 172.7 x 213.3 cm. Photo: courtesy of the artist.

**40. Nicholas de Ville, *Bryan Ferry with Studebaker in
Newcastle-upon-Tyne, 1968.***
Photo: courtesy of de Ville, Ferry and David Enthoven.

rectangle to rectangle – which borrowed their proportions and hue from
the amateur film footage that Abraham Zapruder took of the 1963
Kennedy assassination. Colour stills from this film were reproduced in
Life magazine and this was Lancaster's source.[95] In this instance, the
figurative content of the film has been ignored but the title preserves a
connection with the violent event and, according to Morphet, Lancaster's concern with a particular shape had 'an obsessive character partly
dependent for its operation on an emotional cause (the peculiarly
personal impact of this murder and gratuitous loss)'.[96]

From 1965 to 1966 Lancaster taught at Newcastle but he still
managed to squeeze in a trip to Los Angeles where he and his friend
Hockney stayed in Nick Wilder's apartment. Lancaster then assisted
Hockney to produce a portrait of their host and art dealer by
photographing Wilder in the latter's swimming pool.

During the 1960s, one of Hamilton's and Lancaster's students was Bryan Ferry (b. 1945) who was to found, along with Brian Eno and others, the world-famous rock band Roxy Music in the early 1970s. Ferry studied fine art at Newcastle from 1964 to 1968 and for a time occupied the same premises as Lancaster. As a student Ferry was obsessed by American music and visual culture. In his final year he acquired a flash but rusty American car – a Studebaker – and was photographed posing against it by Nick de Ville. The songs and album imagery of Roxy Music included many American references and the quotational approach that Ferry favoured when writing lyrics was indebted to Hamilton's Pop art.

Talking about the 1972 song *Virginia Plain*, the title of which derived from a painting dated 1964 about a brand of American cigarettes, Ferry remarked:

> The American Dream, that's what the single is all about: dreaming of going to New York and living in an attic and painting. The whole Warhol set-up was fantastically attractive then.[97]

The glamour associated with Warhol's Factory studio in the 1960s was thus able to fire the imaginations of Britons who had never visited it.

Lancaster was later to reside in the United States for an extended period: from 1974 to 1985 he was employed as Jasper Johns's personal assistant. Lancaster returned to live and work in Britain in 1985 (however, at the time of writing he resides in Florida). Two years later he was shocked and upset by the news of Warhol's death. To purge his sorrow, he began to paint small canvases at a rate of one every two days for a year until he had completed 179 of these. Their common starting point was Warhol's famous paintings of Marilyn Monroe. In the words of Marco Livingstone:

> These *Post-Warhol Souvenirs* deconstruct Warhol's icon of Marilyn in seemingly endless permutations, stripping it down to its various components and then reconstituting it in relation to other elements and references drawn from Warhol's own work, from the work of other artists, and from Lancaster's own history and imagination.[98]

Lancaster's pictorial tribute to Warhol was exhibited at the Mayor Rowan Gallery, London, during February and March 1988.

Conclusion

During the post-1945 era Britain began to experience what was called
'the brain drain', that is, the loss of well-educated scientists to other
countries, especially America. They were attracted to the latter by
larger salaries, a higher standard of living, better facilities and more
resources and research opportunities. From the examples of the artists
we have considered, it is clear there was also an 'artist drain' although
some individuals, it should be said, did return to Britain. Most artists
who visited the United States for a time benefited from their stay and
some of them recorded the land and cityscapes of America. The degree
to which British artists became Americanised varied from individual to
individual and in some cases Americanisation only had a short-term
effect. Alan Wood, a British painter and art college lecturer, observed in
1967:

> It is amazing that though quite a number of British artists have got on to the
> US gravy train they have come through it all with ... their British
> individuality intact ... British artists have learned what was to be learned
> from America ... and then progressed in their own way. This is an
> intelligent attitude.[99]

And, of course, the traffic was not just one-way from East to West
because Britain too attracted American artists who took up residence
for varying periods. On the whole, therefore, the to-ing and fro-ing
across the Atlantic widened horizons, enriched both cultures and raised
the level of cultural interaction.

6 Over Here: American Artists in Britain

Since 1945 Britain – especially the capital city, London – has appealed to a number of American artists who have either visited for limited periods or who have remained for decades. Precedents for extended residence were established by the American painters Benjamin West (1738–1820), John Copley (1738–1815), James Whistler (1834–1903) and John Sargent (1856–1925), and by the American sculptor Jacob Epstein (1880–1959). Obviously, the fact that the main language is English made it easier for them to settle in Britain than in other countries on the continent of Europe. American artists who have either visited or lived in Britain since 1945 include: Michael Craig-Martin, Jim Dine, John Dugger, Jann Haworth, Susan Hiller, John Hubbard, Mary Kelly, R.B. Kitaj, Dante Leonelli, Claes Oldenburg, Yoko Ono, Ralph Ortiz, Larry Rivers, Mark Rothko and Ed Ruscha. Some of these artists have had little impact on British art but, as we shall discover, others have had a significant effect, especially those like Craig-Martin, Kitaj and Leonelli who have taught generations of students in British art schools.

American art magazine editors, critics, dealers, patrons and film-makers have also visited or made their home in Britain; for example, Mario Amaya, Gene Baro, Suzi Gablik, Peter Gidal, Clement Greenberg, Jim Haynes, Barbara Reise, Doris Saatchi and Jack Wendler.

Visitors to Cornwall

St Ives, Cornwall, is a fishing and tourist village situated in a part of England noted for the quality of its light and the beauty of its ancient landscape. In the twentieth century St Ives became one of the few significant centres for the production of visual art in England outside London.[1] Different styles and movements have coexisted there. Before 1945 a mixture of abstract and naive art prevailed. Among the artists who lived there were Ben Nicholson, Barbara Hepworth, Naum Gabo, Alfred Wallis, Christopher Wood and the potter Bernard Leach. Contradictions are associated with the art of St Ives, namely, abstract works which are also dependent on nature, which are claimed to be local or regional but which are also regarded as contributions to International Modernism.

During the late 1940s and early 1950s a number of younger artists, working in a wide variety of idioms, took up permanent residence in St Ives or visited during summer months, for instance, Robert Adams, Merlyn Evans, Terry Frost, Roger Hilton, Victor Pasmore, William Scott, John Wells and Bryan Wynter. As explained earlier, Patrick Heron moved to Zennor, near St Ives, in 1956. Peter Lanyon (1918–64) was perhaps the quintessential St Ives artist because he was born there and his lyrical, semi-abstract paintings were inspired by his experience of the sea, sky and moors.

Such was the reputation of the art colony by the sea that several American artists – Jack Bush, Frankenthaler, Hubbard, John Hultberg, Rothko and Tobey – were attracted there during the late 1950s. Critics, curators and dealers – Greenberg, Hilton Kramer, William C. Seitz, Martha Jackson, Bertha Schaefer and Catherine Viviano – also paid visits. The semi-abstract painter John Hubbard (b. 1931) remained for months and returned several times.[2] His early work was influenced by Oriental art and by Abstract Expressionism but later on the experience of landscape became crucial. In 1958 he met Lanyon, a painter whom he recognised as a kindred spirit. After a period spent in Rome, Hubbard lived in London where he taught at the Camberwell School of Art. Then, in 1961, he married and made his home in Dorset. Subsequently Hubbard was to find inspiration in the art of the British painters Samuel Palmer and Turner.

In July 1959 Greenberg was sent to Europe by the French & Co. Gallery of New York to search for promising European artists. After visiting France he travelled to Cornwall where he spent several days with Heron. During this visit he met Sandra Blow, Roger Hilton, John Wells and Bryan Wynter. He then travelled to London to see Anthony Caro.

Rothko, accompanied by his wife and daughter, visited William Scott in Somerset in August 1959. The Rothkos then spent three days in St Ives staying with the Lanyons. Rothko spent most of the time socialising, sightseeing and talking with Davie, Paul Feiler (a painter who lived in Paul near Penzance), Frost, Heron and Wynter. He also viewed local chapels because he was thinking of decorating one.

41. Paul Feiler, *Mark Rothko at Feiler's home – Chapel Kerris, Paul, nr Penzance*, August 1958. On the right are Mell and Mark Rothko and Terry Frost, top left is Peter Lanyon. Photo: courtesy of June Feiler, Mrs S. Lanyon and the Tate Gallery Archive, London.

Rothko had been to Europe before, in 1950, and he was to visit Britain twice more in 1961 and 1966. His affection for Britain was indicated by the fact that he donated nine large paintings, the Seagram Murals, to London's Tate Gallery in 1969. After his suicide in 1970, Scott and Feiler wrote a letter to *The Times* testifying to his importance to British art. So symbolically significant was his visit to Cornwall that it has been the subject of a 1996 display of three Rothkos plus archive material at the St Ives Tate Gallery. Chris Stephens has observed:

> Rothko's stay has entered the folklore of post-war St Ives art history, serving to validate the town's importance as an artistic centre and to assuage any anxieties of parochialism.[3]

Any influence that Rothko had on the St Ives artists predated his visit of course and was the result of the 1956 and 1959 London exhibitions of new American painting. In any case, arguably, it was not a direct influence in the sense of imitation but a stimulus followed by a reaction that confirmed national differences.

The 'white writing' calligraphy of Mark Tobey (1890–1976) is generally thought to have influenced Wynter's painting style. Curiously, Tobey had worked and taught in Britain for seven years (1931–38) before the Second World War at Dartington Hall, the radical, progressive school in Devonshire. Also teaching at Dartington was the British, Neo-Romantic artist, Cecil Collins. It has been claimed, by David Mellor, that Collins' Surrealist habit of automatic drawing in white ink impressed Tobey and that this was the origin of his white writing style.[4] If Mellor is right, then this is a case of an influence which has come full circle.

Heron, in his criticisms of American cultural imperialism written during the 1960s and 1970s, has cited the visits by the Americans to Cornwall as evidence of their respect for British artistic achievements and of the cordial relations that existed between the two camps during the 1950s.

Ronald Brooks Kitaj

Kitaj is a Jewish-American painter, printmaker and bibliophile who has lived in Britain, mostly London, since 1957. (He has also spent some years in the United States teaching.) His desire to come to Europe in order to become an artist dated from a childhood experience of seeing *The Red Shoes* (1948), a British film directed by Powell and Pressburger and starring Moira Shearer as a doomed ballet dancer. Movie culture was to become a vital resource for Kitaj, who was born in Cleveland, Ohio, in 1932, studied in New York and Vienna during the early 1950s and worked sporadically as a merchant seaman. After serving in the US army in Germany and France, he received a GI scholarship which enabled him to study drawing and painting at the Ruskin School, Oxford, and the RCA, London, from 1957 to 1961.

Kitaj's ambition during the late 1950s was to become a 'scholar-painter' and he developed a fascination with the art history methods of iconography and iconology associated with Erwin Panofsky, Aby Warburg and Edgar Wind (the latter taught him at Oxford). At the RCA Kitaj was a contemporary of Boshier, Hockney, Jones, *et al.*, but since he was older and more mature than most British students, he became a role model and adviser. The intelligence, seriousness and discipline with which Kitaj approached the art of painting was important to his fellow students. Kitaj immediately noticed Hockney's artistic abilities and bought a drawing of a skeleton from him for £5 because he thought it 'marvellous'. They quickly became friends. In 1960, feeling dissatisfied with a foray into abstraction, Hockney consulted Kitaj, who advised him that painting was a kind of research and that he should tackle subjects that concerned him most.[5] Hockney later explained:

> The artist who influenced me most strongly I think not just as an artist but as a person, is Ron Kitaj. It's partly because I've always admired his art enormously ... and also because he opened my eyes a great deal and I always think of things beginning from particular moments when I discussed things with him.[6]

And, in 1965, Allen Jones recalled:

> I learned more, I think, about an attitude to painting merely from watching him. I didn't speak to him very much but suddenly I thought this was something vital in comparison to everything else at the college. In other words, the influence wasn't one of imagery but of a dedicated professionalism and real toughness about painting.[7]

Kitaj commuted daily from Dulwich, a suburb in South London, to the RCA in South Kensington. He had bought a house in Dulwich and lived there with his first wife and child. Later on he resided in Kensington and Chelsea. London streets feature in a number of his paintings. Most of Kitaj's paintings reflect a mediated rather than an unmediated experience: scenes with figures are generally constructed by quoting existing images taken from a variety of sources but they also involve his imagination and his knowledge of history, both personal and public. Those of his works which depend upon direct observation of external reality tend to be life drawings and portraits.

An early example of a mediated, history-painting was *The Murder of Rosa Luxemburg*.[8] It was exhibited in the *Young Contemporaries* exhibition of 1961 at the same time as the RCA Pop painters so Kitaj was associated with them in the minds of critics. Subsequently he denied that he was ever a Pop painter and stated that he had no interest in popular music or culture. However, the confusion was to some extent understandable because Kitaj used a mixture of figuration and abstraction, compartmentalised compositions and fragments of images quoted from secondhand, mass media sources (books and journals especially). Where he differed from the British Pop artists was in his greater theoretical sophistication and knowledge of the history and culture of Europe, in particular the lives of major Socialist intellectuals such as Luxemburg (a Jewish and Marxist martyr) and, somewhat later, Walter Benjamin (a major cultural critic and Jewish contributor to the Frankfurt School of Philosophy). Kitaj was more interested in the culture of the past than in the admass environment of the 1960s, consequently he tried to resurrect allegorical and history-painting while simultaneously employing a variety of modernist pictorial techniques. [9]

It should be obvious that the example that Kitaj set the RCA students was markedly different from that set by the Abstract Expressionists appearing in the 1959 Tate exhibition or that set by American mass culture. Since Kitaj was already American, his home-land did not have the exotic aura for him that it had for British art students. In the 1990s Kitaj recalled his days at the RCA:

> Americanism was in the air ... but there was no one in London who could add to what I already knew more or less profoundly, like Hollywood Kulchur, American politics, Action painting ... and, well, American life, art and literature in general. Popular music never interested me and the slick American razzle I grew up with, which was Popping art didn't dazzle me. I fled from it into my own neuroses ... [10]

In 1963 Kitaj's first one-man show at the Marlborough Fine Art, New London Gallery – *Pictures with Commentary, Pictures without Commentary* – was a critical and financial success. The artist's catalogue notes revealed his knowledge of Warburgian iconographic theory and his obsession with word-image interactions.[11] In several instances Kitaj contradicted the 'purity of the medium' and 'purely visual' dictums of 1960s' painting theory by writing on his canvases or by collaging printed matter to their surfaces. In addition he supplied second order writings to assist the viewer in understanding his densely coded puzzle-pictures whose imagery was appropriated from so many sources – Kitaj is the master (some might say victim) of intertextuality – intermingled with references to his own life.

One of those entranced by this exhibition was a student from Walthamstow College of Art, the future film director Peter Greenaway (b. 1942). He later recalled:

> I have the catalogue with my enthusiasms still scribbled – embarrassingly – in the back ... I was at art school and didn't really know what I was doing – I

was repeatedly told my paintings were too literary ... I suddenly saw this body of work that legitimised all I had hopes of one day doing. Kitaj legitimised text, arcane and elitist information, he drew and painted as many as ten different ways on the same canvas, he threw ideas around like confetti, ideas that were both painterliness and direct Warburg quotation; there was an unashamed political passion and extravagant sexual imagery. His ideas were international, far from English timidity and English jokiness ... I often walk around the film-set with a book of Kitaj's paintings under my arm ... [12]

As a result, the style of Greenaway's paintings and films was significantly indebted to early Kitaj.

During the 1960s Kitaj taught at several London art schools – Ealing, Camberwell and the Slade – and so had an impact on several generations of British students and, in some cases, his fellow tutors. Patrick Procktor had first met Kitaj in 1961 at the time of the *Young Contemporaries* exhibition (Procktor, a Slade student, had been one of the organisers). Later he taught with Kitaj at Camberwell and paid social visits to his home where he met other American artists such as Jim Dine. In his autobiography Procktor admits that around 1964 Kitaj was 'an influence and a presence'. He added:

What did impress me was his particularity, his control, so that he could shift from moment to moment, in different texture, in different style and enforce a logic out of it. There was nothing half-hearted about the mixture of styles. I was influenced by that mood ... [13]

In the mid-1970s, when Conceptual art and other, non-painterly kinds of avant-garde art were in vogue, Kitaj was worried by the narrowness of such work; he wanted something more accessible, empirical and social. He became convinced that he should spend more time perfecting his drawing skills and that drawing the human figure should be re-emphasised in the British art community. (In some art schools, it seems, life drawing was being abandoned.) To encourage the latter end he curated an exhibition of figurative drawings and paintings entitled *The Human Clay*, many of which he had selected and purchased for the Arts Council's Collection.[14] Kitaj denied that this was a backward step by declaring that he was moving *forward* to drawing, not back to it. He also pointed out that Matisse and Picasso, the masters of modern art, had been expert in drawing the human body. At the same time, one can argue that Kitaj has always been half-hearted in his commitment to Modernism and many of his portrait and nude drawings look academic. (He was elected to the Royal Academy in 1985, the first American to receive this honour since Sargent.) Nevertheless, his arguments in favour of drawing were welcomed and debated by many British artists and critics.

In his catalogue text for *The Human Clay* Kitaj also used the expression 'School of London' which, as we have seen, had earlier been employed by Heron. Kitaj's expression proved to be influential. Once again it provoked much discussion in the British art world and eventually resulted in thematic exhibitions and books. For example, in 1987 there was a British Council exhibition which toured Europe. It featured paintings by six figurative artists: Michael Andrews, Frank Auerbach, Francis Bacon, Lucien Freud, Kitaj and Leon Kossof. Since all these artists were highly individualistic, the term 'school' was problematic. According to Michael Peppiatt, what these painters shared besides individuality was a commitment to the human figure as the proper subject for art; a disregard for short-term fashions in art; personal and gallery links; long-term residences in London (the city was also part of the subject matter of some of these painters); and a monastic sense of vocation.[15] One could also add high artistic quality.

In a book published in 1989, Kitaj's concept was extended by Alistair Hicks to include artists such as Gillian Ayres, Howard Hodgkin and John Walker.[16] Not everyone was persuaded by the label: in a review of Hicks's book, the art critic Tim Hilton flatly denied there was any such thing as a 'School of London'.[17] Arguably, the label was essentially a marketing tool designed to do for London's artists what the labels 'School of Paris' and 'New York School' had done for the artists of those cities.

During the 1980s Kitaj was increasingly troubled by the question of his national and cultural identity. He began to reflect on his Jewish origins and the significance of the Holocaust and to address these subjects in his paintings. In a 1989 manifesto he introduced the term 'Diasporist Painting' to characterise his own work and that of any other 'displaced' artists whose art reflected the experience of living in 'exile' from their homelands.[18]

The acclaim and respect which Kitaj had mostly enjoyed in Britain ever since his first one-man show culminated in a large-scale retrospective held at the Tate in 1994, which later travelled to Los Angeles and New York. At this point friendly relations with his host nation suddenly soured because several harsh notices were published. The dangers of Kitaj's erudite, literary approach to art were obscurantism, pretentiousness and a failure to fulfil his own ambitious programme. James Hall summed up what happened:

> Few institutional shows by a living artist have been greeted with such blanket derision. Kitaj's attempts at a modern kind of history painting were regarded as vulgar and pretentious ... in the *Independent* he was described as being a small man with a large megaphone ... [in America] most of the reviews were lukewarm at best ... Kitaj has also fallen foul of the political correctness lobby with many Americans finding the work irredeemably sexist.[19]

Naturally, Kitaj was shocked and distressed. Hall continued:

> Kitaj blamed the onslaught on a combination of British philistinism and anti-semitism. [It did not cross his mind, apparently, that the critics might have been right.] He vowed never to show his work in England again, and considered moving back to America. To make matters worse, his wife died soon after the show opened.

Another report claimed that Kitaj blamed the tabloid press for a decline in British culture and the trend towards sensationalism, and that he believed 'education and humanity were dying out in England'.[20] Despite the abrupt decline in Kitaj's reputation in Britain, he was awarded the painting prize at the 1995 Venice Biennale.

Kitaj did exhibit in Britain again – at the 1996 Royal Academy Summer Exhibition. His contribution was a four-panel collage and painting entitled *The Critic Kills*. It featured a portrait of his second wife Sandra Fisher (1947–94), an American figurative painter who had died from a stroke aged 47, anti-modern art remarks made by Hitler, plus a quote from Andrew Graham-Dixon's (the *Independent*'s art critic whom Kitaj dubbed 'Anal-Andy') negative review. The work was signed 'by Ron and Sandra' and priced at £200,000. Kitaj's extraordinary contention was that the bad reviews of 1994 intended to injure him had killed his wife instead.[21] This work, therefore, was a very public attack on the art critics via his own medium of expression.

A second assault on British critics was launched via a magazine produced in Paris entitled *Sandra Two*. A third attack – *Sandra Three* – was mounted at the 1997 RA summer show. This time Kitaj curated a

42. R.B. Kitaj, *The Killer-Critic Assassinated by His Widower, Even,* **1997.**
Oil and collage on canvas, 152.4 x 152.4 cm.
Photo: Prudence Cuming Associates,
reproduced courtesy of Marlborough Fine Art, London.

whole roomful of paintings by 'a geriatric avant-garde', that is, by artist
friends such as Auerbach, Freud, Jones, Hamilton, *et al.* Auerbach's
contribution was a portrait of Sandra Fisher. The centrepiece of this
mini-show was a new painting by Kitaj entitled *The Killer-Critic
Assassinated by His Widower, Even,* whose composition was borrowed
from Manet's famous *The Execution of Maximilian* (1868). Kitaj's
luridly coloured painting with many collaged elements and angry
written comments depicted a monster with an enormous brown head
and a yellow, forked tongue who was being fired at by two avengers, one

of whom was clearly Kitaj. A final defiant gesture was the price Kitaj asked: £1 million!

While the show was in progress Kitaj proclaimed that he was leaving London for good in order to relocate in Los Angeles. 'Hollywood', he declared, 'is in my blood'. (However, he added that he planned to retain a studio in London because his children had been born there and he wanted to keep his friends and enemies in England amused.)[22]

Kitaj's example raises yet again questions concerning national and cultural identity. His admirers tie themselves into knots trying to resolve them when it seems obvious that Kitaj is American *and* Jewish *and* European; in short, he is an example of cultural pluralism and hybridity.[23] Similarly, his art is a fraught mixture of traditional and modern, conservative and radical ingredients.

The sense of rootlessness and homelessness that Kitaj has experienced could also be explained by those familiar with philosophical critiques of modernity as a sign of the alienation that is characteristic of this mode of life, especially that associated with huge, cosmopolitan cities. Kitaj himself has remarked:

> History is full of artists who lived out their lives in places far from their origins ... I would submit that entire milieux in New York, Paris, London, etc. have been profoundly affected by the Alien in their midst and drew infinite aesthetic, even tragic power therefrom ... There's a pattern ... a social history of art as a function of cosmopolitan refuge. These great cities are wondrous safe havens for a transient, alien, vulnerable modern aesthetic.[24]

During the decades when Kitaj lived outside America he seems to have revelled in his 'alien' status. However, it should be noted that he, unlike so many others forced to flee their homelands, was an exile by choice, not by compulsion.

Larry Rivers

One American artist who operated in the zone between Abstract Expressionism and Pop art was Larry Rivers (b. 1923).[25] A versatile individual, he was a jazz musician, painter, poet, film-maker, stage designer, sculptor and printmaker. He developed a distinctive painterly style while studying under Baziotes and Hofmann in the 1940s. In

New York during the 1950s he became acquainted with de Kooning, Guston, Kline and Pollock. In a gesture designed to offend the New York art world, to deflate the seriousness of abstract painting, he produced *George Washington Crossing the Delaware*, (1953), an interpretation of a famous 1850 academic canvas by the German-American Emanuel Leutze depicting an important incident in American history, which Rivers executed in a loose, smudgy style indebted to the work of Gorky.

By the early 1960s Rivers was tackling such popular culture subjects as Camel cigarette packs, Buick car grills, Ford trucks, Dutch cigar boxes and French banknotes in a suave, improvised, Action-painting manner; in other words, his source material was Pop but his rendition was not. Rivers visited Paris and London several times during the 1960s. The British dealer Kasmin saw him in Paris and showed him photographs of Hockney's paintings. Rivers responded favourably to Hockney's work and to tales of his 'mad and interesting' personality. In 1961 Rivers was in London for his marriage to Clarice Price, a Welsh-born teacher of music and art. During a short stay he encountered Kenneth Armitage, Lynn Chadwick, Elizabeth Frink, Sir John Rothenstein, David Sylvester and Joe Tilson. The night Rivers gave a talk on BBC radio, he met William Coldstream who was then head of the Slade.

In May 1962 the Gimpel Fils Gallery gave Rivers his first one-man show in London. He made friends with Frank Bowling who was also being shown by Gimpel Fils. While in London Rivers painted a full-length portrait of one of Britain's leading art critics – *Mr Art (Portrait of David Sylvester)* – and gave talks about his ideas and methods at various venues at one of which he met Hockney. Rivers reports being charmed by Hockney's 'Liverpool' (sic) accent. Subsequently, Rivers wrote a personal letter to the British artist which was published, along with an interview between the two men, in a 1964 issue of *Art and Literature*.[26] The respect between the two artists appears to have been mutual.

Allen Jones also heard Rivers speak and later claimed that Hockney was influenced by Rivers.[27] This opinion has been repeated by Peter Webb, a Hockney scholar. In his memoirs Hockney himself admitted that, during the early 1960s, 'Someone who was an influence on a lot of students was Larry Rivers; he had come to England and a lot of people were interested in his work, which was a kind of seminal Pop art.'[28] Rivers' habit of painting or stencilling letters and words on his

43. Larry Rivers, *Mr Art (Portrait of David Sylvester)*, 1962.
Oil on canvas, 182.8 x 132.1 cm.
Photo: O.E. Nelson, courtesy of the Marlborough-Gerson Gallery, New York,
© Larry Rivers / DACS, London / VAGA, New York 1998.

canvases may well have encouraged Hockney to do the same. Michael Upton, who was then studying at the Royal Academy School, was another young painter whom Peter Phillips recalls being impressed by Rivers (and by Rauschenberg).[29]

44. Larry Rivers, *OK Robert OK Negro*, 1966.
Spray paint, pencil and collage, 59.6 x 50.2 cm. Private collection.
Photo: John Webb. © Larry Rivers / DACS, London / VAGA, New York 1998.

During his third visit to London Rivers became acquainted with the
Tate curator Ronald Alley, the painter Francis Bacon and the critic
John Russell. Coldstream had invited Rivers to be an artist-in-
residence at the Slade. From January to June 1964 Rivers worked in a
Slade studio where he painted *The Greatest Homosexual*, a portrait of
Napoleon (based on a reproduction of David's *Napoleon in His Study*
(1812)) and tutored British students. Among the later were some who
had decided to work collaboratively and to seek an alternative to the art
gallery system; they called themselves Fine-Artz Associates and were
keenly interested in teenage cults and Californian customising.[30]

Rivers was in London again during the winter of 1996–67 sharing a house in Belgravia with Howard Kanovitz, an artist and trombone player. During this period he made a lithograph, with cut-outs and collages, entitled *Robert Fraser's London*. It was produced with the help of the noted British printer Christopher Prater. Rivers also made a mixed-media, full-face and profile portrait of Fraser entitled *OK Robert OK Negro*. The subject matter of these two works indicates a close link between the American painter and the fashionable British dealer.

Jann Haworth and Robert Fraser

Along with Boty and Marisol, Haworth was one of the few women who contributed to the Pop art movement during the 1960s. Haworth (b. 1942) was American – she hailed from the Mecca of America mass culture, Hollywood, where her father Ted worked in the movie business. She studied at the University of California in Los Angeles from 1959 to 1961, and at the Slade from 1962 to 1963. While in London she met the British Pop artist Peter Blake and they married in 1963 (they had two daughters but were divorced in 1981). As described earlier, the couple paid a visit to Los Angeles in the same year. The Pop paintings of Blake and the Pop sculptures of Haworth were clearly different, but both artists were fanatical about detail and handicraft and both venerated popular culture personalities.

Haworth's distinctive contribution to Pop art took the form of life-sized effigies and some smaller dolls, stuffed with kapok, made from fabrics such as satin and stockinette and real clothes. They depicted various characters or social types: cheerleaders, cowboys, geriatrics, maids, movie stars and surfers. While these figures were not as naturalistic as waxworks, they were sufficiently lifelike to be somewhat sinister and disturbing. Among the American subjects that Haworth tackled were W.C. Fields, Shirley Temple, Mae West and the *LA Times* newspaper. *Mae West Dressing Table* (1965) was an illusionistic representation of the Hollywood actress famous for her double-entendres in terms of a head and shoulders relief portrait placed behind a sheet of glass purporting to be a mirror. In fact, the mirror-effect was generated by duplicating objects before and behind the glass.

LA Times Bedspread, which dates from the same year, was a quilted enlargement of a double page spread showing comic strips and

45. Michael Cooper, *Jann Haworth with her 1965 mixed media relief*
'Mae West Dressing Table', 1966.
Photo: courtesy of Adam Cooper.

advertisements. The identity of this object was peculiar because it blended craft, fine art and mass media. Like a painting, it could adorn a wall or, alternatively, it could be serve a practical function as a bed covering. Marco Livingstone comments:

> the images in the individual strip-frames are discernible only as ghostly contours, all colour having been expunged, but they are clearly labelled with the familiar titles of the strips [for example, Dick Tracy and Little Orphan Annie] from which they were copied. A faithfully transcribed advertisement for a pink telephone is literally 'dropped in' as a jarringly realistic note within a surface that otherwise seems virtually abstract in its reticence.[31]

Regarding Haworth's preferred themes, soft materials and sewing skills, Livingstone remarks: 'Haworth brought a specifically feminine perspective to a predominantly male domain in her choice of subject matter and especially in her use of procedures associated with "women's work".'[32]

During the 1960s Robert Fraser (1937–86), the Eton-educated son of the wealthy banker Sir Lionel Fraser, ran a fashionable art gallery at 69 Duke Street, in London's Mayfair. Fraser spent the period 1958 to

1962 in America learning about the art trade. He opened his London gallery in 1962 and four years later it was cited in the famous *Time* magazine issue about swinging London. Fraser specialised in Pop art, both American and British: he showed Barker, Blake, Dine, Hamilton and Oldenburg; Haworth too had solo shows in 1966 and 1969. Fraser was also a key figure in the crossover between the realms of Pop art and pop music that occurred during the 1960s because he was friends with the singer Marianne Faithfull and rock musicians belonging to the Beatles and Rolling Stones. He was instrumental in obtaining record cover commissions for Beatles' LPs for British fine artists.

In 1967 Fraser was paid £1,500 to cover the costs of producing the sleeve design for the Beatles' concept album *Sergeant Pepper's Lonely Hearts Club Band*, which included a paltry fee of £200 for Blake's art direction. Arguably, this record was the most crucial, mixed-media artifact of the 1960s. It featured music of exceptional originality and strangeness, packaged in a highly original and creative fashion. Despite being a complex work of art, it achieved a mass sale of 7 million copies. Recorded while the Beatles explored mind-altering substances such as LSD, *Sgt Pepper* signalled the emergence of a new phase in the development of the culture of the 1960s – psychedelia – which was very different in character from the simple, innocent beat music of the early 1960s when the Beatles all wore the same mod suits and were at the command of managers and media people.

The sleeve design for *Sgt Pepper* was devised by Blake and Haworth working in collaboration with the Beatles, mainly Paul McCartney, and with Gene Mahon and Al Vandenberg of the advertising agency Geer Dubois. Although many people assume the front cover image showing the Beatles surrounded by cultural idols was a collage, it was in fact a three-dimensional tableau staged in a studio involving photo cut-out portraits, waxworks, dolls, plants, etc., which was then photographed by Michael Cooper (1941–73). The cut-out portraits were created by enlarging black and white photos of celebrities to life size and then pasting them on to hardboard sheets. Haworth added colour to some by hand-tinting them. In terms of the famous people represented in the cover image, Europeans and Americans were intermingled without regard to their different achievements: Karl Marx was depicted on an equal footing with Marilyn Monroe. Close to the right-hand edge of the cover were two of Haworth's cloth sculptures depicting an old lady and a female child. The latter rests on the woman's lap and wears a striped shirt with the words: 'Welcome The Rolling Stones, Good Guys.'

According to the record's producer George Martin, Haworth thought of the idea of having the LP's title in the form of civic flower-bed lettering.[33] She also assisted Blake with the creation of the record's Pop art style sheet of *Sgt Pepper* cut-outs (moustache, regimental stripes, etc.) which was inserted into the sleeve. Clearly, Haworth made significant contributions to the cover design but rarely has she received full credit for them.

Following Haworth's last exhibition at the Fraser Gallery in 1969, her work was shown at the Sidney Janis Gallery, New York, in 1971. For these shows she produced some bizarre, three-dimensional, mixed-media constructions whose titles – *Snake-Lady* and *Sorceress* – indicated a shift in the direction of mysticism and womanpower.[34] Haworth has lived in Wellow, Somerset, since 1969 and she founded 'The Looking Glass School' (a private, experimental school for children) there in 1974. Having children of her own brought about a change in her work – a greater emphasis on fantasy. With her husband Peter Blake she participated in the Ruralist movement of the 1970s. Haworth continues to live and create in Britain; however, despite further exhibitions, she has not enjoyed the same success and attention that she did during the Pop art era.

Jim Dine

Another American Pop artist whom Fraser knew and exhibited was Jim Dine. He was born in Cincinnati in 1935 and studied at the University of Cincinnati, the Boston Museum School and Ohio University. By the late 1950s he was living in New York, painting and taking part in Happenings. A versatile artist, Dine's oeuvre eventually encompassed collages, drawings, book illustrations, costume designs, sculptures, poems and prints. 'Pop' was not a very satisfactory label because Dine's art was variously indebted to European Dada, Abstract Expressionism and American Neo-Dada. However, his early paintings generally depicted everyday, domestic subjects and had real objects such as tools, shoes and even washbasins attached to their surfaces. Some works focused on the artist's studio and featured equipment such as brushes, colour charts and palettes.

Dine's art soon became known in Britain via magazine articles and mixed exhibitions of Pop art held in London. Clive Barker, the British Pop sculptor, was to meet Dine via the Fraser Gallery. Barker liked one

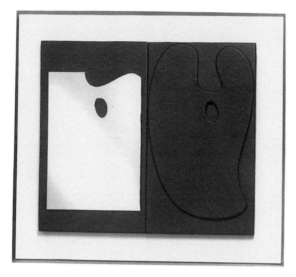

46. Clive Barker, *Two Palettes for Jim Dine*, 1964–65.
Leather and chrome-plated brass, 66 x 76.2 cm.
London: private collection.
Photo: Prudence Cuming Associates, reproduced courtesy of the artist.

of Dine's palette paintings dedicated to Picabia and responded to it by making *Two Palettes for Jim Dine*, (1964–65), one plated with chrome and one covered in leather.

In 1965 Dine was given a one-man show by Fraser and showed work which, according to Cyril Barrett, 'paid tribute to Mary Quant and other aspects of the London scene'.[35] The Tate Gallery acquired the mixed-media work *Walking Dream with a Four Foot Clamp* from the exhibition. In April of the following year Dine and his wife Nancy came to London for a period of two months, so they were in the city during its 'swinging' phase. Dine had been invited to collaborate with the printer Christopher Prater of Kelpra Studio. (This print workshop had been founded by Rose and Chris Prater in 1957. In the 1960s it became noted for its Pop art prints.) Together they made a series of screen-prints entitled *A Tool Box* which was subsequently published by Editions Alecto. (During the 1960s the latter was the leading British publisher of Pop artists. In 1964 it established its own printmaking facilities and studios at 27 Kelso Place, W8, which it later made available to the visiting American artists Oldenburg and Ruscha.)

Besides museums such as the Imperial War Museum and the Natural History Museum, Dine visited Hamley's, the famous toy shop in Regent Street, and he enjoyed watching a Fulham versus Sheffield football match. He was also fascinated by London's fashion and youth culture scene. He and Nancy visited Biba, the fashionable clothes shop in South Kensington, where they found the fabrics and garments 'marvellous and cheap', but the youthfulness of the hippies made him feel like an old man despite the fact he was only 30. He also visited the RCA where he saw student work. In his view there was no doubt that the students 'should be in America'.

Paolozzi and Hamilton were two British Pop artists Dine had contact and discussions with while in Britain. Dine also visited the London home of his fellow countryman R.B. Kitaj where he met younger British artists such as Procktor.

Fraser interviewed Dine for the newly founded magazine *Art & Artists* edited by Mario Amaya.[36] It seems that Dine was relieved to escape the commercialism and pressure-cooker atmosphere of New York. He explained that he felt a greater sense of artistic and personal freedom in Britain because, unlike New York, there were no expectations about what he might create. Moreover, the British art world was more civilised and private, less abrasive and competitive than that of New York. He made similar remarks to the critic Edward Lucie-Smith who thought he was criticising London for being too soft. Lucie-Smith, Gene Baro and Charles Spencer had served on a jury for an exhibition of works by American painters living in Britain to be held at the American Embassy. The selectors, Lucie-Smith remarked,

> felt a little disappointed with the quality of the work submitted, which seemed, too often, to suffer from just those qualities of softness and compromise which Dine denounces among the English. In fact environment seemed to have triumphed over heredity – the kind of painting being done by Americans resident in Britain is related far more closely to the current situation in England than to anything which is now going on in America.[37]

Dine also told Fraser that he had spent a pleasant day with Paolozzi at the latter's rural retreat in the Essex village of Thorpe-le-Soken. As a memento he produced a series of collages from torn paper, string, and watercolour images of hearts, 1930s' advertisements for London buses, steam trains and ocean liners, entitled *Thorpe-le-Soken*. Paolozzi

47. Jim Dine, *Thorpe-le-Soken No. 1*, 1966.
Collage, pencil and watercolour, 76.8 x 55.9 cm.
Photo source: Robert Fraser Gallery, London. © Jim Dine.

supplied Dine with a range of patterns and popular cultural materials with which the American made collages which became known as the *Dine-Paolozzi* series. Regarding the collage-drawings he made in the 1960s, Dine told Constance Glenn:

> I used to walk along the streets of London, kicking up junk, thinking it was really possible to make all the art without ever using the paint, just laying the pieces, scraps, side by side, and creating a surface.[38]

Besides street debris, another source of raw material for collages was wrapping paper with patterns of pink roses sold in Selfridges, the famous Oxford Street department store.

48. Jim Dine, *Dine – Paolozzi No. 1*, 1966.
Collage, 58.4 x 64.8 cm.
Photo source: Robert Fraser Gallery, London. © Jim Dine.

Some of the *Dine-Paolozzi* series included explicit representations of the female genitals and pubic hair. Despite this, Dine claimed – somewhat disingenuously – that the collages were 'asexual'. In September 1966 Fraser mounted a show of Dine's new works: on one wall were drawings of the male penis in various stages of erection; on the opposite wall were drawings of the female organ; one image was deemed to show copulation in progress. Dine later recalled:

> I did a series of drawings depicting male and female sex organs, but I don't see these as pornography. I see them as objects. They represent a very natural part of my style. The object fascinates me. I think of the foot as an object ... To me, sex organs are objects. Powerful objects.[39]

According to the critic John Russell, one source of inspiration for these images was 'the phallic drawings which embellish those unsung galleries of folk art'.[40]

Since Fraser's gallery had a large plate glass window, it was alleged that the drawings were visible from the street. (Fraser claimed they were not.) A member of the public made a complaint to the Metropolitan Police and, as a consequence of their investigation, Dine's works and the catalogues were seized and Fraser was charged under an indecency clause of the Vagrancy Act of 1836. At the conclusion of a court case held in November, Fraser was found guilty and fined £20 plus 50 guineas costs.[41]

Although this time Fraser's punishment was light, the authorities retained an interest in him and his social circle. On 12 February 1967 Fraser was arrested again along with Mick Jagger and Keith Richards following a drug-squad raid on Richards' Sussex home. Fraser was found guilty of possessing hard drugs and he served several months in prison. Richard Hamilton was later to memorialise these events in a series of paintings, prints and posters entitled *Swingeing London '67* (1968–69).

When Dine returned to the United States he spent several months teaching at Cornell University. Then in June 1967, the Dine family (by 1965 Jim and Nancy had three sons) came back to London. Apart from visits to the States and European cities such as Paris, Dine remained in London until 1971 where he concentrated on poetry and printmaking. A fruitful, long-term association was established with Paul Cornwall-Jones who founded the Petersburg Press – specialising in lithographs and etchings – in 1968. The following year Dine held another one-man exhibition at the Fraser Gallery. This time there was no trouble from the police because Dine showed graffiti-style pictures with hundreds of names of people who were important in his life scrawled on them (the so-called 'Name Paintings').

David Bailey, the swinging London photographer, included a portrait of Dine in the 1969 book *Goodbye Baby and Amen: A Saraband for the Sixties* and in 1970 Dine collaborated with the American poet Ron Padgett (b. 1942) on the book *The Adventures of Mr and Mrs Jim and Ron*. How he came to team up with Padgett was explained in a documentary entitled *Jim Dine* (Blackwood Productions, 1970). This film, directed by Christian and Michael Blackwood, also showed Dine at work on large charcoal drawings collaged with bleeding hearts. Dine talked about his attitude to London and its art world and a clip was shown of the new, British, living/singing sculptors Gilbert and George performing *Underneath the Arches* (1969–70).

Dine's visits to Britain and France brought him into closer contact with the fine arts traditions of Western Europe and these had an impact on the direction of his art and upon its iconography. For example, in early 1975 Dine visited an exhibition at the Victoria and Albert Museum about van Gogh's stay in Britain 100 years earlier.[42] Dine was later inspired to produce a series of large drawings after van Gogh just as the latter had made drawings after Delacroix and Millet.

It seems clear that Dine's visits and extended periods of residence in London were stimulating and productive as far as he was concerned. He made friendly contacts with British artists, critics, dealers, art students, printmakers and publishers, and even collaborated with some of them. No doubt they too benefited from their encounter with a rising star of the New York art world.

Yoko and John

Ono (b. 1933), a tiny, Japanese-American woman of tremendous ambition and willpower, became world famous during the late 1960s by marrying the Beatles' singer-guitarist John Lennon (1940–80), but even before she met him she was becoming notorious in fine art and underground circles in New York and London for her contributions to the Fluxus movement and her strange ideas, experimental events, films and exhibitions.[43] Ono came from a wealthy family background but by the early 1960s she was living a poverty-stricken, bohemian existence. Consequently she was constantly on the lookout for affluent people willing to sponsor her art. Accompanied by her second husband Anthony Cox (a film-maker) and their daughter Kyoko, Ono first came to London in September 1966 in order to take part in the Destruction in Art Symposium (DIAS), an international event which Gustav Metzger and John Sharkey had organised. Two other Americans who contributed were Al Hanson and Ralph Ortiz.

For the DIAS Ono performed *Shadow Piece* in a Notting Hill Gate playground on 13 September. It involved drawing around the bodies of people lying on a cloth with a view to capturing and collecting the shadows of everyone in the world. Further performances included *Cut Piece* (in which members of the audience were invited to cut off her clothes with a pair of scissors – a striptease that was also a critique of such shows) which took place at the Africa Centre, the Jeanette Cochrane Theatre, London and the Bluecoat Chambers, Liverpool, between September 1966 and March 1967.

There is no doubt that Ono actively sought publicity to further her career even though much of the media coverage she attracted was mocking and denigratory. One project that excited public attention and provoked censorship was *Film No 4: Bottoms* (1966–67), a documentary shot with the help of Tony Cox, which showed in close-up 365 naked, moving bottoms belonging to people in the London art scene.

Much of Ono's art was balanced on a knife-edge between fatuity and profundity; to many it seemed absurd, slight and shallow, but her ideas had a strange power and persistence. There were several reasons why her artworks appeared insubstantial: they did not conform to the traditional conventions of painting or sculpture; they were often ephemeral; many required the active participation of the viewer to complete them; and they stressed absence – the realm of the invisible – as much as presence – the realm of the visible.

In June 1967 Ono enhanced London's street culture by organising a 'be in' on Parliament Hill Fields, a slope overlooking London ideal for kite flying. The art critic Jasia Reichardt reported that, in response to a flyer issued by Ono, about 250 people turned up, some wearing elaborate costumes.[44] For several hours they danced, played music, burned incense sticks and generated soap bubbles while Ono sat on the grass knitting. The police arrived and were baffled by the innocence and apparent purposelessness of the gathering. Eventually they departed after issuing a warning that kite flying was illegal.

Ono's first London exhibition was held at the Indica Gallery and Bookshop in November 1966. Indica was partly funded by Paul McCartney and Peter Asher (of the duo Peter and Gordon) and it was managed by Barry Miles and John Dunbar who, via his wife the pop singer Marianne Faithfull, had contacts with the Beatles and Rolling Stones. Lennon first met Ono at a preview of the Indica show entitled *Unfinished Paintings and Objects*. Lennon and Ono became friends when they discovered that they both enjoyed playing 'mind games'. In the late 1950s Lennon had been an art student at Liverpool Art College and, although he dismissed most avant-garde art as 'bullshit', he was sufficiently intrigued by contemporary art to attend exhibitions once the Beatles had moved from Liverpool to southern England.

Ono's second exhibition, entitled *Half-a-Wind Show*, was held at the Lisson Gallery in October 1967 – four months after the release of the

Beatles' *Sgt Pepper* LP – and displayed household objects and furniture sawn in half and painted white (white was Ono's favourite 'colour'). The idea conveyed was that humans are only half complete. Lennon was the second half that Ono was seeking. He sponsored the show to the tune of £5,000.

Another show, entitled *You Are Here*, was mounted by Lennon at the Fraser Gallery in July 1968. It consisted of a number of street charity collection boxes in the form of children or animals plus a white circular screen with the tiny inscription 'You are here' in the centre. John and Yoko also released 365 helium-filled, white balloons with invitations to those who found them to reply to Lennon.

Ono and Lennon became lovers in May 1968 and, after divorcing their respective partners, were married in Gibraltar in March 1969. They embarked on an intense romance which was also a remarkable artistic collaboration encompassing super-8 mm films, musical recordings and concerts, and public events and campaigns. Their union represented a convergence of East and West and the realms of avant-garde aesthetics and popular culture. One of the first fruits of their musical experiments was the LP *Unfinished Music No 1: Two Virgins*, released in November 1968. This proved highly controversial mainly because of the album's cover photographs depicting John and Yoko as naked as Adam and Eve.

Wrapping objects in order to disguise and defamiliarise them was a tactic devised by the Surrealists. In August 1967 Ono applied this technique first to the lion sculptures in Trafalgar Square and then in December 1968 by coming on the stage (along with Lennon) of the Albert Hall during the *Alchemical Wedding* event in a bag. The use of white or black bags enabled Yoko and John to appear in public without being seen. 'Bagism' also made the point: 'The essential is hidden from the eye.'

Living with Yoko encouraged John to resume drawing.[45] Portraits, nudes and oral sex with Yoko supplied the subject matter. Some of his erotic images were turned into lithographs by Curwen Studios and issued in an edition of 300 packaged in white plastic bags. An exhibition of Lennon's explicit lithographs was mounted by the London Arts Gallery, New Bond Street, in January 1970. Predictably, Scotland Yard raided the show and took away eight images which they considered to be indecent. A prosecution followed under an act dating back to 1839 but it proved unsuccessful.

Lennon's wealth enabled Ono to fulfil many of her artistic projects while she in turn showed him that artistic, personal and political growth was possible outside the context of an all-male band.[46] However, she became a hate figure – a Dragon Lady – to many Britons because they blamed her for being a 'Jap', being older than Lennon, a pretentious con artist who could not sing (Ono's vocals included screams and sighs) and, above all, for 'stealing' Lennon and thereby breaking up the Beatles. The latter charge was unfair because by the late 1960s the band had ceased touring and each member was seeking to develop in individual directions. Yoko reacted to vilification and demonisation with Zen-like fortitude:

> You see, when all that hate energy was focused on me, it was transformed into a fantastic energy. It was supporting me. If you are centred and you can transform all this energy that comes in, it will help you.[47]

Ono was a pioneer of 'Concept art' which, as its label suggests, emphasised ideas, the imagination and language more than craft skills and physical objects appealing to the sense of sight. *Grapefruit*, a book of her Concept or instruction pieces – the earliest dating from 1953 – was published in Britain in 1970.[48] Lennon's popular song, *Imagine* (1971), reflects the influence of Ono's stress on the power of thought and the effect of Ono's feminism can also be detected in Lennon's song, *Woman is the Nigger of the World* (1972).

Both Lennon and Ono were opposed to the Vietnam war and war in general as a way of settling humanity's disputes. Their pacifism led to the 'bed-in' protest held in the Amsterdam Hilton hotel during their honeymoon which was reported by the world's press, to the song *Give Peace a Chance* (Plastic Ono Band, 1969) and the billboard campaign *War is Over! If you Want It*. (Twelve cities around the world displayed the anti-war posters at Christmas 1969.) It also resulted in them being watched by the FBI and being treated as dangerous subversives. The couple did lend their moral and financial support to many causes and political struggles.

Realising that they would be subject to intense media attention, John and Yoko decided to harness it for their own ends – hence the bed-in. By issuing their own posters they made use of advertising media to 'sell' ideas rather than consumer goods. By commissioning Nick Knowland to make *Film no 6: Rape* (1969) – a harrowing story of a woman persecuted by a film crew – they supplied a critique of the intrusiveness of the news media. In these ways they anticipated much of the media-based art of the 1980s.

**49. *John Lennon and Yoko Ono with 'War is Over!' poster,*
London, December 1969.**
Photo: Keystone Press/Getty Images, London. © Hulton Getty.

Initially Lennon had trouble obtaining a visa to enter the United
States because he had a drugs possession conviction on his record.
However, the couple did move to New York in 1971 and later
purchased an apartment in the Dakota Building close to Central Park.
For some years Lennon had to fight a legal battle against deportation.
His application for permanent residency was at last approved in 1976.
Lennon enjoyed living in New York because it was in effect the capital
of the American 'empire', it had a constant 'buzz' and he felt safe to
walk the streets.

On 8 December 1980 Lennon was shot dead by a supposed fan –
Mark Chapman – outside the Dakota Building. Because of the easy
availability of guns in America and the extreme behaviour of socially
dysfunctional individuals who worship/hate celebrities, a famous
person is far more likely to be stalked and murdered there than in

Britain. It is highly likely, therefore, that if Lennon had not met Ono and had made his home in London rather than New York, he would still be alive today. Had this been the case, however, the creative partnership between John and Yoko would never have occurred and their son Sean would not have been born.

Following Lennon's death, Ono became one of the world's richest, most famous and respected widows. Eventually she resumed her artistic and musical activities and by dint of many exhibitions in America and Europe she gradually achieved widespread recognition as a fine artist.[49] In the view of some critics, Ono's example and Concept art has been an influence and inspiration to young women artists working in Britain during the 1990s.

Of all the American artists who came to Britain during the mid-1960s Ono had the greatest impact in the realms of avant-garde art, rock music, feminism, sexual liberation and radical politics. Simply by 'bagging' Lennon she entered the consciousness of most of the population; indeed, she astonished and divided the nation.

Oldenburg and London

Another leading American Pop artist who spent time in London during the mid-1960s shortly after Dine was Claes Oldenburg (b. 1929). Since his father was a Swedish diplomat, much of Oldenburg's youth was divided between Scandinavia and the United States. (Oldenburg officially became an American citizen in 1953 at the age of 24.) After studying art, literature and drama at Yale University, he attended The Art Institute of Chicago from 1953 to 1954. Two years later he moved to New York where he produced collages and expressionist, figurative drawings and paintings. By the end of the decade he was performing in Happenings. His reputation as an innovative, humorous and erotic Pop sculptor and creator of environments was established during the early 1960s. Many of his works represented everyday, manufactured objects such as typewriters, washstands and hamburgers, but Oldenburg altered their scale by enlarging them and, by changing their materials, he made them soft rather than hard or hard rather than soft. Since he wanted his art to reach a wide audience, he was keen to design enormous public sculptures such as the metal, red-painted head of Mickey Mouse, *Geometric Mouse – Scale X* (Houston, Texas, 1974).

Despite Oldenburg's Scandinavian heritage and the influence of European artists such as Dubuffet, Duchamp and Klee, his Pop sculptures were imbued with American vitality and vulgarity; they were responses to the material abundance in America, the energy and debris of New York's streets, as well as his admiration for American popular culture. According to the critic Barbara Rose, in his direct, instinctive approach to making art Oldenburg rejected 'the idealist aesthetics of European art ... in favour of the empirical values of American pragmatism'.[50]

After a period of time spent in Stockholm, Oldenburg travelled to London. His first extended visit lasted two months – October–November 1966 (he had spent four days walking around the city a few months earlier). He made use of a studio provided by Editions Alecto in order to produce additional works for a one-man show held at the Fraser Gallery during November and December. The works in question included plans for the three-dimensional multiple *London Knees 1966*, drawings and collages based on his responses to the city and to British light-switches and electric wall-plugs, sculptures such as *Fag-ends*, and various proposals for public monuments. According to Oldenburg, to make monuments in a new city was 'to use that city as a studio'.[51]

Oldenburg once explained how he acclimatised to a strange city:

> During the first two or three weeks in a new city, I try to visit as many places as possible, and be taken around by people who live there and know the city. I listen to what they say about it. Also, I try to read every newspaper and magazine on sale. I sketch a lot. And I observe the food.[52]

London's street life fascinated him and he was astonished by the traffic congestion and the density of the crowds of shoppers in Oxford Street and Regent Street. Hans Hammarskiöld, a Swedish photographer, snapped him in Oxford Street carrying a sculpture in the form of a huge tube of toothpaste. This work – *Tube* (1964) – appeared in the Fraser show. Hammarskiöld also documented Oldenburg posing as a 'living sculpture' on an empty plinth near Grosvenor Square.

In contrast to America, he found detail and smallness 'a cultivation of obstacles'. While moving around he scanned the city searching for icons of symbolic value. Like the majority of tourists, Oldenburg visited Piccadilly Circus with its landmark bronze fountain by Sir Alfred Gilbert topped by a winged archer/angel popularly known as 'Eros', and he acquired postcards and photographs which formed the grounds for

**50. Hans Hammarskiöld, *Claes Oldenburg in Oxford Street,
London, carrying 'Tube' (1964)*, 1966.**
Photo: H. Hammarskiöld, Sweden.

collages such as *Drill Bit in Place of the Statue of Eros* and *Lipsticks in
Piccadilly Circus*. Using imagery snipped from advertisements, Oldenburg substituted phallic forms such as a giant drill bit (literally and
metaphorically a screw) and a cluster of red lipsticks for the Eros
fountain (lipsticks were both feminine and phallic). Red, Oldenburg
noticed, was a prominent colour in London: there were red buses and
underground trains, etc. The drill bit and a design for a single tube of
lipstick were intended to rise and fall with the level of the River
Thames which echoed the ebb and flow of sexual desire. Oldenburg's

substitutions were acts of modernisation but the erotic connotations of the original sculpture were retained; indeed, they were made more explicit. His aim was to replace old, idealistic symbols of love with new, non-idealistic ones.

The mid-1960s was an era of sexual liberation or permissiveness, and Oldenburg – like Dine before him – was to find the ambiance of London erotic. A scribble-like sketch in crayon and watercolour of circular light-switches depicted from the front and the side were simultaneously breast-like and phallic. He was intrigued by the different types of switches he encountered in London rooms – travellers invariably notice small variations in material culture from one country to another. He made a plaster model of a square switch which he planned to cast in metal. He imagined a multiple consisting of patterned English wallpaper with unconnected light-switches attached magnetically so that they could be moved around.

Paris was a female city while London – according to Oldenburg – was a male city. Compared to Stockholm, which was hard and dry, London was a wet city.[53] London was all about coming in and going out: the flow of water in the Thames and in people's ear and throat passages – due to colds – and the smokers who inhaled and exhaled. Oldenburg became conscious of particular parts of the body: the ear, the knee and the navel. Frequent trips in London's black taxi cabs gave him the idea for an intimate *Taxi Monument*, that is, an interior lamp in the shape of a human ear. It was to be made from reddish plastic and would light up when rubbed.

Oldenburg has recalled how he became aware of knees, his own and women's:

> I use my body to feel and come to know a city. In London I constantly felt cold in my knees – they always ached. It was aggravated by having to squat in those small English cars. 1966 was also the time of knee exhibitionism because of the mini-skirt, especially when 'framed' by boots. Oxford Street was a sea of knees. So knees were on my mind; and since knees are doubles, I found myself collecting examples of doubles ... [54]

For the knees multiple – issued by Editions Alecto in 1968 – Oldenburg cast the sawn-off legs of a mannequin in latex (so that they would be as squeezable as flesh) and coloured them ivory to match the hue of the Elgin Marbles in the British Museum.[55] In addition he proposed a massive, double knees monument taller than St Paul's Cathedral for

**51. Claes Oldenburg, *Proposed Colossal Monument in the Form of Knees,
on the Victoria Embankment, London*, 1969.**
Detail of a photo-collage, 26 x 40 cm.
Photo: reproduced courtesy of the artist. © Claes Oldenburg.

the Victoria Embankment placed in such a way that it related to the
towers of the Battersea Power Station, and a single knee monument for
the Thames Estuary.

To Oldenburg, London seemed like a giant toilet that was flushed
out daily by the tidal waters of the Thames. This prompted him to
imagine a monument in the form of two colossal ballcocks made from
highly reflective copper floating alongside the Houses of Parliament.
Rods would connect them to the centre of one of the bridges spanning
the Thames. (Clearly, the *Thames Ball* monument was based on the
float in a toilet's cistern.) According to Gene Baro, 'The float
monument would be buoyant and brilliant and would supply Londoners with the sun.'[56] It was visualised in 1967 via crayon, ink and
watercolour on two picture postcards. John Stezaker (b. 1949) is a
British artist who has specialised in collage since the 1970s. Following
Oldenburg's precedent, he too has made use of the brightly coloured
postcards of London sold to tourists.

London also struck Oldenburg as a city of columns and column-like forms. By bending, twisting and softening such forms he evoked human anatomy. He has remarked:

> Still another thing I noticed by being aware of my body was the London preoccupation with the throat, mouth and cigarettes. Lots of ads picture people coughing and smoking. I mated this preoccupation with the constant presence of columns and proposed *Colossal Fag-ends for Hyde Park*.[57]

Party-goers were surprised to see Oldenburg collecting cigarette butts or, as Britons call them, fag-ends. He had seen an anti-smoking poster depicting them which suggested the possibility of transforming something unpleasant into something beautiful. Oldenburg perceived sculptural potential in such smelly waste: he was intrigued by the different forms the cigarettes had after being stubbed out. There was a hard/soft conjunction too: the filter section was hard, the rest of the cigarette soft. He made small-scale sculptures from actual fag-ends and he also envisaged multiples with ashtrays overflowing with fag-ends. Another idea – sketched in crayon and watercolour – was for a monument in Hyde Park consisting of fag-ends which were giant twisted cylinders lying horizontally, like broken columns or tree trunks, on the grass. Oldenburg had seen Hyde Park after a violent storm had felled many trees.

The fag-end motif proved very fertile and when Oldenburg returned home he made a series of fag-end/ashtray drawings, models and sculptures in various materials well into the 1970s.[58] Damien Hirst (b. 1965) exhibited an enormous white ashtray full of British butts in his New York one-man show in 1996. Thus the most fashionable British artist of the 1990s paid a tribute to Oldenburg's work inspired by his 1966 London trip.

Five other monumental proposals which arose from Oldenburg's stay in London were: (1) a diagonal gear-shift to replace Nelson's column in Trafalgar Square. Given the square's constant traffic congestion, he considered a gear-shift column appropriate to the site. The idea was that the gear-shift would move suddenly, every quarter of an hour, through four positions in order to scatter the pigeons in the air. The movements would echo the thousands of gear changes drivers made when circumnavigating the square; (2) a metal rear-view mirror taken from the front wing of an automobile, enlarged and placed on the base of Nelson's column, to enable the city to look at itself and its history; (3) a mini-monument or pavement obstacle (1967) entitled *Fallen Hat*, a memorial to Adlai Stevenson (the American Democratic politician who had died in a London street in 1965) and to a friend of Oldenburg's who had died from a heart attack in London in 1966. A man's hat made from bronze was to be set in a pavement slab so that pedestrians would trip over it; (4) a London square in the form of objects left on a gentleman's night table: a carnation, lighter, cufflinks, a clasp with money and a wristwatch, all resting on an invitation card the size of the square. The face of the watch, Oldenburg suggested, could be a pool of water in which the hands slowly turned; (5) a huge knife slicing through a terrace in Regent Street as if it were a pat of butter.

Clearly, if Oldenburg's monuments had been built they would have drastically altered the existing fabric of London, and some of them approached the condition of architecture rather than sculpture by being conceived as figurative buildings. For example, a giant drum kit for Battersea Park was intended to function as a pleasure palace. The result of enlarging a three-pin extension plug was a house raised on stilts. A building in the form of a vast office machine was planned in place of the high tech Post Office Tower which had opened in 1965.

Oldenburg returned to London again in June 1969 in order to install *Bedroom Ensemble II* (1969), a replica of his celebrated environment *Bedroom Ensemble I* (Los Angeles, 1963), with its weird kitsch and anamorphic furniture, at the *Pop Art Redefined* survey show held at the Hayward Gallery. A retrospective of his work was mounted by the Tate in the summer of 1970 and a short documentary – *The Great Ice-cream Robbery* (Maya Films, 1971) – directed by James Scott, was made at this time: in it Oldenburg was seen at the gallery, at parties, delivering lectures and filming with a super-8 mm camera.

In the 1960s none of the public monuments which Oldenburg envisaged for London were constructed – they were too enormous, fantastic, vulgar and transgressive for the taste of most Britons and no funds were available. However, there did come a time when one of his schemes was realised but it happened in the north of England rather than in the south; this was the *Bottle of Notes*, situated in Central Gardens, Middlesborough, Cleveland. This civic landmark cost £130,000 and leans like the Tower of Pisa, as if stuck in the sand by a receding tide. It was conceived in 1986, erected in 1993 and was designed in collaboration with Oldenburg's second wife Coosje van Bruggen (b. 1942, Groningen, The Netherlands). The 35 ft high and 12 ft diameter sculpture has a bottle shape made from an open network of

**52. Claes Oldenburg and Coosje van Bruggen, *Bottle of Notes*,
Central Gardens, Middlesborough, 1993.**
Steel painted blue and white, 10.6 x 3.6 m diameter.
Photo: *Evening Gazette*, Teeside.

steel, painted blue and white, in the form of handwriting. The two
artists selected short quotes from Captain Cook's journal (Cook was
born locally) and the overall concept derived from seafarers' bottles
with model ships inside and notes or messages set adrift in bottles.[59]
The Italian critic Germano Celant has suggested that the bottle
sculpture is 'an instrument of communication between two cultures',
hence it is a work especially appropriate to the theme of this book.[60]

In the decades since the 1966 Fraser exhibition, Oldenburg's art has been much shown in Britain – an 'anthology' of his work was presented at the Hayward Gallery in June–August 1996 – and there are many publications available about it, therefore it is familiar to most British artists and art students. While it would be an arduous task to trace all the instances of the influence of Oldenburg's work on British artists, he has been such a major figure in the history of modern sculpture since 1960 that there is little doubt that many examples could be found. Furthermore, it is evident from the account given above that Oldenburg made imaginative proposals for the transformation of London and has enhanced the visual culture of north-east Britain.

Michael Craig-Martin

Craig-Martin was born in Dublin in 1941.[61] From 1945 to 1966 he lived mainly in the United States where, during the 1960s, he studied painting at Yale University. He obtained a teaching post in Britain in 1966 and took up permanent residence in London a few years later.

While an art student in the United States Craig-Martin was influenced by Minimal art, particularly that of Robert Morris. Like so many others he developed from Minimalism into Conceptualism but his approach differed from that of Art & Language by being object- rather than language-based. Over the years Craig-Martin has employed many diverse materials and everyday objects: plywood boxes, mirrors, milk bottles, buckets, venetian blinds, housepaints, clipboards, neon lights, and so on. All his works are extremely precise and professionally presented. Obscurity, blurs, blood and guts have no place in his art. He draws the outlines of such mundane things as lightbulbs, chairs and ladders in coloured tape on walls but not scenes of human suffering, torture or war.

Since his art is squeaky clean and cerebral it lacks the popular appeal of Hockney's and the sensuous attraction of Hodgkin's. Conceptual art is appreciated primarily by art world intellectuals. If Craig-Martin is known to people beyond the art world, then it is for his thought experiment, *An Oak Tree* (1973), which was first exhibited at the Rowan Gallery, London, in April–May 1974. This work consists of: (1) a small shelf, made of glass, attached to a wall by metal brackets nine feet from the ground; (2) upon which stands, in the centre, a plain drinking glass two-thirds full of water; (3) a printed text, red in colour, in leaflet form entitled *An Interview with Michael Craig-Martin*; and (4), the title *An Oak Tree*. What the artist asserts is that, by some miracle akin to those performed by certain holy men, he has managed to transform the glass of water into an oak tree even though the viewer's eyes cannot confirm this claim.

During the 1970s *An Oak Tree* was scorned by such figures as Fyfe Robertson (a television journalist) and Giles Auty (a critic) as the epitome of charlatanism. As far as younger British artists are concerned, Craig-Martin's Conceptual masterstroke is a suitable subject for art world in-jokes. At the *New Contemporaries* exhibition, held at the Camden Arts Centre, London, in July 1996, a group of northern artists calling themselves Leeds United (after the football team of that name) parodied *An Oak Tree* by exhibiting many glass shelves with different kinds of drinking glasses resting on them placed at different heights on the wall. Scattered on the floor below were a number of empty spirit bottles – the result of an opening night drinking bout performance. The title of the installation was *Felled 1966*; it was described by the artists as 'the remains of an ancient deciduous forest'.

Craig-Martin has lived and worked in Britain for decades now but still speaks with an American accent. Some critics regard his work as American but inflected by British politeness. He exhibits in plush Cork Street galleries and his works are to be found in the collections of the world's major museums. Besides being an artist, he is an influential tutor at Goldsmiths College (in 1994 he was appointed to the Millard Chair of Fine Art), an art school which, during the 1980s, trained many of the young turks of the British art world. In addition, Craig-Martin has curated exhibitions and written articles for art magazines. Although some critics claim he is radical and subversive, he is in reality a valued member of the British arts and media establishment: he regularly appears as a pundit on television arts programmes and he serves as a trustee of the Tate Gallery. It would be hard to overestimate the influence that Craig-Martin wields on the London art scene.

7   Criticism and Resistance

After the Second World War the United States took on the roles of the world's policeman and relief agency and tried to exert its power globally in order to secure the future for capitalism rather than for communism. Outside the communist bloc, it had many successes. However, as Leon F. Litwack has observed:

> In its attempts to reorder the world, the United States came to discover that the influence it could command, based on its superior economic and military power, was far less that it had assumed. The world refused to conform to American ideals and expectations. Nations might be inspired by the American example, they might aspire to the same material plenty, but they were determined to resolve their conflicts and problems within their own cultures, needs, and aspirations.[1]

There were many Britons who regretted and resisted the process of Americanisation that they witnessed during the 1940s and 1950s. These anti-American feelings have been summed up by Bevis Hillier:

> There was the sour feeling that America had entered the war late, and only after the direct assault on Pearl Harbour: a feeling which the American 'How we won the war' movies after the war did little to dissipate. There were unforgiving husbands whose wives had taken up with American servicemen billeted in England; there were even unforgiving wives who resented certain Americans' attempts to make them unfaithful – for this was the Unpermissive Society. The complaint: 'They're over-dressed [over-paid?], over-sexed, and over-here' was a popular joke. Above all, there was the indecent richness of America: the food parcels sent with the kindest intention but grudgingly received by people who hated 'accepting charity'; the larger-than-life tourists with technicolour space-age cars whose silver-finned tails blocked the pavement when parked at right-angles; the steady flow into Britain of American pop culture – first chewing gum and bubble gum, later horror comics, rock'n'roll, Elvis the Pelvis, and jukeboxes. Teachers ... called the invading culture 'brash', 'trash' and ... 'slick'.

Anti-American feeling reached its height in the late fifties, when the huge brazen American Embassy was put up among the quiet Georgian and Victorian mansions of Grosvenor Square.[2]

The embassy that Hillier mentions was designed by the Finnish-American architect Eero Saarinen (1910–61) and was constructed between 1958 and 1961. It is a rectangular block consisting, from the first floor upwards, of emphatic rectangular window frames arranged in four horizontal bands. The fortress-like facade is crowned by a huge bronze sculpture of a threatening eagle by the Polish-American sculptor Theodore Roszak (1907–81).

53. Michael-Ann Mullen, *Detail of the American Embassy, London, with Eagle Sculpted by Theodore Roszak*, 1998.
Photo: courtesy of M-A. Mullen / Format Photographers.

In the space of one chapter it will not be possible to document every instance of criticism of, and resistance to, American power since 1945, therefore only a few, disparate examples will be considered.

Horror Comics

The importation of American mass culture was a matter of particular concern to the British because of its persuasive power and its appeal to impressionable groups such as children and teenagers. American service-men stationed in Britain were an early source of supply of comic books which they passed on to British children. Comics were also sold in news-agents and on market stalls. The story of the public outcry that occurred regarding American or 'American-style' crime and horror comics – which in many cases were aimed at adults rather than youngsters – has been described in detail by Martin Barker in his 1984 book, *A Haunt of Fears*, therefore only a summary will be supplied. [3]

British adults perceived that the American comics their children were reading were full of repulsive tales with scenes of sadistic violence, quasi-pornographic representations of women's bodies, an obsession with death and murder, and the glamorisation of criminals and fascistic forms of power (Superman, for example). There was a concern that the depiction of certain crimes was causing copycat behaviour in Britain. The visual dimension of the comics led to the charge that they were contributing to illiteracy despite the fact, as Barker has pointed out, that some strips contained as many as 2,000 words. He has also defended the comics against the charge of immorality by showing that most stories did relay moral messages.

In April 1950 the British, National Strip Cartoon Weekly the *Eagle* (Hulton Press) was founded by the Reverend Marcus Morris as a direct response to the 'spiritual sickness' of the American comics. Its aim was to provide an attractive, colourful, but wholesome and educational alterna-tive promoting Christian values. (A sister comic aimed at females was called *Girl*.) Its main strip – a space epic starring Dan Dare and his alien enemy the Mekon – drawn by Frank Hampson, featured a white, British hero modelled on RAF pilots. The *Eagle* achieved sales of 800,000 but, as a result of competition from television, it folded in 1969.

From 1949 to 1955 a concerted campaign was mounted against American-style comics by an alliance of teachers, journalists, librarians, parsons, psychologists, trade unionists and politicians, which resulted in an Act of Parliament, the Children and Young Persons (Harmful Publica-tions) Act (1955), which in turn resulted in the banning of American comic books. Participants in the campaign came from both ends of the political spectrum: some were Conservatives while others were commu-nists. The latter used the campaign as one weapon in a general attack upon America because, of course, it was the primary example of the cap-italist system and it was anti-Soviet. In his researches Barker discovered that the cultural division of the Communist Party of Great Britain had been heavily implicated in the anti-comics campaign. A 1951 issue of

Arena – the Party's cultural journal – was entirely devoted to 'the American threat to British culture'.[4] As Barker noted, it was odd that internationalists committed to world revolution should have decided to defend a national tradition of art based on a heritage conception of culture.

Meanwhile, as we saw in Chapter 2, in Dover Street other left-wing intellectuals – members of the ICA and Independent Group – were collecting American magazines and mass media images and showing positive appreciation of them. A meeting held at the ICA on 20 January 1955, at which Alloway spoke, even discussed horror comics but, unfortunately, no record of the proceedings seems to have survived. It is safe to assume, however, that the comics were subject to a thoughtful evaluation, not a knee-jerk dismissal.

Kasmin's Distaste for American Mass Culture

For the majority of British teenagers during the 1950s, America was a promised land and the source of entertaining movies and dynamic rock music. However, as the case of John Kasmin – the future art dealer – demonstrates, there were some who reacted negatively. (Kasmin, the son of Polish parents, was educated in Oxford.) In 1991 he told Allen Jones:

> What I objected to was the Americanising of everything. Some people saw America as glamour. I saw it as chewing-gum ... I loved Stuart Davis ... but I didn't like the celebration of consumerism ... I hated all those things [Coca-Cola, Elvis Presley]. Johnny Rae [sic] singing *Cry* [a hit in 1952] – my sister used to play it. And there was the cult of the motor-car. I didn't like the look of American motors. Nor did I drive ... [5]

No doubt Kasmin agreed with the opinions of the cultural analyst Richard Hoggart who, in his famous study of British working-class life, *The Uses of Literacy* (1957), disparaged what he called 'jukebox boys' with American slouches who wasted their youth listening to American records in milk bars.[6]

Later, in the 1960s, Kasmin ran a fashionable gallery in New Bond Street which showed both British and American contemporary art. He made several trips to the United States and he mounted exhibitions of the work of such American painters as Frankenthaler, Louis and Noland. Kasmin's dislike of American mass culture meant that he did not appreciate Pop art in either its British or American forms (although he did show Hockney and Richard Smith). It seems clear that Kasmin would not have considered representing Hamilton, Dine or Oldenburg. Fortunately, Robert Fraser was more open-minded.

Incidentally, another Briton who could not stomach American Pop art was Herbert Read. He dismissed it as 'tedious nonsense' and when the trustees of the Tate Gallery proposed in 1967 to purchase Roy Lichtenstein's *Whaam!* for £5,000 he, along with Barbara Hepworth, voted against its acquisition. Read was upset when he was outvoted.

One thing Kasmin did admire about middle-class Americans was their willingness to take a risk by purchasing contemporary art, unlike their English counterparts who, in Kasmin's judgement, were 'too nervous ... not involved'.[7] It has been estimated that 80 per cent of wealthy Americans are willing to buy art whereas only 20 per cent of wealthy Britons are prepared to do so.

Negative Reactions to Abstract Expressionism

As we have seen, during the 1950s the high culture of America in the form of Abstract Expressionism was admired by progressive British artists but it was also criticised and resisted by Neo-Romantics, Royal Academicians and the popular press.

Given that Keith Vaughan's paintings were rooted in the Classical and Romantic traditions of European and British art, his reaction to the Abstract Expressionists on view at the Tate in 1956 was bound to be unfavourable, although he did warm a little to Guston's 'squashy, sensuous drip'. In 1975, thinking about people who had provided him with intellectual stimulus, he recalled that Guston had been 'perhaps the last real challenge'. His verdict on Action painting reveals an acute consciousness of what he perceived to be its limitations:

> Its main sources were anarchy and decoration. Its achievement was to show how much could be done with so little. Its failure was that it brought no disciplines, no restrictions which would enable growth. It offered the artist perfect freedom, the kiss of death ... Since it had no aesthetic it had to substitute historical or dramatic values – the painting as a record of an event, the artist as hero unarmed before his canvas. Such fantasies can appeal to a society deeply frustrated by having its spiritual problems transposed into economic ones.[8]

These remarks were penned in 1961 after Vaughan had been to the United States. A decade later, following a visit to a Rothko exhibition at the Hayward Gallery in February 1972, Vaughan wrote dismissively: 'Feeble stuff. Large decor. Boring to paint and to look at.'[9] Two years later, in November 1974, he arrogantly noted: 'Looked at some pictures of Jackson Pollock. Some are still good. Though I could do better. Scale, energy and nerve is all one requires.'[10]

Predictably, the popular press's reaction to the Abstract Expressionists showing in London in the late 1950s was contemptuous. *Reynolds News* carried an article by 'a psychoanalyst' with the headlines: 'Save me from the Great String Spider Webs, This is not Art – it's a Joke in Bad Taste.'[11] The *Daily Telegraph* – a right-wing paper – maintained that the new American painting was 'utterly degenerate, lucrative muck'. Even sections of the specialist art press were dismissive; for example, G.S. Whittet, the editor of *The Studio* – then a drab, theoretically naive periodical – judged the American paintings to be 'unrelated to visual life, divorced from humanism ... examples of non-art for non-art's sake'.[12]

Alloway, the supporter of American art and mass culture, devoted an entire article to an examination of the reviews of the 1959 *New American Painting* show.[13] His conclusion was that most criticisms were confused, ill-informed and inaccurate. He also found instances of anti-Americanism and even anti-semitism.

In Chapter 3 the negative reaction to Tachisme and Action painting on the part of the RCA tutor John Minton during the 1950s was mentioned. Another RCA tutor who felt threatened by the influence of these movements on his students was Ruskin Spear (1911–90), a conventional portrait and landscape painter who showed regularly in the Royal Academy's annual, summer exhibitions. Years later, in 1970, Spear depicted Barnett Newman standing in front of *Who's Afraid of Red, Yellow and Blue III* (1966–67), a vast vermilion abstraction divided by blue and yellow vertical 'zips'. Spear's portrait was based on a 1968 photograph and was entitled *Homage to Barnett Newman and Alexander Liberman*. (The title was inscribed on the surface of the canvas. Liberman was the photographer.) In fact, this painting was not intended as a homage but as a sarcastic comment. Spear was irritated by Newman's paintings because he considered them 'banal, ludicrous, second rate' and because he thought Newman, the man, was 'self-satisfied'.[14] Newman died in July 1970 shortly after the portrait was completed

**54. Ruskin Spear, *Homage to Barnett Newman
and Alexander Liberman*, 1970.**
Oil on canvas, 213 x 122 cm. Private collection.
Photo: Alex Seago, reproduced courtesy of Mary Spear.

and Spear was then complimented by admirers of the American for
the speed with which he had responded to the news!

By placing a portrait in front of an abstraction Spear was, in effect,
seeking to restore the primacy of figuration over abstraction, while
simultaneously exploiting the fame of the subject. In the late 1950s he
had applied exactly the same reactionary tactic to William Green –
witness *A Young Contemporary (William Green)* (1958) – who was
then a media celebrity.

Heron's Critique of American Art and Criticism

Patrick Heron, having praised in print the new American painting when it first appeared in London, gave up art criticism in order to devote himself to painting. In July 1959, while living in Cornwall, he was visited for the second time by Greenberg who in his arrogant way sought to persuade Heron to make compositional changes. Greenberg wanted Heron to bunch forms in the centre of his canvas leaving empty space around them instead of placing them in such a way as to call attention to the edges. Heron refused this advice because by then he objected to the simplicity and symmetry of so many American paintings and he advocated, as a necessary next step, the *re-complication* of the picture surface.[15] Within a few years, Heron was to note, both American critics and painters had become edge-conscious. Naturally Heron claims credit for this change.

By the early 1960s Greenberg was backing the American Post-Painterly Abstractionists. Once Heron had become familiar with their work, he began to have reservations about its originality and quality. In addition he became aware of the 'ruthless promotional techniques' underpinning the international success enjoyed by American artists. Heron came to resent the nationalistic boasting of Greenberg and his followers. Clearly, they had not read Eric Knight's handbook, *A Short Guide to Great Britain*, issued by the War and Navy Departments in Washington to every GI on their way to Britain during the Second World War, which warned: 'The British do not like boasting and showing off.'[16] Since many Britons are (or were) modest, reticent beings who are embarrassed to blow their own trumpets – and this is judged to be a major difference between them and Americans – Heron had to steel himself to make his critical thoughts about the Americans public. At the ICA in July 1965, during a discussion about Morris Louis and Post-Painterly Abstraction, he dared to do so by attacking Greenberg and by claiming that he (Heron) had invented vertical stripe painting in 1957, that is well before Louis. There was an uproar and Heron was howled down. As he later argued, it seemed as if the British art world had become completely cowed and brainwashed by American hype, so much so that questioning the chronological priority of American art was inconceivable. It is not unusual for weak individuals and nations to develop such a strong identification with more powerful people and states that they become incapable of independent thought.

Heron maintained that the extravagant claims made by the Americans – and reiterated by compliant British critics such as Alloway and Paul Overy – had resulted in a totally one-sided account that failed to credit the innovations of his generation of British artists. Younger artists were thus kept in the dark about the latter's achievements, especially since the walls of the Tate were being dominated by American art. Examining the history of the interaction between British and American art, Heron was driven to the conclusion that certain British artists had, via exhibitions held in New York, influenced American ones rather than vice versa. Heron's arguments were later developed in print in a trio of articles published in *Studio International* over the period 1966–70.[17]

Then, in October 1974, the *Guardian* newspaper printed three, full-page, illustrated articles by Heron charging the Americans with cultural imperialism.[18] It was remarkable that a national, daily broadsheet was willing to devote so much space to an art world issue. To 'prove' his thesis that British artists had influenced the Americans, Heron juxtaposed illustrations of paintings from both countries. Unfortunately the grey, newsprint reproductions gave little idea of the quality of the originals. Furthermore, since no measurements were supplied, readers had no idea if two images of similar size on the page were, in reality, comparable in size. There were indeed many cases of formal similarity between the British and American paintings but this in itself did not prove an influence because artists on both sides of the Atlantic could have reached similar conclusions at roughly the same time. Even if an influence could be proved without doubt, or was admitted, the result in the hands of an American artist might well have been better than in the hands of a British one.

In spite of these reservations, there does seem to be a case to answer, one which American art historians could investigate: which paintings by British artists were shown in New York? When were they shown and who saw them? Are any influences or borrowings acknowledged by American artists and critics? If so, then the history of American art since the 1940s will need revising. What Heron was seeking – mutual recognition and reciprocity (that is American museums should display British art to the same extent that British museums displayed American art) – was surely not unreasonable.

Latham's Attack on Greenberg

Another Briton who was to become critical of the ideas and judgements of Greenberg was John Latham. The latter's most notorious assault on a book was his *Still and Chew* event of 1966–67 which involved the partial destruction and distillation of Greenberg's *Art and Culture* (1961). This influential collection of essays by America's most prestigious formalist art critic was much read by students in the 1960s, including those at St Martin's where Latham taught part time. The book became a prime target because Latham considered its title pretentious and because Greenberg's emphasis on space and form conflicted with his own emphasis on time and event.

Greenberg had earlier dismissed Latham's book reliefs in a postcard to the artist as 'patly Cubist'. He had visited Britain in 1965 to chair the jury at the John Moores Liverpool Exhibition where work that Latham had submitted was rejected. The critic looked down on most contemporary British art because he considered it was in 'too good taste', so Latham decided to invert the comment to see if Greenberg 'tasted good'.

55. *Clement Greenberg as he appeared in an Open University*
Arts TV programme, 1983.
Photo: reproduced courtesy of Nick Levinson,
the BBC and the Open University, Milton Keynes.

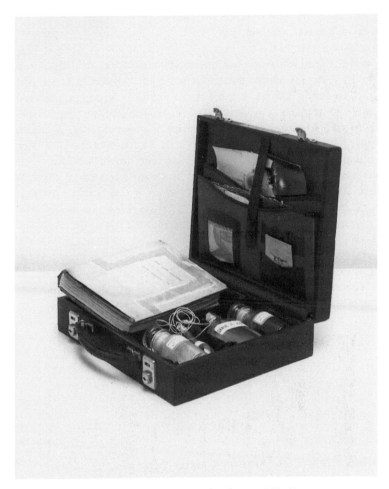

56. John Latham, *Art and Culture*, 1966–69.
Assemblage: leather case containing book, letters, photostats, etc., and labelled
vials filled with powders and liquids, 7.9 x 28.2 x 25.3 cm.
New York: The Museum of Modern Art collection, Blanchette Rockefeller
Fund (purchased 1970). Photo: The Museum of Modern Art, New York.

The *Still and Chew* event was held in August 1966 at Latham's
home in Holland Park. Barry Flanagan, then a sculpture student at St
Martin's, helped to organise it. Guests chewed pages torn from a copy
of *Art and Culture* borrowed from the art school's library. About

one-third of the book received this treatment. When well chewed, the soggy pages were spat out into a flask, then immersed in 30 per cent sulphuric acid until the solution was converted to a form of sugar. This was neutralised by the addition of sodium bicarbonate. An alien culture – yeast – was introduced and the mixture left for months to ferment until, in May 1967, an overdue notice marked 'very urgent' arrived from the art school's librarian. Latham distilled the liquid and transferred it to a glass phial in the shape of a drop of water, labelled it and returned 'the essence of Greenberg' to the library. As a consequence of this action, he was dismissed from his teaching post.

Latham performed an alchemical-like transformation in order to distil the book's essence but in such a way as to neutralise its potency. If he had engaged Greenberg at the level of theory, he would have stepped outside the role of the artist and into the role of the critic. His riposte was all the more striking because it took the form of a semi-public event and because it engaged with Greenberg's text, as befits an artist, in a literal, material manner.

Subsequently, Latham assembled the phial of essence, bottles of liquid and powder, what remained of Greenberg's book, letters and other documents relating to the event and placed them in a black leather case. This assemblage – now entitled *Art and Culture* – was later acquired by MoMA in New York and came to be regarded by certain critics as a key example of Conceptual art. The willingness of MoMA to buy *Art and Culture* indicated that the Americans had a sense of humour and that they regarded Greenberg and Latham as significant figures.

Riley's Distaste for American Business Methods

A common European opinion of Americans is that they are crass materialists obsessed with the accumulation of wealth and in its pursuit are willing to commercialise and commodify everything, to subject everything – even fine art – to the hard sell. A prime example of this occurred in the case of the work of Bridget Riley during the mid-1960s.

Riley (b. 1931) was brought up in Cornwall, educated at Cheltenham Ladies' College, and studied at Goldsmiths and RCA during the period 1949–55. In the early 1960s she developed a form of painting which became known as Optical or Op art and which, as explained earlier, involved the manipulation of black on white patterns to trigger reactions in the viewer's retinas. Many of Riley's paintings were characterised by tensions between flat surface and illusionary depth and by contrasts between areas of repose and disturbance.

Her work became known in the United States during 1964 as a result of its appearance in exhibitions and articles in *Time* and *Life* magazines. Then, from February to April 1965, a large-scale, mixed exhibition of Op art entitled *The Responsive Eye*, curated by William C. Seitz, was held at MoMA, New York. (It then travelled to St Louis, Seattle, Pasadena and Baltimore.) Two 1964 paintings by Riley, *Current* and *Hesitate*, were featured. *Current*, which was in MoMA's permanent collection, was reproduced on the front and back covers of the catalogue and *Hesitate* was owned by Larry Aldrich, a dress manufacturer and art collector. Aldrich had established a Museum of Contemporary Art in Ridgefield, Connecticut, in 1964 and Riley's work had appeared in its opening exhibition.[19] (*Hesitate* has since returned to Britain and is now in the Tate Gallery's collection.)

At the same time as the MoMA show, Riley was given a solo exhibition by the Richard Feigen Gallery in New York. Thus the public and private sectors operated in parallel to promote Riley. She flew to the United States in order to attend the exhibitions. Later she recalled:

> I was driven from the airport down Madison Avenue, and to my amazement I saw windows full of versions of my paintings on dresses, in window displays, everywhere.

One might have expected her to have been flattered and exhilarated by this homage but no, her reaction was:

> My heart sank. What happened is that someone who was connected with the Museum of Modern Art and who was also a dress manufacturer had bought a painting of mine and made dresses based on it which other people in the fashion world immediately picked up on ...

and at MoMA she found that

> ... about half the people there were wearing clothes based on my paintings and I tried to avoid having to talk to the people who were the most completely covered in 'me'. There was one member of the MoMA council who was so furious that he said 'So, you don't like it? We'll have you on the back of every matchbox in Japan!'[20]

57. Larry Aldrich (seated) with Young Elegante designer Morton Myles and four models wearing Op art dresses. The model on the right is wearing a dress the design of which derived from Bridget Riley's *Hesitate* (1964).
Photo source: *American Fabrics*, spring 1965.

In 1966 Riley also told Prudence Fay that 'Aldrich kept inviting her to his showrooms "for a surprise". When she finally went, he triumphantly wheeled out a rack of dresses printed with the complete image of her *Hesitate*. As if bestowing an accolade, he offered her the first.' [21]

Op art's eye-dazzling patterns proved irresistible to fashion, graphic, shop window and textile designers in the United States and in Britain and soon they were reproduced everywhere. Fine artists surely benefited from this explosion of interest and free publicity, but Riley did not welcome the instant celebrity. Her distaste at the transformation of her fine art into applied art – which she regarded as falsification and disfigurement – was somewhat odd given the fact that she herself had previously been willing to work for business, that is, for the advertising agency J. Walter Thompson for six months and on a part-time basis, where – I understand – she had helped to develop the Woolmark trademark, an Op design in black and white.

However, she did have several legitimate objections, one of which was that her permission had not been sought. Some American artists were sympathetic to her plight. Barnett Newman, for instance, took her to see his lawyer but they discovered that artists in America had no copyrights,[22] so Aldrich had not broken any American law. To remedy matters, a Bill to amend the law of the New York State was introduced in 1967 and, according to Newman, it was dubbed 'Bridget's Bill'. Ever since 1965 Riley has been hyperconscious of her copyrights: over the years she has taken legal action against Gilbey's Gin, Nestlé and Harrods for the 'vulgar plagiarism' of her work.[23]

A second, aesthetic objection Riley had was that her abstract designs had been created for flat surfaces and not for rounded bodies and fabrics with folds. Riley told Fay:

> If manufacturers and designers appreciated the principle on which my images are based, and re-applied them to dresses, they'd get something different and perhaps quite marvellous. But they just lift them wholesale, and on the most superficial level. So nothing has any unity. I've yet to see an Op fabric which is wearable. I think they're ugly beyond belief.[24]

A third objection was that commercial exploitation had hindered serious aesthetic appreciation of her paintings because 'The public can't come fresh to them.'[25] On her return to Britain Riley wrote an article for *Art News* in which she explained her artistic intentions to the American public. She also complained that she had left America with feelings of 'violation and disillusionment' because her art had been 'vulgarized in the rag trade', and because 'an explosion of commercialism, bandwagoning and hysterical sensationalism' had prevented its proper appreciation: 'Virtually nobody in the whole of New York was capable of the state of receptive participation which is essential to the experience of looking at pictures.'[26] Again this was odd given that Riley later informed Jonathan Aitken that 'Op is very much a proletarian art; as long as you have a pair of eyes, you can see it. It will do as much for you as the art historian or the big critic.'[27]

In a 1966 article Lawrence Alloway, the British-born critic then living in New York who was sympathetic to Pop art and popular culture, reflected on the reception of Seitz's exhibition and Riley's complaints. Alloway maintained that Op art had evoked a widespread public response in America which had not been shared by art critics and the art press. Riley's negative reaction, he thought, stemmed from the violation of a desire for a humanist tradition of an intelligent, sensitive, numerically small audience on whom an artist can count for understanding. In one way or another Miss Riley's complaint echoes the complaints of American art critics, most of whom disliked the show (including her work), but they shared her assumption of a small congenial audience. On this basis they resented the large-scale public attention given to the artists in *The Responsive Eye*.[28]

What Riley did not acknowledge in her *Art News* article was the financial benefit she gained from the American enthusiasm for her Op art: her Feigen show was sold out by the opening day! Riley must have known that the Feigen Gallery was a profit-seeking business and that her paintings – offered for sale – were commodities, albeit luxury ones. However, she did not gain any royalties or fees from the rag trade reproduction of her abstractions.

There are real physical and aesthetic differences between paintings made by hand and designs generated by mechanical processes. There is a contrast between one-off and batch-production objects and they reach the public via different distribution systems. Hence the cultural distinction that is normally drawn between the fine and the applied arts, between painting and graphic design, is rooted in material differences, but there are also economic-value and cultural-status reasons: it is important to many artists to maintain a distinction so that artworks-as-expensive-commodities are not confused with cheaper, mass produced goods which inevitably have a lower cultural prestige.

The distress Riley experienced in reaction to American commercial exploitation was surely due to the threat that the latter posed her high status as a fine artist and thus to the sales of the unique, highly priced goods that she was producing. One sees the same logic at work in perfume marketing: manufacturers of expensive brands refuse to allow downmarket shops to sell their bottles on the grounds it would undermine the upmarket, 'exclusive' image and value of their brand.

Riley began to use colour in 1967 and by dint of developing her pictorial vocabulary she has enjoyed a financially successful and critically acclaimed career. The events associated with her 1965 New York trip, therefore, do not seem to have harmed her or prevented the art world from treating her work seriously.

As a mid-1960s' fashion, Op design quickly became exhausted as a consequence of over-exposure and dilution. In any case, interest in it was not likely to last long, given that it appealed to the retina more than the mind.

British Reactions to America and the Vietnam War

During the 1960s many Britons became disillusioned with the United States because of its cultural imperialism and its involvement in Vietnam's savage civil war. For example, Herbert Read, during a trip to the Far East in 1965, complained about the all-pervasive influence of America. It was, he declared, 'ruthless and ugly ... the madness of a rootless, deeply alienated technocracy'. The war in Vietnam in particular aroused his disgust and he felt unwilling to go to the USA again while the conflict persisted.

The atrocities and violence committed by American weaponry and troops were vividly revealed by documentary photographs and by television news footage and this produced revulsion in both America and Europe. The war divided the American people and caused unrest and violence at home. Michael Sandle (b. 1936), a British sculptor, was in Berkeley, California, during the late 1960s and witnessed riots in which American police beat up student demonstrators and shot at them with rubber bullets. This experience informed sculptures on the theme of war – such as *A Twentieth Century Memorial* (1971–78) – that he was to make later.

Another shocking incident occurred in the United States in May 1970, that is, the shooting by National Guardsmen of students – four of whom died – on the campus of Kent State University, Ohio, during a protest against the war in Vietnam. In England Richard Hamilton took a photograph of a television transmission of a student-made, 8 mm film and turned this into a screenprint which was published in an edition of several thousand. The content of the print was stark: it simply showed the bloody body of a male victim lying on the ground. The student depicted – Dean Kahler – was not in fact killed but he was paralysed as a consequence of spinal injuries.

Hamilton decided to 'layer many transparent layers of colour over each other to build up the image from the overlaps and fringes'.[29] It was a difficult technical procedure and many prints were ruined.[30] (4,000 were eventually issued and sold for the low price of £15. The prints were first exhibited at Studio Marconi, Milan, in January 1971.)

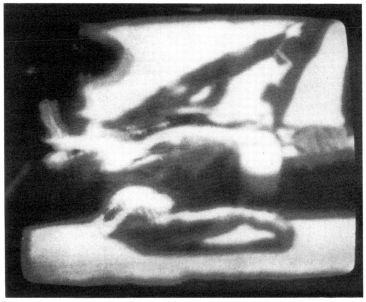

58. Richard Hamilton, *Kent State*, 1970.
Screenprint, 67.2 x 87.2 cm. Published by Dorothea Leonhart, Munich,
in an edition of 5,000. © Richard Hamilton 1998. All rights reserved DACS.

The final image was blurred and abstracted to indicate its mediated
character and it was enclosed within the rounded shape of a television
screen to acknowledge its source. In a statement that Hamilton wrote
at the time, he limited himself to a dry and detailed account of the
passage of visual information, via various communication systems and
media, from the USA to the UK, rather than giving an expression of
personal disgust at the event itself.[31]

During the 1950s Hamilton had been a Labour Party member and a
CND supporter, therefore he was an artist with political commitment
and social awareness. His fascination with American mass culture had
been primarily anthropological, and that of a knowing consumer, but
the Kent State print showed that Hamilton was not unaware of, or
indifferent to, the negative aspects of American society.[32]

In London some artists began to participate in mass protests – such
as the one mounted by 25,000 demonstrators outside the American
Embassy in 1968 – and to make art which made angry criticisms. One
such artist was Peter Kennard. He was born in London in 1949 and

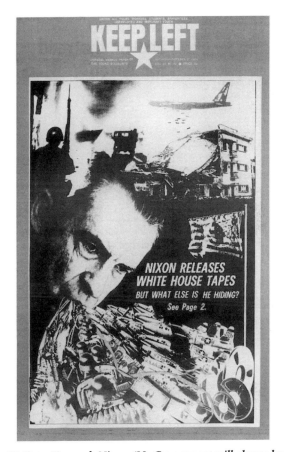

59. Peter Kennard, *Nixon: 'My Government will always be dedicated to World Peace'*, 1973.
Photomontage used on the cover of *Keep Left* (official weekly paper of the Young Socialists), Vol. 22, No. 43 (27 October 1973).
Photo: reproduced courtesy of the artist.

trained as a painter at the Byam Shaw School of Art and the Slade from 1965 to 1970. (He also attended the RCA from 1976 to 1979.) Although Kennard drew and painted, he tended to prefer photographs and reproductive media because they were cheap, understood by a wide public and could be published and distributed in many forms. Gradually Kennard became noted as a left-wing political artist and photomontagist working in the tradition of John Heartfield.[33]

During the mid-1960s Kennard became radicalised by media coverage of the Vietnam war. A sketchbook drawing dated 1965 proposed a Vietnam memorial cross and in 1970 he produced a print concerning the Kent State killings. In the early 1970s a stream of photomontages followed which attacked American military aggression. An example was *Nixon* – a complex amalgam of images – published on the cover of *Keep Left* in 1973. Normally Kennard's montages appeared in the press rather than in art galleries and they had a strong black and white contrast for greater emphasis and to aid clarity when reproduced. Many American artists, of course, also made works critical of America's involvement in the Vietnam war. That involvement ended in 1973 when President Nixon signed a ceasefire agreement.

British Artists versus Disney

Multinational corporations such as Walt Disney and McDonalds with headquarters in America are so rich, well organised and powerful that they exercise a global reach. For instance, they can afford to employ teams of lawyers to ensure that they receive payment for any use of their copyrighted imagery (so-called 'character-merchandising') and to limit or suppress any adverse criticism of their activities. The image of the cartoon character Mickey Mouse has been employed in a critical way by the British sculptor Michael Sandle, the painter John Keane and the muralist Brian Barnes (of the Wandsworth Mural Workshop).[34] Barnes and his team of helpers included images of Mickey Mouse and Walt Disney as part of a Community mural entitled *Morgan's Wall* or *The Good the Bad and the Ugly* (London, Battersea Bridge Road, 1976–78, destroyed in 1979). They were protesting against a proposal to build a Disneyworld in Battersea instead of vital housing and other social amenities for local people on low incomes. Threatened by Disney's lawyers, the British artists responded with defiance by mounting a street theatre performance in which a Disney character tried unsuccessfully to prevent the completion of the mural. The event was filmed as part of the documentary *Morgan's Wall* (Arts Council/ Liberation Films, 1978) and so reached a wider audience.

Political and community murals appeared in considerable numbers both in Europe and North America during the 1970s. However, the fact that this kind of art concerned local urban issues, aimed to nurture community values and assist social change, was part of the physical fabric of a neighbourhood and avoided commodification meant that it was significantly different from most fine art. It was national without being nationalistic; it was local but still took note of external forces – such as those emanating from American corporations – acting upon small, British communities.

Community artists sought an alternative to current fashions in art and the marketing/collecting/exhibiting of art via the gallery/museum system, therefore they had no interest in exhibiting in New York or seeking the approval of American critics and curators. They did take an interest, however, in historical examples of public art in the Americas, namely the achievements of the Mexican muralists Orozco, Rivera and Siqueiros, and the murals painted in the United States during the 1930s via the Works Progress Administration scheme.

This chapter has discussed some British artists and critics who have attacked American cultural, economic and military imperialism. However, their efforts were dwarfed by the heroic struggles waged by the women who protested for years against the presence of American nuclear missiles at the Greenham Common airbase and by Dave Morris and Helen Steel who fought a long legal battle against the fast food giant McDonalds.[35]

8   The Decline of American Influence and the Rise of BritArt

In 1996 the British art critic Adrian Searle remarked: 'Today, Manhattan looks as provincial – and as parochial – as everywhere else.'[1] To explain how this situation came about we need to review the history of British reactions to Minimal art and the subsequent emergence of Conceptual art.

After Pop art and Modernist sculpture, the next movement which had a significant impact during the 1960s was Minimal art. Although this movement was international in the sense that it had adherents in several countries, it was generally deemed to be American because of the major contributions made by such American artists as Carl Andre, Dan Flavin, Donald Judd, Sol LeWitt, John McCracken, Agnes Martin, Robert Morris, Ad Reinhardt, Robert Ryman, Tony Smith and Frank Stella.

Initially, Stella's pared down, monochrome, 'stripe' paintings dating from 1959 became known in Britain via illustrations in American books, catalogues and magazines. Kasmin gave him one-man shows in 1966 and 1968, and then a larger exhibition was held at the Hayward Gallery in 1970. Examples of American Minimalism were also displayed in the strangely named show *The Art of the Real*, curated by E.C. Goossen, mounted at the Tate in April 1969. In the same month the British journal *Studio International* published a thematic issue entitled 'Aspects of Art called "Minimal"' guest edited by the American critic Barbara Reise, which featured the work of Andre, Flavin, Judd and Smithson. In New York in 1968 Gregory Battcock edited an important collection of articles entitled *Minimal Art: A Critical Anthology* which was published in Britain the following year. Caro was virtually the only British sculptor discussed in this overwhelmingly American text and he was a Modernist sculptor rather than a Minimalist.

In the event few British artists were willing to commit themselves to the extreme programme of reduction and exclusion, to the stark

PLUTO ✦ PRESS

Please tell us which book you have purchased

....

☐ Yes please add me to your mailing list.
My subject interests are:

....

☐ Please send me the current catalogue

The last catalogue I received was ....

Name..................

Position..................

Institute..................

Address..................

....

....

.... Postcode..................

VISIT THE PLUTO PRESS WEB-SITE AT
http://www.leevalley.co.uk/plutopress

PLUTO PRESS
FREEPOST ND 6781
LONDON
N6 5BR

simplicity and use of identical, mass-produced units that American Minimalists were willing to embrace. Perhaps only Alan Charlton, Peter Joseph, Bob Law and William Turnbull produced work of comparable severity. Law became notorious in the 1970s for his virtually blank, all-white or all-black, canvases. There was also the immigrant artist Rasheed Araeen (b. 1935) – who came to Britain from Pakistan in 1964 – who worked in a Minimalist idiom, constructing abstract lattice structures in metal, between 1965 and 1972.

Minimal art had a minimal appeal to the British public. Exhibitions by Andre and Judd in London galleries during the 1970s were generally deserted and the dealer Nicholas Logsdail complained about the lack of British buyers. The Carl Andre 'bricks' affair in 1976 – a 'scandal' whipped up by the tabloid press about the 'waste' of public money on the purchase of Andre's *Equivalent VIII* – 120 American firebricks – by the Tate Gallery – at least resulted in Minimalism entering the public's consciousness. As a comment on the affair, one British critic produced a photomontage of 'the bricks' with a male thug throwing one brick out of the picture space towards the viewer; the caption sardonically declared: 'American Culture is Good for You!'

60. John A. Walker, *American Culture is Good for you!*, 1976.
Photomontage printed on a postcard, edition of several hundred.

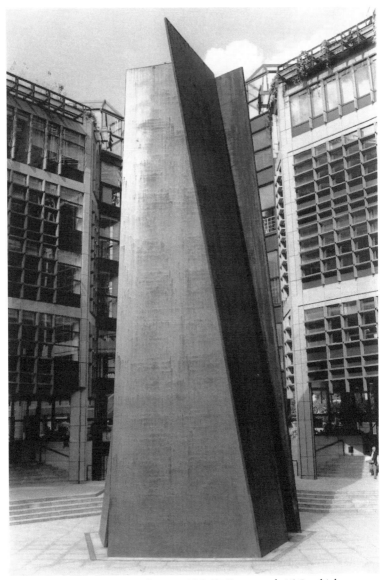

61. Richard Serra, *Fulcrum,* **1986–87.** Rusty steel, 16.5 m high.
London: near Broadgate Circle. Photo: Roderick Coyne.

A Robert Morris (b. 1931) installation at the Tate (April–June 1971),
proved more popular with the public because it included an audience

participation 'assault course' consisting of ramps, rollers, ropes and tunnels which excited young, athletic visitors. So enthusiastic and active did they become, in fact, that immense noise was generated, exhibits were destroyed and accidents occurred. Fearing serious injuries, the Tate's curator, Michael Compton, felt compelled to close the show for a time. It seems that Morris had misjudged the British: he had assumed that they would be far more inhibited and sedate than turned out to be the case.[2]

The largest public manifestation of American Minimalism (some critics would say Post-Minimalism) in Britain is Richard Serra's *Fulcrum* (1986–87), a 200 ton, 55 ft high construction made from rectangles of rusty steel propped up against one another, situated in Broadgate, near Liverpool Street station, London. (Broadgate, a huge complex of offices by the property developer Sir Stuart Lipton, has a scattering of sculptures intended to add a veneer of culture to a business zone. One of them, *The Rush Hour Group*, is by the American Pop sculptor George Segal.) Strangely Serra's metal monument has been accepted by Londoners with equanimity or indifference whereas his *Tilted Arc* (1979–81), located in Federal Plaza, Manhattan, aroused such hostility from New Yorkers that a campaign was mounted for its removal, which was eventually successful in 1989.

'Art by telephone' was another description of Minimalism because artists could simply order by phone materials they wanted – bricks, steel plates, neon tubes, etc. – from industrial companies. Particular pieces were also generated by means of written sets of instructions which, like food recipes and musical scores, could be executed by people other than the artist. The conceptual element inherent in all art was thus foregrounded and this enabled a further development of avant-garde art to occur, namely, Conceptual art. Many British Conceptual artists perceived Minimalism as the 'degree zero' of art and they began by pushing the conventions of Minimalism to even more extreme, and absurd, conclusions. Consequently, American Minimalism was more significant to British Conceptualists than to the majority of British painters and sculptors.

Victor Burgin can be cited as an example of the critical response to Minimalism by British artists. Burgin was born in Sheffield in 1941 into a working-class family. After studying at the RCA from 1962 to 1965, he travelled to the United States and spent two years at the graduate Art and Architecture School of Yale University. Judd, Morris and Reinhardt were three of the artist-teachers Burgin encountered. He listened to what they said in lectures and read what they wrote in magazines like *Artforum* but while doing so he felt dissatisfied with the narrowness of the concerns of the Americans – one lecture was all about the difference between flat and rolled steel! He also detected logical contradictions which he considered could only be solved, if at all, at the level of thought. At the same time Burgin was wrestling with the implications of Greenberg's theories about art and with the ideas of Michael Fried, Greenberg's acolyte.

Burgin came to the conclusion that he had discovered questions and problems that the next, younger generation of artists – his own – had to address. Thus American Minimalism did not so much influence him as prompt the search for 'the next step' and for an art which had social content and a wider public appeal.[3] Subsequently, Burgin became noted as an artist using photographs plus texts for political purposes and as a theorist employing psychoanalysis and semiotics to decode imagery. His artistic output was mostly self-subsidised from his earnings as a lecturer in British art colleges and polytechnics. During the 1980s another brain drain occurred: Burgin moved to the United States to teach at the University of California. Others who left for America were the artist Conrad Atkinson and the writers/theorists Rosetta Brooks, T.J. Clark, Dick Hebdige, John Tagg and Peter Wollen.

Art & Language

A major force within Conceptual art during the late 1960s and the 1970s was the group called Art & Language (A & L).[4] Essentially its founder members were artist-friends who shared certain concerns and who were prepared to work collaboratively on what they regarded as a series of learning projects. Their collaboration began in 1966 but the group was not formally constituted until two years later. Writing in 1997, the British art critic John Roberts contended that Conceptual art 'began out of violence, the violence of American imperialism and the Vietnam war'. However, he went on to argue that this was not manifested in political imagery attacking the United States but in 'an iconophobia', a rejection of imagery (though they did in fact still use diagrams and photos): 'As if the spectacle of violence could only be challenged by de-aestheticising the visual.'[5]

British participants in A & L included Terry Atkinson, David Bainbridge, Michael Baldwin, Harold Hurrell, Philip Pilkington, Mel Ramsden, David Rushton, Paul Wood and the art critic and historian Charles Harrison. Eventually, A & L expanded and became trans-Atlantic in character. American participants included Sarah Charlesworth, Michael Corris, Dan Graham, Preston Heller, Joseph Kosuth, Christine

Kozlov, Andrew Menard, Sol LeWitt, Mayo Thompson and Lawrence Weiner, as well as the Australians Ian Burn and Terry Smith, an art historian who obtained a Harkness Scholarship to visit New York. Membership of A & L fluctuated continuously; at its peak around 50 people were involved.

British art education was a prime source of dissatisfaction to future members of A & L because of its low level of intellectual discourse and self-understanding. Baldwin was expelled while a student and later on several members of A & L were sacked from their posts as art school tutors because their second-order theoretical questioning was found so subversive by other staff committed to the production of first-order things – 'visible, tangible objects' – such as paintings and sculptures. It is perhaps not surprising therefore that A & L became aggressive and set out to cause trouble in an art world that they considered blighted by careerism, greed and money and befuddled by ideas that were idealist (Hegelian) rather than materialist (Marxist).

As art students in the early 1960s the British founders of A & L realised that they could not make a significant contribution to the development of fine art until they had come to terms with the ideology of Modernism exemplified by American art and criticism. In Britain their situation was doubly provincial: many of them came from the Midlands and the North, and they had studied and were teaching in art schools outside of London. They were provincial in terms of the geography of their homeland and, since they knew that the power base of the art world was now New York, they realised that all British art was provincial in relation to that city.

Pop art was an influential movement during the 1960s but A & L had a dismissive attitude to Pop and to British art college tutors such as Hamilton whom they deemed to be in thrall to American mass culture. Such people, A & L observed, wore 'Americanised tee-shirts and basketball boots'. It was an 'appearance cultivated by certain art school teachers keen to regard the Americanisation of the world with unambiguous gratitude'.[6] Leading members of the Independent Group were also rubbished as 'halfwits who based their reputations on their efforts to persuade us that Coca-Cola is a social amenity'.[7]

Unable to obtain clarification from their art school tutors, the future members of A & L came to terms with Modernism/American art in two ways: firstly, by scrutinising exhibitions of recent American art in Britain and articles published in American art magazines; and, secondly, by making forays to New York. The shows that they considered significant were

Johns's and Rauschenberg's at the Whitechapel in 1964, as well as exhibitions of new American art at the Kasmin and Fraser galleries. The articles that they thought important were those written by Greenberg, Fried, Judd, Morris and Smithson appearing in such journals as *Arts* and *Artforum*. Subsequently, they discovered that more useful critical tools were to be found in the writings of the philosopher Ludwig Wittgenstein and the historian of scientific revolutions Thomas S. Kuhn (an American) rather than in the art press.

Visits to New York occurred as follows: at Easter time 1966 Baldwin (b. 1945), then aged 20, went there with a letter of introduction to Ivan Karp, a dealer employed by the Castelli Gallery. As a result, Baldwin met or saw the work of Pop artists such as Dine, Lichtenstein, Oldenburg and Rosenquist, and Minimal artists such as Flavin, Judd and Stella. Highlights of his trip were a performance by Rauschenberg and Alex Hay given at the Judson Theatre and a show of Stella's paintings at Castelli's. Charles Harrison and Fred Orton commented: 'Such direct experience tends to have a demythologising effect' and Baldwin was surprised to find that, apart from Judd, 'few of the American artists seemed capable of articulating what they were doing'.[8] During the summer of 1967 Terry Atkinson (b. 1939) visited New York where he met Andre, LeWitt and Smithson.

There was mutual interest and support between the British and American artists: Smithson borrowed material from Baldwin for one of his articles and was instrumental in the publication of statements by Baldwin in *Arts* magazine during 1967. Later on, the British artists were to publish essays by the Americans in their journal.

Mel Ramsden, born in England in 1944, studied at Nottingham art school in the early 1960s but then moved to Australia where he met Ian Burn (1939–93). For a time they returned to live in London but in 1967 they moved to New York where they founded – with Roger Cutforth – the Society for Theoretical Art, which in turn was incorporated into the expanded A & L. In America, during 1967 and 1968, Ramsden made a series of 'Conceptual' paintings; for example, *Secret Painting*, which consisted of a black square with the following statement placed alongside: 'The content of this painting is invisible; the character and dimension of the content are to be kept permanently secret, known only to the artist.' The American artist John Baldessari, based in Los Angeles, was making very similar paintings at the same time. In 1971 Ramsden visited the British branch of A & L for an extended period. Eventually, in 1976, he left

New York altogether to take up residence in Oxfordshire where the British wing of A & L was located.

During the mid-1960s the representative art of Modernism was Minimalism. However, by 1967 the future members of A & L had come to regard it as 'largely incoherent and theoretically empty'.[9] Much of the early work of A & L, therefore, was a critique of the principles of Minimalism and jokes at its expense. They produced a great deal of talk and writings strongly influenced by British linguistic philosophy until eventually their discourse became a kind of collective process which challenged the individualistic ethos and marketing of most art. In May 1969 they began to publish a journal called *Art-Language* which, for a short while, was subtitled 'Journal of Conceptual Art'. The articles featured in the magazine discussed the concept 'art' and blurred the distinction between work by artists and work by critics. Eventually, analysis of the concept 'art' was extended to the broader socioeconomic context in which it was marketed and so a gradual left-wing politicisation occurred within A & L – see, for example, the contents of the American journal *The Fox* (three issues 1975–76)).

One might assume that the rejection of painting and sculpture and the adoption of language as the primary means of expression would preclude collectors being interested in their work but some German, French and Swiss dealers and publishers purchased work or paid A & L members retainers. In London the dealer Robert Self, and Logsdail of the Lisson Gallery, gave A & L shows while in New York Seth Siegelaub functioned as an 'alternative' dealer/publisher. A charitable foundation called Change Inc., established by Rauschenberg, was a source of funds for A & L activities in America.

The best known American artist associated with A & L was Joseph Kosuth (b. 1945) who, for a time, acted as the American editor of A & L's journal. His *One and Three Chairs* – a photo, a text and a real chair – was a seminal piece though there were those who doubted the accuracy of its early date – 1965. Harrison (b. 1942), an assistant editor of the British journal *Studio International,* visited New York in April (and September) 1969 where he met Kosuth. As a result, Kosuth was able to publish his influential, two-part essay, 'Art after Philosophy', in *Studio International* in October and November 1969. Later on, Kosuth aroused the anger of the British members of A & L because they felt he was a careerist and opportunist, that is, he promoted himself as an individual artist rather than being willing to submerge his identity and name in group projects.

During the early 1970s exchanges and communications across the Atlantic persisted and A & L publications appeared and exhibitions were mounted both in Europe and the United States. But due to ideological, political and personal differences, resignations, expulsions and factional schisms eventually occurred. In Britain Terry Atkinson withdrew in order to pursue an independent career as a socialist painter. Disagreements between the British and American branches of A & L resulted in the dissolution of the latter. Strategies were adopted by A & L (UK) in order to exclude Kosuth and those participants in A & L (US) – Mel and Paula Ramsden, Mayo Thompson and Christine Kozlov – who wanted to continue moved to England in 1977. Membership of A & L was drastically reduced. Harrison and Orton conclude their account of this period of internal strife as follows:

> With the dissolution of the New York base a major, if historically necessary, source of distraction was finally removed from A & L. None of those left on their feet has since experienced a moment's regret.[10]

Thompson was a rock musician and record producer who had helped found the band Red Crayola in Texas in 1966. In May 1981 a reconstituted Red Crayola issued the LP *Kangaroo?* with lyrics by A & L. One song – *A Portrait of Lenin in the Style of Jackson Pollock* – began as follows:

> Jackson Pollock was the artist of the Marshall Plan,
> He broke the ice for artists when the Cold War began,
> He was the leading artist of the New York School,
> He was the action painter who rebelled against the rules ...

During the late 1970s and early 1980s Baldwin, Harrison and Ramsden contributed written and televisual material to the content of the Open University's distance learning course *Modern Art and Modernism* (1983), an art history survey which started with Manet and concluded with Pollock. American artists and scholars also contributed to the course material and Greenberg was interviewed on camera by the British art historian T.J. Clark.

As a result of reflections on the causes and genesis of painting, on the nature of painting as expression and representation, and musings about the competences that viewers needed in order to 'read' modern works, A & L began to make 'first-order' objects, that is, stencil and

62. Art & Language, *Portrait of V.I. Lenin in the*
Style of Jackson Pollock, IV, 1979.
Enamel paint on paper, 61 x 61 cm.
Photo: courtesy of A & L and the Lisson Gallery, London.

drip-paintings such as *Portrait of V.I. Lenin in the Style of Jackson Pollock, IV* (1979) which retrospectively attempted a shotgun marriage between the two major styles – Abstract Expressionism and Socialist Realism – of the opposing sides of the Cold War. A & L recognised that these hybrid, ideologically incompatible pictures were 'a "monstrous stylistic détente" between two supposedly antagonistic parts of a mutually reinforcing pair'.[11]

The songs and paintings demonstrated that, despite A & L's withdrawal from the New York art world, some of its members were still seeking to settle accounts with American abstract art and art criticism of the 1940s and 1950s, and with the ideological struggle between the capitalist and communist systems. The artists and critics of the 1950s discussed in earlier chapters could hardly have envisaged or predicted the emergence of such peculiar history-paintings.

As one might expect, the past achievements of A & L are much contested by current members and ex-members. In 1996 Atkinson and Kosuth responded to A & L's version of the history of the group by founding A & L II after taking legal advice in New York regarding their right to use the name. They thus attempted to restore the trans-Atlantic connection which had been broken off two decades earlier.[12]

The Call to Renew a National Tradition

Alan Bowness, the British critic who wrote the 1967 article about the 'invasion' of American art into Britain during the 1950s, later regretted its impact on British art. In 1978 he remarked:

> I must admit to watching rather sadly the way in which British artists in particular simply accepted this cultural domination of American art ... There is a basic lack of confidence that has allowed people to succumb to the cultural imperialism that went with the American artists; and it's only now that because of what has followed begins to look rather hollow that one can see really that British society is quite different from American society. There *is* an Englishness to English art, and I think it is extremely important to resist the American takeover of modernism which seems to have happened ... I believe that national traditions are extremely important.[13]

Another British critic, Peter Fuller, came to share Bowness's sentiments. In 1988 he wrote:

> The degree to which British art suffered, from the late 1950s to the late 1970s, from the corrupting influence of American fashions can hardly be over-emphasised. Heron was amongst those who began to open our eyes to the way in which the American achievement, such as it was, was far more dependent upon prior British discoveries than had hitherto been assumed. More generally, it could be said that undue emphasis upon American work led to the tragic eclipse of an indigenous sensibility whose influence is discernible from the time of Turner and Constable, to the achievements of Moore and Sutherland; this tradition was based upon an imaginative response to natural form, indeed the whole world of nature.[14]

Fuller died in a car accident in April 1990. One can be certain, however, that were he alive today the BritArt phenomenon discussed below would not have met with his approval, that it would not have constituted the renewal of the 'indigenous sensibility' that he sought.

One would never guess from Fuller's emphasis on nature that he had spent most of his adult life in urban environments, including the poor East London borough of Hackney, or that his very livelihood as a critic depended upon the concentration of cultural resources typical of a metropolis. There was a refusal to recognise that for the majority of the British people and artists their lived experience is urban, not rural: since 1850 most Britons have lived in towns and cities and thus their behaviour reveals that they prefer city life to rural life. One can also point to British artists who have recorded urban life more than the countryside: Hogarth, Atkinson Grimshaw, L.S. Lowry, Sickert, the Camden Town Group, and so on. The example of John Latham shows that it is perfectly possible for an artist to live in a city for decades while at the same time representing nature – providing nature is defined as the whole cosmos rather than just landscape. Although Latham is a British citizen, his art is not limited by national boundaries or concerns.

Another aspect of twentieth-century life that Fuller disliked was the presence and power of the 'Mega-Visual', that is, the mass media (despite this, he wrote for the press and appeared on television). They have become a second nature that rivals first-order nature. It was this reality that the British Pop artists responded to in the 1950s and 1960s. (Fuller detested Hamilton's work.)

Earlier, in 1986, Fuller had attacked the internationalism of modern art and cited, approvingly, John Ruskin's claim that 'All great art, in the great times of art, is *provincial.*'[15] According to Fuller, a weakness of British art in the 1930s had been 'a too great an obsession with "international" forms and varieties of modernism'. What British artists should have attended to more was their national tradition because, paradoxically, 'A genuinely "universal" art in the late 20th century can only begin with what [Kenneth] Clark called a "profound intimacy" with particular places, persons and traditions.' One wonders how Hockney fits this schema. One place he knows well and has depicted over many years has been Los Angeles: is he, therefore, British or American? Did Fuller wish to prevent British artists from emigrating or living abroad? Certainly he believed that Morley had been ruined by his move to the United States.

Ignoring the complexity and diversity of the United States and its polyglot population, Fuller declared, in 1987: 'American culture is irredeemably base and spiritually bankrupt.'[16] Such blanket condemnations are absurd. In my view, American influences were, in many instances, beneficial and stimulating for British art and music. Consider the example of the Beatles: the beat group began in the 1950s by imitating American rock'n'roll but by the 1960s they were generating their own music and lyrics based on their own lived experiences of Britain and Germany (and later India), which they then successfully exported to America. (Even *Sgt Pepper* drew inspiration from the Beach Boys' *Pet Sounds* album.) This example demonstrates that an initial dependence upon American culture can be transformed by British creativity into a cultural triumph with international appeal.

Whatever one's conclusion concerning America's positive or negative effects, such trans- and inter-cultural phenomena are bound to occur unless one country can erect a total barrier to communication, trade and travel. (When Japan attempted to do this in the nineteenth century, the barrier was broken in 1853–54 by a US Navy squadron under the command of Commodore Perry.) Given the present ease and speed of communication, freight and travel systems, and the ever-increasing globalisation of industry by multinational businesses, it is now extremely difficult for one nation or culture to exclude outside influences. And when the relationship between one culture and another is unequal – that of a large, strong power versus a smaller, weaker power – then the latter has little room for manoeuvre. Discrimination is always possible, that is, selecting what is useful and beneficial, rejecting what is deleterious. Counter-measures, such as quota systems, can also be introduced and, as we have seen, criticism, resistance and transformation are always possible too. But the reality is that one cannot expect the powerful not to exert their power.[17]

Given this situation, it was inevitable that America and its art and mass culture would have a significant effect upon British art and artists during the period when Europe was recovering from the effects of the Second World War.

The 1970s and 1980s

It is clear from the history of A & L, Vic Burgin and others, that by the late 1960s some young British artists were subjecting American art and criticism to a rigorous critique in order to emancipate themselves from their influence. A situation of equality and cooperation was signalled by the early trans-Atlantic phase of A & L. (Similarly the Punk rock movement of the mid-1970s occurred in both New York and London at roughly the same time and there were interactions between the two scenes.) However, the British attacks on Kosuth which were followed by the termination of the American branch of A & L amounted to a declaration of independence. By the mid-1970s, British post-Conceptual artists were saying that they did not need to look to America any more, that in their judgement New York was now as 'provincial' as anywhere else. Of course, New York was and continues to remain a crucial art centre but even within America its importance has been diminished by the blossoming of art scenes in cities such as Boston, Chicago, Houston, Los Angeles and San Franciso.

In 1975 Michael Corris also pointed out that the art galleries of New York were supported by 'a strong international market' and that it was 'the overseas market network' which had enabled Conceptual artists to survive in New York at a time when there was 'virtually no financial support for that work in America'.[18] He went on to argue that since New York had become 'a distribution point first and foremost' it need not continue to be the centre of the production of art. In other words, artists could live and work elsewhere while still exhibiting and gaining sales and reviews in New York. But Corris also predicted that 'the media (mediacentric production)' would allow 'the New York City Art World Market to expand virtually at will, to appropriate the existing culture abroad for its own gain'. What Corris was drawing attention to were the flows of goods and information across the globe. Since the development of the Internet, information flows have expanded exponentially and resulted in a measure of decentralisation.

By the 1970s Europe had fully recovered its affluence and European art had recovered its confidence. European cities such as Amsterdam, Barcelona, Basel, Berlin, Frankfurt, London, Madrid, Milan, Paris, Rome and Stuttgart had become important art centres again in which many new public museums and private galleries had been established. The major exhibitions of contemporary art taking place in Kassel, Germany, and Venice, Italy, attracted entries and visitors from all over the world. If America's most famous artist at this time was Andy Warhol, Europe could boast Joseph Beuys. The two artists met in 1979 and the following year Warhol produced silk-screened portraits of Beuys – *Diamond Dust Beuys* – in recognition of the star status of his great rival.

The resurgence of Europe is gradually causing a re-evaluation of European art as against American art. Nicholas Serota, Director of the Tate Gallery, remarked in 1996:

> I think it's still taking us a while to recognise that much of the best modern art made in the last 30 years has been made in Europe more than America. And as we look forward over the next 20 years, it's going to be as much in Asia as it is in North America.[19]

There remained one example of New York's visual culture which influenced young Britons to a considerable extent, namely the graffiti writers or spraycan painters who 'bombed' the subway trains and city walls with their tags and murals in the 1970s and 1980s. As a result of books and television programmes devoted to this subcultural practice, and Pop music video promos featuring graffiti murals as backgrounds, many male youths in British cities such as Bristol and London became graffiti writers. Of course, the artistic status and value of graffiti was and remains contested: while some people respect and admire it as a form of subcultural or grass-roots art, there are others – usually those in authority representing the majority of citizens – who regard it as a form of vandalism of public property that has to be outlawed and stamped out. The latter think of subway graffiti not as a valuable American import but as a foreign plague. At the same time, the work of American artists influenced by street graffiti to some degree, such as Basquiat and Keith Haring, was assured a warm welcome in London's art galleries.

That a new equality between Europe and the United States existed in terms of the visual arts was signalled by the 1980 Royal Academy show, *The New Spirit in Painting*, which featured a mix of American and European paintings (38 painters were represented, around a quarter of whom were American). The popularity of 'Neo-Expressionistic' and/or 'Trans-Avant-Garde' painting in Germany, Italy and Scotland meant that American critics and dealers paid much more attention to Europe than they had done for some time.

Also important was the founding of the Saatchi collection and gallery in St John's Wood, London, which opened in 1985, by Charles Saatchi and his then American wife Doris (they have since divorced). Charles was born in Baghdad in 1943 into an Iraqi-Jewish family which came to Britain in 1947. During the 1960s Charles worked for advertising agencies as a copywriter, a trade he learnt in the United

63. *Street graffiti, London*, 1988. Photos: Anna Groom.

States. By spending millions derived from an advertising agency with global ambitions, the Saatchis rapidly established a huge, eclectic collection of contemporary art. At first they bought American art – Judd, Schnabel and Warhol for instance – and then European art – Baselitz, Clemente, Kiefer – but later Charles bought more and more British artists, both established and unknown. The scale of his holdings in British art was demonstrated by the *Sensation* exhibition which filled the galleries of the Royal Academy in the autumn of 1997.[20] In Charles Saatchi Britain at last acquired a patron of new art comparable to the wealthiest and most adventurous of American collectors. There are some critics who believe that Saatchi's influence is baneful but no one doubts that his lust for art and his purchasing power have transformed the British art scene.

During the 1980s, even in America, the tide of critical opinion seemed to shift away from American art towards British art. The Australian-born critic Robert Hughes, who had worked in Britain during the 1960s and then emigrated to the United States to become *Time* magazine's art correspondent, increasingly questioned the quality of recent American art – for example, he penned attacks on Basquiat, Koons and Schnabel – and wrote monographs in praise of the British painters Auerbach and Freud. Hughes judged the latter to be 'the greatest living realist painter'. Despite his residence in the media centre of New York, Hughes found that commissions for television arts series came from the BBC in London, not from CBS or NBC even when, as in the case of *American Visions* (1997), the subject matter was the history of American art. (This series was in fact a BBC/Time-Life co-production.)

The rapid rise of the Asian 'tiger' economies meant that the differential between them and the United States was reduced and within America itself there was racial strife, severe inequalities and social fragmentation. Instead of a melting pot, America became a patchwork of ghettos. This is why, Hughes argued in his television series, so much recent American art had been concerned with questions of identity.

Hughes concluded his tie-in book to the television series by remarking that the visual arts in America were fatigued and the vanguard myth of progress was played out. He added: 'Cultures do decay; and the visual culture of American modernism, once so strong, buoyant, and inventive, and now so harassed by its own sense of defeated expectations, may be no exception to that fact.'[21]

The 1990s and BritArt

During the 1990s the yBa (young British artists) or BritArt phenomenon occurred. Artists such as Dinos and Jake Chapman, Mat Collishaw, Tracey Emin, Douglas Gordon, Marcus Harvey, Damien Hirst, Gary Hume, Sarah Lucas, Marc Quinn, Sam Taylor-Wood,

Gillian Wearing and Rachel Whiteread attracted much public and media attention both at home and abroad. Hirst rivalled Warhol and Koons in terms of his shock tactics, publicity savvy, acceptance of the commodity nature of art and willingness to work in a variety of media. (Unlike Riley, he had no scruples about the commercial exploitation of his art.) A 1987–88 Saatchi Gallery exhibition entitled *New York Art Now*, which included works by Bickerton, Gober and Koons, had some influence on the new generation. A massive historical survey mounted by the Royal Academy – *American Art in the Twentieth Century: Painting and Sculpture 1913–1993* – in 1993 also facilitated a re-evaluation. But by May 1996 amusing reports were appearing in British newspapers about a Hirst show in New York, which included dead cows pickled in formaldehyde, which was causing a stir in the art world, worrying the city's health authorities and prompting protests from animal-rights activists.

Many of the yBas had studied under Craig-Martin at Goldsmiths and learnt the importance of self-promotion, marketing and business sponsorship. These artists were no longer hesitant about the economic dimension of art nor held back by a British sense of modesty or inferiority. The kind of 'in your face' aggression and vulgarity previously associated with Punk performers like Johnny Rotten and Sid Vicious, and with British football lager louts marauding across Europe, was manifest in some of their works and self-images – see Taylor-Wood's (b. 1967) photographic self-portrait showing her with panties and bare thighs, plus a T-shirt emblazoned with the words 'Fuck, Suck, Spank, Wank'. A far cry from the image of the English gentlewoman conveyed to Americans by British costume drama films and television series based on the novels of Jane Austen.

Furthermore, BritArt was trumpeted abroad in the brash way previously associated with American salesmanship: for example, the title of a survey show curated by Richard Flood was *'Brilliant!' New Art from London* (Minneapolis, Walker Art Center; Houston, Contemporary Arts Museum, 1995–96). The cover photo of this show's catalogue depicted buildings in Bishopgate, City of London, after a massive IRA bomb blast (10 April 1992) had wrecked them and killed two people. The appropriation of this particular photo implied: 'What a tough and exciting place we come from.' Even the violence perpetrated by the IRA, it would seem, could be mobilised to promote BritArt overseas.

Today, if press reports are to be believed, it is British art and London which now rule the roost, not American art and New York. In 1997

64. Cover of the catalogue for *'Brilliant!' New Art from London*, 1995.
Minneapolis: Walker Art Center.
Image for cover supplied by Mat Collishaw.

Norman Rosenthal, exhibition secretary of the Royal Academy, was reported as saying: 'For the first time this century, London is where it is at on the art scene, without rival.'[22] A sceptic who doubts the veracity of such claims might well conclude that, via the use of bragging and the hard sell, the British art scene of the 1990s reveals the extent to which it has absorbed the crudest of American values without, apparently, realising that it has done so.

Despite one's reservations about the marketing methods and quality of BritArt, Britain's future survival depends upon the creativity of its artists and scientists. Nineteenth-century Britain was the the work-shop of the world and the hub of an empire. But since the loss of its empire and the decline of its heavy industries, Britain has come to rely more and more on scientific discoveries, technological inventions and creative or cultural industries – art, architecture, theatre, product design, fashion, advertising, animation, film and television, rock and Pop music, tourism – and these in turn have depended upon the art school system and the creativity, innovation and hard work of its people, especially those from the working and lower-middle classes, and from ethnic minorities and immigrant groups.[23]

David Puttnam and Neil Watson have also stressed the importance of visual culture in the new age of information and argued that 'the distinguishing characteristics of any nation or community today lie in the quality of its intellectual property ... the ability of its people to use information and intelligence creatively to add substance and value to global economic activity, rather than just quantity'.[24]

Those who share the late Peter Fuller's view that there is a national tradition of art in need of renewal, should appreciate that borders between nations are porous and that modern nations themselves are composed of different tribes and subcultures. A historian of British art remarked: 'What makes British art so quintessentially British is the fact it has been created by people of so many different origins: not only Welsh, Scottish, Irish and English but also French, German, Flemish and Dutch ...'[25] In reality, therefore, all such cultures are hybrid and plural rather than homogeneous and singular. America's fine arts and mass culture are still tremendously important to the inhabitants of the British Isles but Britain – especially London – is now a far more multiracial and multicultural society than it was in the 1940s and influences come from around the globe, not just from Europe or the United States.[26] If the British-born artists and designers of today have a native genius it is surely their receptivity to other cultures, their inclusivity and syncretic ability to produce something new from sources both ancient and modern, both indigenous and foreign.

Notes

Introduction

1. The term 'British' has been preferred to 'English' in order to include Scottish architects and artists.
2. For one account of the Americanisation of British life see Francis Williams, *The American Invasion* (London: Anthony Blond, 1962).
3. Much of the factual information contained in this book has already been published but in many, scattered sources. One of the few publications addressing this topic was 'British and American Art: The Uneasy Dialectic', *Art & Design*, Vol. 3, Nos. 9–10 (1987), which took its theme from a symposium held at the Tate Gallery on 27 June 1987 entitled 'Interchanges: British and American Painting 1945–87' organised by the London-based British American Arts Association. A transcript of the proceedings is held in the Association's library. See also Thomas Kellein, 'It's the Sheer Size: European Responses to American Art', *American Art in the Twentieth Century: Painting and Sculpture 1913–1993*, eds C.M. Joachimides and N. Rosenthal (London: Royal Academy of Arts/Munich: Prestel Verlag, 1993), pp. 187–94.
4. A. Brighton, 'Since '62: The Last Twenty-five Years', *Exhibition Road: Painters at the Royal College of Art*, ed. Paul Huxley (Oxford and London: Phaidon, Christie's and the Royal College of Art, 1988), p. 55.
5. M. Baxandall, *Patterns of Intention: On the Historical Explanation of Pictures* (New Haven and London: Yale University Press, 1985), p. 59.
6. See Correlli Barnett's brutal analysis of Britain's parlous post-war situation in *The Lost Victory: British Dreams, British Realities 1945–50* (London and Basingstoke: Macmillan, 1995).
7. See G. Steiner, 'The Archives of Eden', and the responses to this article by various Americans, *Salmagundi*, Nos 50/51 (Fall/Winter 1980–81), pp. 57–253 and 'America as the Archive of Eden', *Times Higher Educational Supplement* (6 March 1981), pp. 12–13.
8. For an overview of the activities of the CIA in Europe see *Dirty Work: The CIA in Western Europe*, eds Philip Agee and Louis Wolf (London: Zed Press, 1978); especially relevant to this text is Richard Fletcher's essay, 'How CIA Money Took the Teeth Out of British Socialism', pp. 188–200.
9. For an illuminating analysis of the phenomenon of cultural imperialism see John Tomlinson, *Cultural Imperialism* (London: Pinter, 1991).

1   First Encounters with Post-war America and American Culture: the 1940s

1. Robert Kudielka, *Robyn Denny* (London: Tate Gallery, 1973), p. 18.
2. This quotation appears in *The Undeclared War: The Struggle for Control of the World's Film Industry*, by David Puttnam and Neil Watson (London: HarperCollins, 1997), pp. 148–9.
3. 'Vera Lindsay in Discussion with Michael Sandle', *Studio International*, Vol. 178, No. 914 (September 1969), pp. 80–83.
4. E. Paolozzi, 'Notes from a lecture at the Institute of Contemporary Arts, 1958', *Uppercase*, No. 1 (1958), reprinted in *Eduardo Paolozzi*, by Diane Kirkpatrick (London: Studio Vista, 1970), pp. 120–30.
5. Carol Hogben and Elizabeth Bailey, 'About the Prints: The Artist Talking at an Interview', *Bunk* (London: Victoria and Albert Museum, 1973), unpaginated.
6. Ibid.
7. E. Paolozzi, 'Retrospective Statement', *The Independent Group: Postwar Britain and the Aesthetics of Plenty*, ed. David Robbins (Cambridge MA and London: MIT Press, 1990), pp. 192–3.
8. Kudielka, *Robyn Denny*, p. 18.
9. Information on Read is largely derived from James King's biography *The Last Modern: A Life of Herbert Read* (London: Weidenfeld & Nicolson, 1990). See also the chronology in *Herbert Read: A British Vision of World Art*, eds Benedict Read and David Thistlewood (Leeds: Leeds City Art Galleries, The Henry Moore Foundation/London: Lund Humphries, 1993), pp. 146–66.
10. James King, *The Last Modern*, p. 229.
11. Read remarked: 'One of the most curious characteristics of this people is their complete misunderstanding of democracy. They do not believe in *equality*, but in "equality of *opportunity*". They confess that again and again, with pride, without realising that "equality of opportunity" is merely the law of the jungle, that they are not egalitarians but opportunists ...' Ibid., pp. 229–30.
12. *Horizon*, Vol. 20 (October, 1949), pp. 268–84. *Horizon* was published from January 1940 to December 1949.

2   The ICA, the IG and America During the 1950s

1. Anne Massey is a British design historian who has researched the history of the ICA and IG in great depth and so my summary is indebted to her writings, in particular, the article 'Cold War Culture and the ICA', *Art & Artists*, No. 213 (June 1984), pp. 15–17, and the chapter 'Cold War Culture' in her book, *The Independent Group: Modernism and Mass Culture in Britain 1945–59* (Manchester and New York: Manchester University Press, 1995), pp. 62–71.
2. J. King, *The Last Modern*, p. 258.
3. A detailed account of the competition is supplied by Robert Burstow,

'Butler's Competition Project ...', *Art History*, Vol. 12, No. 4 (December 1989), pp. 472–96.

4. See Burstow's painstaking examination of the complex machinations behind the competition: 'The Limits of Modernist Art as a "Weapon of the Cold War": Reassessing the Unknown Patron of the Monument to the Unknown Political Prisoner', *Oxford Art Journal*, Vol. 20, No. 1 (1997), pp. 68–80.

5. Munsing was an active and influential arts official. His parents were immigrants from Russia. He grew up in Detroit and then worked as a designer in New York. During the Second World War he served in an army unit, searching for stolen works of art in Europe. Later he established the 'America Haus' programmes of exhibitions and cultural events in Berlin and Munich. After his move to London, Munsing organised shows of work by American artists such as Paul Jenkins, Philip Pavia and Ben Shahn, as well as mixed exhibitions. During the following two decades he built up a collection of contemporary art for the National Museum of Fine Art in Washington and ran the 'Art in Embassies' scheme for the State Department. He retired in 1976 but still acted as a consultant for the American Association of Museums. He died of cancer in 1994. An obituary appeared in the *New York Times*, Cultural section (8 December 1994), p. 22.

6. See A. Massey and P. Sparke 'The Myth of the Independent Group', *Block*, No. 10 (1985), pp. 48–56; A. Massey, 'The Independent Group', *Burlington Magazine*, Vol. 129, No. 1009 (April 1987), pp. 232–42; L. Alloway and others, *Modern Dreams: The Rise and Fall and Rise of Pop* (Cambridge, MA and London: MIT Press, 1988); D. Robbins (ed.), *The Independent Group: Postwar Britain and the Aesthetics of Plenty* (Cambridge, MA and London: MIT Press, 1990); A. Massey, *The Independent Group: Modernism and Mass Culture in Britain 1945-59* (Manchester and New York: Manchester University Press, 1995).

7. Banham, quoted in J. King, *The Last Modern*, p. 270.

8. See Carol Hogben and Elizabeth Bailey, 'About the Prints: The Artist Talking at an Interview', *Bunk* (London: Victoria and Albert Museum, 1973) and Rosemary Miles, *The Complete Prints of Eduardo Paolozzi: Prints, Drawings, Collages 1944-77* (London: Victoria and Albert Museum, 1977).

9. U.M. Schneede, *Eduardo Paolozzi* (London: Thames & Hudson, 1971), p. 5.

10. J. Stirling, 'Retrospective Statement', *The Independent Group*, ed. David Robbins, p. 195.

11. E. Paolozzi, 'Retrospective Statement', *The Independent Group*, ed. David Robbins, p. 193.

12. C. Rowe, 'Introduction', *James Stirling: Buildings and Projects*, eds Peter Arnell and Ted Bickford (New York: Rizzoli, 1984), p. 18.

13. J. Stirling, 'Acceptance of the Royal Gold Medal in Architecture 1989', *Architectural Design*, Nos 7/8 (1980), A.D. Profile No. 29, p. 6.

14. The following summary is taken from G. Holroyd's 'Retrospective Statement' in *The Independent Group*, ed. David Robbins, pp. 189–90.

15. Ibid.

16. Peter Smithson and others, 'Eames Celebration', *Architectural Design*, Vol. 36 (September 1966), pp. 432–71.

17. P. Kirkham, *Charles and Ray Eames: Designers of the Twentieth Century* (Cambridge MA and London: MIT Press, 1995), p. 347.

18. A. and P. Smithson, *Without Rhetoric: An Architectural Aesthetic 1955–72* (London: Latimer New Dimensions, 1973), p. 42.

19. A. and P. Smithson, 'Cluster City: A New Shape for the Community', *Architectural Review*, Vol. 122, No. 730 (November 1957), pp. 333–6.

20. P. Smithson, 'Just a Few Chairs and a House: an Essay on the Eames-Aesthetic', *Architectural Design*, Vol. 36 (September 1966), p. 433.

21. Pat Kirkham, interview with Alison Smithson, 1991, quoted in *Charles and Ray Eames*, p. 240.

22. A. Smithson, 'And Now Dhamas are Dying Out in Japan', *Architectural Design*, Vol. 36 (September 1966), pp. 447–8.

23. A. and P. Smithson, *Without Rhetoric*, pp. 44–7.

24. A. and P. Smithson, 'Personal Statement 1: But Today we Collect Ads', *ARK*, No. 18 (November 1956), pp. 49–52.

25. P. Smithson, 'Letter to America', *Architectural Design*, Vol. 28 (March 1958), pp. 93–7, 102.

26. Ibid.

27. Ibid.

28. *The Independent Group*, ed. D. Robbins, p. 194.

29. See Charlotta Kotik and others, *The Expendable Icon: Works by John McHale* (Buffalo, NY: Albright-Knox Gallery, 1984).

30. These articles were: 'Hommage à Chrysler Corp' (1958), 'Persuading Image' (1960), 'Popular Culture and Personal Responsibility' (1960), 'An Exposition of $he' (1962) and 'Urbane Image' (1963). Several are reprinted in Hamilton's *Collected Words 1953–82* (London and New York: Thames & Hudson, 1982).

31. It it printed in *Collected Words 1953–82*.

32. James L. Reinish, 'An Interview with Lawrence Alloway', *Studio International*, Vol. 186, No. 958 (September 1973), pp. 62–4.

33. L. Alloway, 'Personal Statement', *ARK*, No. 19 (Spring 1957), pp. 28–9.

34. T. del Renzio, 'Pioneers and Trendies', *Art & Artists*, No. 209 (February 1984), pp. 25–8.

35. In 1961 Alloway returned to the United States for good. After a period of teaching at Bennington College, Vermont, he became a curator at the Guggenheim Museum in New York (1962–66). A stream of exhibitions, articles and books on virtually all aspects of American art then followed. The subject of one of his publications – an analysis of the iconography of violent American films (*Violent America: The Movies 1946–64* [1971]) – Alloway acknowledged was indebted to the kind of discussions that had taken place at IG meetings. Thus, IG ideas had proved 'developable'. From 1963 to 1971 he wrote art criticism for *The Nation*, performed an editorial role for *Artforum* (1971–76), and from 1968 to 1981 he was employed as Professor of Art History at the State University of New York, Stony Brook, Long Island. Alloway died in New York in January 1990 at the age of 63. His wife Sylvia has donated Alloway's collection to an American museum, see the catalogue: *From Blast to Pop: Aspects of Modern British Art, 1915–1965*, by Richard A. Born and Keith Hartley (Chicago: David and Alfred Smart Museum, University of Chicago, 1997).

36. L. Alloway, 'City Notes', *Architectural Design*, Vol. 29 (January 1959), pp. 34–5.
37. R. Banham, 'The Atavism of the Short-Distance Mini-Cyclist', *Living Arts*, No. 3 (1964), pp. 91–7.
38. R. Banham, 'Who is this Pop?', *Motif*, No. 10 (Winter 1962–63), pp. 3–13.
39. R. Banham, 'How I Learnt to Live with Norwich Union', *New Statesman and Society*, Vol. 67 (6 March 1964), pp. 372–3.
40. R. Banham, *Theory and Design in the First Machine Age* (London: Architectural Press, 1960).
41. Two anthologies of Banham's articles have been published. See R. Banham, *Design by Choice*, ed. Penny Sparke (London: Academy Editions, 1981), and *A Critic Writes: Essays by Reyner Banham*, eds Mary Banham and others (Berkeley and Los Angeles: University of California Press, 1997).
42. R. Banham, 'Vehicles of Desire', *Art* [London] No. 1 (1 September 1955), p. 3.
43. R. Banham, 'Detroit Tin Revisited', *Design 1900–1960: Studies in Design and Popular Culture of the 20th Century*, ed. T. Faulkner (Newcastle-upon-Tyne: Newcastle Polytechnic, 1976), pp. 120–40.
44. Nigel Whiteley has written a perceptive critique of the IG's acceptance of expendability: 'Toward a Throw-Away Culture: "Style Obsolescence" and Cultural Theory in the 1950s and 1960s', *Oxford Art Journal*, Vol. 10, No. 2 (1987), pp. 3–27. Whiteley maintains that, 'In the 1950s and 1960s the protagonists of expendability as cultural theory were ambiguous, vague or accommodating about its political implications.'
45. Printed in *Lessons from America: An Exploration*, ed. Richard Rose (London: Macmillan, 1974), pp. 67–91.
46. In the early 1960s Philip Johnson invited Banham to New York for a weekend to engage in a public debate. More extended visits during 1964 and 1966 were made possible by a Graham Foundation scholarship. His 1969 book, *The Architecture of the Well-Tempered Environment*, was mainly about American buildings. In 1968 he visited Los Angeles where, much to his chagrin, he was at first terrified by its urban sprawl. However, he soon adjusted and as a result of this visit he gave a series of talks on British radio and wrote a book entitled *Los Angeles: The Architecture of Four Ecologies* (1971) and made a film for BBC Television – *Reyner Banham Loves Los Angeles* (1972) – directed by Julian Cooper.

Banham also crossed the Atlantic in order to attend several of the International Design Conferences that were held annually in Aspen, Colorado. In 1974 he edited a compilation of IDCA papers. In 1976, after years of teaching architectural history at University College, London, Banham took up full-time residence in the United States. He taught the history of art and architecture at universities on both the East and West Coasts. In 1980 Banham moved to the West Coast to teach at the University of California, Santa Cruz, which is near several American deserts. Banham's attraction to this type of landscape resulted in a 1982 book entitled *Scenes in American Deserta*. Three years spent in Buffalo – a city noted for its industrial buildings – inspired Banham's last major publication *A Concrete Atlantis: U.S. Industrial Building and European Modern Architecture 1900–25* (1986), in which he brought to bear his knowledge of two cultures. Banham died in March 1988 soon after being appointed to the chair in Architectural Theory and History at New York University.

47. R. Banham, 'Arts in Society: Representations in Protest', *New Society*, Vol. 13, No. 345 (8 May 1969), pp. 717–18, reprinted in *Arts in Society: A 'New Society' Collection*, ed. Paul Barker (London and Glasgow: Fontana/Collins, 1977), pp. 61–6.
48. *The Independent Group*, ed. David Robbins, p. 245.
49. Banham, 'Arts in Society: Representations in Protest'.
50. del Renzio, 'Pioneers and Trendies'.

3 The Impact of Abstract Expressionism During the 1940s and 1950s

1. Fred Orton identifies the individuals involved as a fraction of the ruling class he calls 'the business liberals' who were internationalist in outlook. This group was opposed by another class fraction, a nationalist 'old guard', who favoured isolationism for America. See 'Footnote One: The Idea of the Cold War', *Avant-Gardes and Partisans Reviewed*, by Fred Orton and Griselda Pollock (Manchester and New York: Manchester University Press, 1996), pp. 205–18.
2. H. Namuth, 'Jackson Pollock', *Portfolio, The Annual of the Graphic Arts* (Ohio: 1951).
3. In fact, there were three schools in contention: the Schools of Paris, New York and London – in 1949 Patrick Heron wrote an article claiming there was a 'School of London', therefore he proposed the idea long before R.B. Kitaj. See P. Heron, 'The School of London', *New Statesman and Nation* (9 April 1949), p. 351. In this article Heron cited Ben Nicholson, Hepworth and other St Ives' artists (!), Victor Pasmore, Francis Bacon, Lucien Freud, Matthew Smith, Graham Sutherland, plus several Neo-Romantic artists and the sculptor Robert Adams. He added: 'The School of London is remarkable for its variety.' For a thoughtful account of the battle of the schools see Margaret Garlake, 'Between Paris and New York, Critical Constructions of "Englishness" c1945–60', *Art Criticism since 1900*, ed. Malcolm Gee (Manchester & New York: Manchester University Press, 1993), pp. 180–98.
4. Francis was born in San Mateo, California in 1923. He was a pilot in the Second World War and began to paint after an accident confined him to a hospital bed. He started to make Rothko-like abstractions in 1947. After studying painting at the University of California at Berkeley, he travelled in 1950 with his artist wife Muriel Goodwin to Paris. There he met the modern masters Léger and Giacometti, the Tachist painter Riopelle and the critics Georges Duthuit, Patrick Waldberg and Michel Tapié. (The French artists he admired most were Monet and Bonnard.) Other American artists in Paris during the 1950s were: Norman Bluhm, Larry Calcagno, Claire Falkenstein, Shirley Goldfarb, Al Held, Shirley Jaffe, Ellsworth Kelly, John Franklin-Koenig, Joan Mitchell, Kimber Smith, Bill and Betty Rivers,

and Jack Youngerman. The first article citing Francis by a British critic was one by Herbert Read published in *Quadrum*, No. 1 (May 1956). Read also wrote the catalogue introduction to Francis's first, one-man show held in London at Gimpel Fils in 1957. Francis was resident in Paris until 1962 when he returned to live in California. He died in 1994. See Peter Selz, *Sam Francis* (New York: Abrams, 1975); Eric de Chassey and others, *Sam Francis, Les Années Parisiennes* (Paris: RMN/Editions du Jeu de Paume, 1995). On the relationship between Paris and New York see *Paris – New York* (Paris: Centre Georges Pompidou, 1977) and essays in *Reconstructing Modernism: Art in New York, Paris and Montreal 1945-64*, ed. Serge Guilbaut (Cambridge MA and London: MIT Press, 1990).

5. H. Read, 'An Art of Internal Necessity', *Quadrum*, No. 1 (May 1956), pp. 7–22.

6. See P. Guggenheim, *Out of This Century: Confessions of an Art Addict*, rev. edn (New York: Universe Books, 1979), p. 344.

7. A. Bowness, 'Notes on the Paintings of Alan Davie', *Alan Davie* (London: Lund Humphries, 1967).

8. Conversation with the author, August 1997.

9. A. Davie, 'Notes by the Artist', *Alan Davie: Catalogue of an Exhibition of Paintings and Drawings from 1936-58 ...* (London: Whitechapel Art Gallery, 1958), pp. 6–7. Also, in an unpublished interview with Middlesex University student Linda Myers in March 1992, Davie complained that the American influence upon him had been exaggerated. He remarked: 'A lot of us were throwing paint around at the same time as Pollock without having heard of him.' When Davie saw the early Pollocks it was their extension of Surrealist automatism and primitivism which interested him. He also stated that by the time he spent a weekend with Pollock in 1956 the latter had given up drip painting because 'he knew he was at a dead end'.

10. W. Scott and A. Bowness, 'Biographical Notes', *William Scott: Paintings, Drawings and Gouaches 1938-71* (London: Tate Gallery, 1972), p. 71.

11. P. Heron (Report on American Cultural Imperialism), *Guardian* (11 October 1974), p. 10.

12. R. Alley, *William Scott* (London: Methuen, 1963), unpaginated.

13. R. Melville, 'Exhibitions', *Architectural Review*, Vol. 113 (April 1953), pp. 272–3; and 'Action Painting: New York, Paris, London', *ARK*, No. 18 (Autumn 1956), pp. 30–3.

14. Letter to the author, 11 March 1997. Del Renzio no longer has a copy of his lecture notes. See also his article 'Pioneers and Trendies', *Art & Artists*, No. 209 (February 1984), pp. 25–8.

15. J. Pollock, [Answers to a Questionnaire], *Arts & Architecture*, Vol. 61, No. 2 (February 1944), p. 14.

16. In 1960 Alloway wrote: 'American art is not an exotic national style. It is the mainstream of modern art, which used to run through Paris.' Thus the 'mainstream' seems to be mobile and have specific geographical locations at different times rather than being dispersed equally across the globe. L. Alloway, 'Size Wise', *Art News and Review*, Vol. 12, No. 17 (September 1960), p. 2.

17. R. Araeen, 'The State of British Art: A Debate, Session 3: The Multinational Style', *Studio International*, Vol. 194, No. 989 (February 1978), p. 103.

18. C. Greenberg, '"American-Type" Painting', *Partisan Review*, Vol. 22, No. 2 (Spring 1955), pp. 179–96.

19. P. Heron, *The Changing Forms of Art* (London: Routledge & Kegan Paul, 1955), pp. xi, xiii–xiv, 222, 246.

20. Greenberg's visits to Europe up to 1959 were as follows: April–June 1939, visited England, France, Italy and Switzerland; summer 1954, visited England, France, Italy, Switzerland; July 1959, visited France, London and St Ives.

21. P. Heron, 'The Americans at the Tate Gallery', *Arts*, Vol. 30, No. 6 (March 1956), pp. 15–17.

22. The exhibition was *Some Paintings from the E.J. Power's Collection* (ICA, March 1958). Part of Heron's review is reprinted in *Patrick Heron*, ed. Vivien Knight (Hatfield and London: John Taylor and Lund Humphries, 1988), pp. 32–3.

23. P. Heron, *Guardian* (11 October 1974), p. 10.

24. P. Heron and B. Read, 'A Conversation between ...', *Herbert Read: A British Vision of World Art*, eds Benedict Read and David Thistlewood (Leeds: Leeds City Art Galleries, The Henry Moore Foundation/London: Lund Humphries, 1993), p. 144.

25. B. Taylor, 'Abstract Colour Painting in England: The Case of Patrick Heron', *Art History*, Vol. 3, No. 1 (March 1980), pp. 115–28.

26. P. Heron, 'The Ascendancy of London in the Sixties', *Studio International*, Vol. 172, No. 884 (December 1966), pp. 280–1.

27. Barnett Newman and Dorothy Seckler, 'Interview', *Art in America*, Vol. 50, No. 2 (Summer 1962), pp. 83, 86–7.

28. James Hyman, 'A "Pioneer Painter": Renato Guttuso and Realism in Britain', *Guttuso* (London: Whitechapel Art Gallery, Thames & Hudson/Palermo: Novocento, 1996), pp. 39–53. According to Anne Massey, 'It is misleading to characterise the art of the early 1950s in terms of a polarisation between realism and abstraction' because 'the main critical debate was concerned with the issue of international modernism as opposed to a national school of painting.' 'The Independent Group: Toward a Redefinition', *Burlington Magazine*, Vol. CXXIX, No. 1009 (April 1987), p. 234.

29. J. Berger, *New Statesman and Nation* (January 1956).

30. J. Steyn, 'Art and Conflict 1: Realism versus Realism', *The Atomic Yard: Aspects of British Culture c 1957, Works by John Goto*, John Goto and others (Cambridge: Kettle's Yard Gallery, 1990), p. 15.

31. R. Melville, 'Exhibitions', *Architectural Review*, Vol. 118, No. 703 (July 1955), p. 50–3.

32. R. Melville, 'Exhibitions', *Architectural Review*, Vol. 119, No. 742 (May 1956), pp. 267–8.

33. R. Melville, 'Exhibitions', *Architectural Review*, Vol. 120, No. 716 (September 1956), pp. 185–6.

34. R. Melville, 'Exhibitions', *Architectural Review*, Vol. 125 (May 1959), pp. 355–7.

35. L. Alloway, 'Introduction to "Action"', *Architectural Design* (January 1956), p. 30.

36. See, for example, *Eight American Artists: Paintings and Sculpture* (York:

City of York Art Gallery, 1957), originally organised by the Seattle Art Museum and circulated by the USIA; and *Modern American Painting 1930–1958* (York: City of York Art Gallery, 1960), originally devised by the City Art Museum of St Louis, Missouri and then circulated by the USIS, US Embassy, London.

37. Denny interviewed by Alex Seago in 1989. See Seago's *Burning the Box of Beautiful Things: The Development of a Postmodern Sensibility* (Oxford: Oxford University Press, 1995), p. 97.

38. Del Renzio, letter to the author, 11 March 1997.

39. L. Alloway, 'Some Notes on Abstract Impressionism', *Abstract Impressionism* (London: Arts Council of Great Britain, 1958). See also: L. Finkelstein, 'New look: Abstract Impressionism' *Art News*, Vol. 55, No. 1 (March 1956), pp. 36–9, 66–8, and E. Corbett, *Abstract Impressionism* (South Hadley, MA: Mount Holyoke College, 1957).

40. L. Alloway, 'Art in New York Today', the *Listener*, Vol. LX, No. 1543 (23 October 1958), pp. 647–8.

41. L. Alloway, 'Sign and Surface: Notes on Black and White Painting in New York', *Quadrum*, No. 9 (1960), pp. 49–62.

42. Jones, quoted by Marco Livingstone, commentary to plate two, *Allen Jones: Retrospective of Paintings: 1957–1978* (Liverpool: Walker Art Gallery, 1979).

43. N. Wallis, 'At the Galleries: Heroes of the Day', *Observer* (9 November 1958).

44. J. Berger, 'Jackson Pollock', *Permanent Red: Essays in Seeing* (London: Methuen, 1960), pp. 66–70.

45. D. Hockney, *David Hockney by David Hockney: My Early Years*, ed. Nikos Stangos (London: Thames & Hudson, 1976), p. 41.

46. Phillips, quoted in, *Retrovision: Peter Phillips Paintings 1960–82*, by Marco Livingstone (Liverpool: Walker Art Gallery, 1982), p. 17.

47. For a discussion of de Kooning and Monroe see Griselda Pollock, 'Killing Men and Dying Women ...', *Avant-Gardes and Partisans Reviewed*, by F. Orton and G. Pollock (Manchester and New York: Manchester University Press, 1996), pp. 221–94.

48. On Norman Lewis see Ann Gibson, 'Norman Lewis in the 'Forties', *American Abstract Expressionism*, ed. David Thistlewood (Liverpool: Liverpool University Press and Tate Gallery Liverpool, 1993), pp. 53–76. See also: Valerie J. Mercer, *African-Americans in Paris, 1945–65* (New York: Studio Museum of Harlem, 1996).

49. J. Berger (Statement in), *The Forgotten Fifties*, by Julian Spalding and others (Sheffield: Graves Art Gallery, 1984), p. 46.

50. M. Kozloff, 'American Painting During the Cold War', *Artforum*, Vol. 11, No. 9 (May 1973), pp. 43–54; E. Cockcroft, 'Abstract Expressionism, Weapon of the Cold War', *Artforum*, Vol. 12, No. 10 (June 1974), pp. 39–41. (See also John Tagg, 'American Power and American Painting: The Development of Vanguard Painting in the United States since 1945', *Praxis*, Vol. 1, No. 2 (Winter 1976), pp. 59–79.) Cockcroft's facts and arguments have been challenged by Stacy Tenenbaum, see 'A Dialectical Pretzel: The New American Painting, the Museum of Modern Art and

American Cultural Diplomacy' (London: Courtauld Institute, MA Thesis, 1992). Robert Burstow has also claimed it was unlikely that CIA operatives were behind the 1956 and 1959 exhibitions because the abstract art included in them was too radical for their tastes. See 'The Limits of Modernist Art as a "Weapon of the Cold War": Reassessing the Unknown Patron of the Monument to the Unknown Political Prisoner', *Oxford Art Journal*, Vol. 20, No. 1 (1997), pp. 68–80. Further discussion of the complexities of MoMA's involvement has been provided by Michael Kimmelman's 'Revisiting the Revisionists: The Modern, Its Critics, and the Cold War', *The Museum of Modern Art at Mid-Century: At Home and Abroad*, ed. John Elderfield (New York: MoMA, 1994), pp. 39–55.

51. For a full account see Taylor D. Littleton and Maltby Sykes, *Advancing American Art: Painting, Politics, and Cultural Confrontation at Mid-Century* (Tuscaloosa, Alabama & London: University of Alabama Press, 1989).

52. D. and C. Shapiro, 'Abstract Expressionism: The Politics of Apolitical Painting' (1977), *Pollock and After: The Critical Debate*, ed. Francis Frascina (London: Harper & Row, 1985), pp. 135-51.

53. L. Jackson, *The New Look: Design in the Fifties* (London: Thames & Hudson, 1991), pp. 66–70.

54. N. Lynton, 'British Art and the New American Painting', *Cambridge Opinion*, No. 37 (2nd edn January 1964), pp. 9–13. A. Bowness, 'The American Invasion and the British Response', *Studio International*, Vol. 173, No. 890 (June 1967), pp. 285–93.

4 Abstraction and Pop in Britain During the 1960s

1. Bruce Glaser, '3 British Artists in New York', *Studio International*, Vol. 170, No. 871 (November 1965), p. 179.

2. D. Thompson, *Robyn Denny* (Harmondsworth, Middx: Penguin Books, 1971), p. 22.

3. R. Coleman, 'Introduction', *Situation: An Exhibition of British Abstract Painting* (London: RBA Galleries, 1960), p. 4.

4. See the letter 'Amateurs in Art' signed by twelve British artists which appeared in the *Sunday Times*, June 1963. It is reprinted in David Mellor and others', *The Sixties Art Scene in London* (London: Barbican Art Gallery/Phaidon Press, 1993), p. 91.

5. See Mellor, *The Sixties Art Scene in London*, p. 47.

6. P. Fuller, 'An Interview with Anthony Caro' (1978), *Beyond the Crisis in Art* (London: Writers & Readers, 1980), p. 197.

7. Linda Saunders (ed.), 'Clement Greenberg with Peter Fuller', *Modern Painters*, Vol. 4, No. 4 (Winter 1991), p. 25.

8. Fuller, 'An Interview with Anthony Caro', p. 198.

9. L. Alloway, 'Interview with Anthony Caro', *Gazette*, No. 1 (1961), p. 1.

10. For an account of *24 Hours* see 'Anthony Caro', *The Tate Gallery 1974–6* (London: Tate Gallery, 1978), pp. 74-6.

11. Fuller, 'An Interview with Anthony Caro', p. 198.

12. R. Whelan and others, *Anthony Caro* (Harmondsworth, Middx: Penguin Books, 1974), p. 72.

13. C. Greenberg, 'Anthony Caro' in *Anthony Caro*, by R. Whelan and others, pp. 87–93. (An essay first published in *Contemporary Sculpture*, Arts Yearbook 8, 1965, pp. 106–9.)

14. P. Fuller, 'The Visual Arts', *Modern Britain: The Cambridge Cultural History of Britain: Vol 9, Modern Britain*, ed. Boris Ford, paperback edn (Cambridge: Cambridge University Press, 1992), p. 139. This book was first published in 1988 with the title *The Cambridge Guide to the Arts in Britain: Since the Second World War*.

15. Source of information: interview between David Mellor and Tim Scott, July 1992; see Mellor, *The Sixties Art Scene in London*, p. 102.

16. Johns and Rauschenberg were included in the 1962 *Vanguard American Painting* (London: USIS Gallery, American Embassy) but they did not have individual shows in London until 1964 at the Whitechapel.

17. A small survey show of American Neo-Dada and Pop was *The Popular Image* held at the ICA during October–November 1963. Dine, Indiana, Johns, Lichtenstein, Oldenburg, Ramos, Rauschenberg, Rosenquist, Warhol and Wesselman were represented. Subsequently, Londoners were able to view the work of some of these artists in more depth as a consequence of one-man shows held in public and private galleries: Dine and Oldenburg at the Robert Fraser Gallery in 1966; Lichtenstein at the Tate and Warhol at the Rowan Gallery in 1968; and Oldenburg at the Tate in 1970. *Pop Art Redefined* – an international historical survey – was mounted by the Hayward Gallery in 1969. The book/catalogue accompanying this show included two chronologies which charted in parallel the developments of Pop in Britain and the United States. See John Russell and Suzi Gablik, *Pop Art Redefined* (London: Thames & Hudson, 1969).

18. Mellor and others, *The Sixties Art Scene in London*, p. 142.

19. 1989 Blake interview with Marco Livingstone; see the latter's *Pop Art: A Continuing History* (London: Thames & Hudson, 1990), pp. 251–2.

20. In 1964 Boshier was awarded a Peter Stuyvesant Foundation bursary which he used to visit California where he met up with Hockney, his old RCA buddy. From 1980 to 1993 Boshier lived, worked and taught in Houston, Texas. In 1996, while in London, he told Roger Berthoud:

> When I went to Texas I was regenerated, really revitalised. It was a new place, a totally different culture, there were these palm trees, everybody loved art, which is a change from here, everyone was enthusiastic, and they gave me a studio. Whenever you go anywhere, for the first few months, maybe even years, everything is very fresh, you've got the eye of an outsider. My first works were to do with looking at Texas culture: for instance, I did a series of paintings de-machoing the cowboy. Then I broadened out to look at American – and Mexican – culture.

See R. Berthoud, 'Finally back in the Swing', *The Times* (26 March 1996). Besides the Texas cowboy, Boshier's American subjects encompassed the Ku Klux Klan, a Dan Flavin exhibition, the oil industry, New Orleans and the cityscape of Houston. See Lynn M. Herbert, Marti Mayo (curators) and Guy Brett (essay), *Derek Boshier: The Texas Years* (Houston: Contemporary Arts Museum, 1995). However, the pictorial style he employed – a crude expressionism – was different from his 1960s' canvases and could no longer be described as Pop.

Boshier enjoyed material success in Texas: he bought a colonial-style house with a splendid garden to which he added a swimming pool. In the 1990s Boshier returned to live in England for a while but, at the time of writing, he is living in California.

21. I am grateful to Sue Watling, author of an MA Dissertation with the title *Why Are There No Great Women POP Artists?*, for information about Boty.
22. See Boty's remarks to Nell Dunn in *Talking to Women* (London: MacGibbon & Kee, 1965), p. 16–17.
23. See Phillips's remarks in Bruce Glaser, '3 British Artists in New York', *Studio International*, Vol. 170, No. 871 (November 1965), pp. 178–83.
24. Phillips, quoted in, *Retrovision: Peter Phillips Paintings 1960–82*, by Marco Livingstone (Liverpool: Walker Art Gallery, 1982), p. 17.
25. M. Amaya, *Pop as Art: A Survey of the New Super Realism* (London: Studio Vista, 1965), p. 132.
26. Phillips, quoted in *Retrovision*, p. 34.
27. Phillips, quoted in Glaser, '3 British Artists in New York', p. 183.
28. Hockney interviewed by Bragg in 'Bragg on America', *The South Bank Show* (London Weekend Television, 1997), a two-part series transmitted on 26 January 1997 and 2 February 1997.
29. Burra (1905–76) was an English, Surrealist-influenced watercolourist and illustrator who visited America several times both before and after the Second World War. He first went to New York in 1933 where he stayed in Harlem and the Lower East Side for several months. In 1937 he visited Boston, in 1953 Cape Cod and in 1955 New York and Boston. He was a close friend of the American poet Conrad Aitken. His ink drawing *Funfair* (1928–29), depicting a Coney Island scene, was made before he had been to the United States. Burra was subsequently to become noted for his images of the movie star Mae West, Harlem streets, striptease joints, dance halls, jazz nightclubs and Boston bars. Although verging on caricature, Burra's depictions of the black populace of Harlem are surely exceptional, and exceptionally positive, images from a white, English artist. See Andrew Causey and George Melly, *Edward Burra* (London: Arts Council of Great Britain/Hayward Gallery, 1985).
30. Information on Barker stems from an interview conducted in August 1997.
31. *Sunday Times* Colour Section, 8 April 1962. Journalists noted that, due to America's influence, Britain was acquiring computers, health clubs, jukeboxes, supermarkets and ten-pin bowling. One thing the Yanks would never succeed in Americanising, a native remarked, was the English weather!
32. Tilson, interview with Alex Seago, 1989, quoted in *Burning the Box of Beautiful Things: The Development of a Post-Modern Sensibility*, by A. Seago (Oxford: Oxford University Press, 1995), p. 139.

5 The Lure of America: British Artists in the United States

1. A. Seago, *Burning the Box of Beautiful Things: The Development of a Postmodern Sensibility* (Oxford: Oxford University Press, 1995).

2. This was the name of the company that arranged Hockney's flight to New York in 1961; it is inscribed inside *The Arrival*, an etching from the series *A Rake's Progress* (1961–63). See *David Hockney, Paintings, Prints and Drawings 1960–1970* (London: Whitechapel Art Gallery, 1970), p. 80.

3. R. Francis, 'Mixing Oil and Water', the *Independent* Magazine (15 September 1990), p. 44.

4. K. Kertess, 'On the High Sea and Seeing of Painting', *Malcolm Morley*, by Catherine Grenier and others (Paris: Centre Georges Pompidou/Editions ARPAP, 1993), p. 233.

5. See Melvin Maddocks and the editors of Time-Life Books, *The Great Liners* (Amsterdam: Time-Life Books, 1978), pp. 159–60.

6. A. Lewis, 'Morley and Modernism', *Art Monthly*, No. 70 (October 1983), pp. 3–5.

7. Ibid.

8. T. Castle, 'The Paint Drain', *Art Monthly*, No. 48 (July–August 1981), pp. 11–13.

9. P. Fuller, 'The Lady's not for Turner', *Art Monthly*, No. 82 (December–January 1984–85), pp. 2–6.

10. M. Livingstone, 'Essay', *Richard Smith: The Green Gallery Years 1960–63*, eds Frances Beatty and Samuel Trower (New York: Richard L. Feigen & Co., 1992), p. 11.

11. Seago, *Burning the Box of Beautiful Things*, p. 194.

12. H. Cohen, quoted in, John Richardson, *Harold Cohen: Paintings 1960–65* (London: Whitechapel Art Gallery, 1965), p. 9.

13. 'A Conversation', *Richard Smith: The Green Gallery Years 1960–63*, p. 37.

14. R. Smith, 'Trailer: Notes Additional to a Film', *Living Arts*, No. 1 (1963), pp. 28–35.

15. 'A Conversation', *Richard Smith: The Green Gallery Years 1960–63*, p. 33.

16. R. Morphet, 'Diary entry for 19 November 1962', quoted in *The Sixties Art Scene in London*, by David Mellor and others (London: Barbican Art Gallery and Phaidon Press, 1993), p. 131.

17. B. Glaser, '3 British Artists in New York', *Studio International*, Vol. 170, No. 871 (November 1965), pp. 178–83.

18. B. Adams, 'Cosmetic Abstractions', *Art in America*, Vol. 80, No. 10 (October 1992), pp. 118–21.

19. B. Robertson, 'Preface', *Richard Smith: Paintings 1958–66* (London: Whitechapel Gallery, 1966).

20. Ted Castle, 'Richard Smith in New York', *Art Monthly*, No. 29 (September 1979), pp. 8–9.

21. Cited in Malcolm Yorke, *Keith Vaughan: His Life and Work* (London: Constable, 1990), p. 170.

22. K. Vaughan, *Journals 1939–77* (London: John Murray, 1989), pp. 103–16.

23. Patrick Procktor, *Self-Portrait* (London: Weidenfeld & Nicolson, 1991), p. 87.

24. Yorke, *Keith Vaughan*, p. 188.
25. Ibid., p. 191.
26. Vaughan, *Journals*, p. 116.
27. Yorke, *Keith Vaughan*, p. 210.
28. Newman died on 4 July 1970. Heron's affectionate memories of Newman were published in *Studio International*, Vol. 180, No. 925 (September 1970), p. 70.
29. D. Lewis and others, *Terry Frost* (Aldershot: Scolar Press, 1994), p. 84.
30. P. Davies, 'Notes on the St Ives School, *Art Monthly*, No. 48 (July–August 1981), p. 7.
31. M. Tooby, 'Introduction', *The Presence of Painting: Aspects of British Abstraction 1957–1988* (London: South Bank Centre, 1988), p. 5. (Touring exhibition 1989.) Tooby's information came from Frost via an interview.
32. Lewis and others, *Terry Frost*.
33. J. Hoyland, *Hans Hofmann: The Late Paintings* (London: Tate Gallery, 1988), p. 9.
34. C. Harrison, 'London Commentary', *Studio International*, Vol. 177, No. 911 (May 1969), pp. 238–40.
35. For more on Latham see: J.A. Walker, *John Latham – The Incidental Person – His Art and Ideas* (London: Middlesex University Press, 1995).
36. W.C. Seitz, *The Art of Assemblage* (New York: MoMA, 1961).
37. L. Lippard, 'New York Pop', *Pop Art*, by L. Lippard and others (London: Thames & Hudson, 1966), p. 72.
38. J. Ruddock, *CND Scrapbook* (London: Optima, 1987), p. 9.
39. Ibid., p. 23.
40. C. Self, statement in *Tate Gallery Biennial Report 1972–74* (London: Tate Gallery, 1974), p. 231.
41. C. Finch, 'Colin Self', *Art International*, Vol. 20, No. 4 (April, 1967), pp. 27–31.
42. 'Colin Self and David Hockney Discuss their Recent Work', *Studio International*, Vol. 176, No. 906 (December, 1968), p. 277.
43. C. Self (statement), *Studio International*, Vol. 174, No. 892 (September 1967), pp. 88–9.
44. For a review see William Feaver, 'London: Unruly Selfs', *Art News*, Vol. 85, No. 9 (November 1986), pp. 50–1.
45. C. Self, *Colin Self's Colin Selfs* (London: ICA, 1986), p. 23.
46. Ibid., p. 49.
47. Ibid., p. 26. For more on Self's 1980s' work and his views on art and life see *The Tate Gallery Illustrated Catalogue of Acquisitions 1984–86* (London: Tate Gallery, 1988), pp. 270–82.
48. The information about Hockney which follows derives mainly from Peter Webb's detailed biography *Portrait of David Hockney* (London: Chatto & Windus, 1988).
49. Ibid., p. 42.
50. Ibid., p. 43.
51. M. Glazebrook, 'David Hockney: An Interview', *David Hockney: Paintings, Prints and Drawings 1960–70* (London: Whitechapel Art Gallery, 1970), p. 11.

52. Webb, *Portrait of David Hockney*, p. 193.
53. 'It's Much too Dull in Bradford', *Evening Standard* (19 December 1963).
54. Webb, *Portrait of David Hockney*, p. 90.
55. Ibid., p. 64.
56. A. Causey, 'Mapping and Representing', *David Hockney*, ed. Paul Melia (Manchester and New York: Manchester University Press, 1995), p. 98.
57. Melia, 'Showers, Pools and Power', *David Hockney*, p. 67.
58. Causey, 'Mapping and Representing', *David Hockney*, p. 100.
59. Ibid., pp. 94–5.
60. Procktor, *Self-Portrait*, p. 46.
61. Ibid., p. 126.
62. Ibid., p. 85.
63. 'Peter Blake in Hollywood', *Sunday Times* Magazine (15 November 1964), pp. 27–31.
64. P. Blake, *Some Explanations and Thoughts Toward my Exhibition at the Tate Gallery* (London: Tate Gallery, 1983), leaflet to accompany his Tate Gallery retrospective and catalogue, p. 2.
65. See David Bourdon, 'Art: The Mod Artists', *The Village Voice* (16 December 1965), p. 17.
66. M. Livingstone, *Retrovision: Peter Phillips' Paintings 1960–82* (Liverpool: Walker Art Gallery, 1982), p. 42.
67. Glaser, '3 British Artists in New York', p. 180.
68. Laing, quoted in A. Mackintosh, *Gerald Laing* (Edinburgh: Scottish National Gallery of Modern Art/Scottish Arts Council, 1971), p. 12.
69. Statement in *Gerald Laing: Paintings and Sculpture: 1963–83* (Coventry: Herbert Art Gallery, 1983), unpaginated.
70. R. Banham, 'Notes Towards a Definition of US Automobile Painting as a Significant Branch of Mobile Heraldry: Illustrations by Gerald Laing', *Art in America*, Vol. 54 (September 1966), pp. 76–9.
71. Ibid., p. 79.
72. Mackintosh, *Gerald Laing*, p. 26.
73. 'Giles Auty interview with Gerald Laing', *Gerald Laing 1963–1993: A Retrospective*, by Ian Carr, David Mellor and Giles Auty (Edinburgh: Fruitmarket Gallery, 1993), p. 45.
74. Mackintosh, *Gerald Laing*, p. 32.
75. 'Giles Auty interview with Gerald Laing', p. 45.
76. On *Hybrid* see G. Laing and P. Phillips, 'Hybrid Consumer Research Project', *ICA Bulletin*, No. 151 (October 1965), pp. 17–18. L. Alloway, 'Hybrid', *Arts*, Vol. 40 (May 1966), pp. 38–42. Gene R. Swenson, 'Hybrid, A Time of Life', *Art and Artists*, Vol. 1, No. 3 (June 1966), pp. 63–5. G. Laing, 'Hybrid', *Control Magazine*, No. 8 (August 1974), p. 15.
77. Laing and Phillips, 'Hybrid Consumer Research Project', *ICA Bulletin*, p. 18.
78. Livingstone, *Retrovision: Peter Phillips*, p. 50.
79. 'Art: Market Research Produces a Consumer-Determined Sculpture', *Life*, Vol. 60, No. 20 (20 May 1966), pp. 71–2, 74, 77.
80. Laing, 'Hybrid', *Control Magazine*, p. 15.
81. John Kasmin and Allen Jones, 'Kasmin/Jones: a Dialogue', *Modern Painters*, Vol. 4, No. 3 (Autumn 1991), pp. 58–9.

82. P. Webb, interview with Jones, in P. Webb and others, *The Erotic Arts*; (London: Secker & Warburg, 1975), p. 371.
83. Marco Livingstone and Richard Lloyd, *Allen Jones Prints* (Munich and New York: Prestel-Verlag, 1995), p. 17.
84. J. Coplans, 'An Interview with Allen Jones', *Artforum*, Vol. 3, No. 7 (1965), pp. 19–21.
85. Cited in Livingstone and Lloyd, *Allen Jones Prints*, p. 21.
86. 'Kasmin/Jones: a Dialogue', *Modern Painters*, pp. 58–9.
87. Jones, quoted by Livingstone, commentary to plate 26, *Allen Jones* (1979). Max Kozloff cannot recall writing an article entitled 'English Go Home'. He thinks the article in question was 'The British in Buffalo', *The Nation* (14 December, 1964), pp. 474–5, in which he mentioned Boshier and Jones, and then observed that such British artists risked becoming satellites of American art.
88. Other artists from British colonies who also spent time in the USA were: Avinash Chandra, Iqbal Geoffrey, Donald Locke, Ahmed Parvez, Francis Souza and Aubrey Williams.
89. For information on Bowling see: Frank Bowling and Bill Thompson, 'A Conversation between Two Painters', *Art International*, Vol. 20, No. 10 (December 1976), pp. 61–7. Rasheed Araeen, *The Other Story: Afro-Asian Artists in Post-War Britain* (London: Hayward Gallery, 1989); Mel Gooding, 'Grace Abounding: Bowling's Progress', *Third Text*, No. 31 (Summer 1995), pp. 37–46.
90. In fact, there were two Factories: the first was located on the fifth floor of 231 East 47th Street above a garage and the second was on the fifth floor of 33 Union Square West.
91. F.L. Guiles, *Loner at the Ball: The Life of Andy Warhol* (London, New York: Bantam Press/Transworld Publishers, 1989), p. 212–13.
92. M. Lancaster, 'A Collective Portrait of Andy Warhol', *Andy Warhol: A Retrospective*, ed. Kynaston McShine (New York and London: Museum of Modern Art/Hayward Gallery, 1989), p. 430.
93. R. Morphet, 'Mark Lancaster: Paintings 1965–67', *Art & Artists*, Vol. 2, No. 3 (June 1967), pp. 24–33.
94. Ibid.
95. *Life*, Vol. 61, No. 22 (25 November 1966), pp. 40–8.
96. R. Morphet, 'Mark Lancaster's Painting since 1967', *Studio International*, Vol. 177, No. 912 (June 1969), pp. 270–3.
97. Barry Lazell and Dafydd Rees, *Bryan Ferry and Roxy Music* (London and New York: Proteus Books, 1982), p. 36.
98. M. Livingstone, 'Mark Lancaster: Unmasking Andy's Marilyn', *Art & Design*, Vol. 4, Nos 3/4 (1988), pp. 65–9.
99. A. Wood, 'The Ascendancy of London' (letter), *Studio International*, Vol. 173, No. 886 (February 1967), p. 64.

6 Over Here: American Artists in Britain

1. On the St Ives School see D. Val Baker, *Britain's Art Colony by the Sea* (London: George Rowland, 1959); 'Notes on the St Ives School. Peter Davies talks to four leading members', *Art Monthly*, No. 48 (July–August 1981), pp. 3–8; T. Cross, *Painting the Warmth of the Sun: St Ives artists 1939–75* (Guildford: Hodge and Lutterworth, 1984); P. Davies, *The St Ives Years* (Wimbourne Bookshop, 1984); *St Ives 1939–64: Twenty-Five Years of Painting, Sculpture and Pottery* (London: Tate Gallery, 1985).

2. On Hubbard see George Monkland, 'John Hubbard, American Abstract Painter', *The Studio*, Vol. 161, No. 817 (May 1961), pp. 180–1 and Peter Fuller, 'John Hubbard' (1986), *Peter Fuller's Modern Painters: Reflections on British Art*, ed. J. McDonald (London: Methuen, 1993), pp. 232–43.

3. See Chris Stephens, *Mark Rothko in Cornwall* (St Ives: Tate Gallery, 1996), 14 page booklet; Adrian Searle, 'When Mr Gloom Came to Play', *Guardian* (14 May 1996), pp. 10–11; Simon Morley, 'Yanks', *Art Monthly*, No. 198 (July–August, 1996), pp. 9–12.

4. D. Mellor (ed.), *Paradise Lost: The Neo-Romantic Imagination in Britain 1935-55* (London: Barbican Art Gallery and Lund Humphries, 1987), p. 16.

5. P. Webb, *Portrait of David Hockney* (London: Chatto & Windus, 1988), p. 23.

6. Hockney, quoted in *David Hockney: Paintings, Prints and Drawings 1960–1970* (London: Whitechapel Art Gallery, 1970), p. 9.

7. John Coplans, 'An Interview with Allen Jones', *Artforum*, Vol. 3, No. 7 (April 1965), pp. 19–21.

8. For an analysis see J.A. Walker, 'Kitaj's Memorial to a Socialist Martyr', *Studies in Iconography*, Vol. 13 (1989–90), pp. 258–62.

9. Jim Aulich, the author of an illuminating article on Kitaj, has remarked:

    ... he blends an acute historical awareness with a contradictory technical achievement which parallels Post-Modernist pluralism while at the same time pursuing the emancipatory and utopian ideal inherent in Modernism. He carries out a quest for a lost universality which he is unable to resolve within the discourse of the European tradition. This is ... a reflection of his own cultural insecurity.

    'The Difficulty of Living in an Age of Cultural Decline and Spiritual Corruption: R.B. Kitaj 1965–70', *Oxford Art Journal*, Vol. 10, No. 2 (1987), pp. 43–57.

10. 'Kitaj Interviewed by Richard Morphet', *R.B. Kitaj: A Retrospective*, ed. R. Morphet (London: Tate Gallery, 1994), p. 44.

11. R.B. Kitaj: *Pictures with Commentary, Pictures without Commentary* (London: Marlborough Fine Art, New London Gallery, 1963).

12. Greenaway, quoted in Alan Woods, *Being Naked Playing Dead: The Art of Peter Greenaway* (Manchester and New York: Manchester University Press, 1996), pp. 105–6.

13. P. Procktor, *Self-Portrait* (London: Weidenfeld & Nicolson, 1991), p. 77.

14. R.B. Kitaj, *The Human Clay: An Exhibition Selected by R.B. Kitaj* (London: Arts Council of Great Britain, 1976), Hayward Gallery and then touring.

15. M. Peppiatt, *A School of London: Six Figurative Painters* (London: British Council, 1987).

16. A. Hicks, *The School of London: the Resurgence of Contemporary Painting* (Oxford, Phaidon, 1989).

17. T. Hilton, 'Unknotting the Old School Tie', *Guardian* (26 July 1989), p. 46.

18. R.B. Kitaj, *First Diasporist Manifesto* (London and New York: Thames & Hudson, 1989).

19. J. Hall, 'After the Fall, the Prize', *Guardian* (13 June 1995), p. 8.

20. A. L., 'London: "Teflon Ron" Takes on Brit Crits', *Art News*, Vol. 93, No. 7 (September 1994), pp. 60–2.

21. See Michael Billington, 'Bloody Barbs', *Guardian* (7 June 1996), pp. 2–3. For an obituary of Sandra Fisher see Thomas Meyer, 'Obituary: Sandra Fisher', *Modern Painters*, Vol. 7, No. 4 (Winter 1994), pp. 109–11.

22. Charlotte Wiggens, 'Struck Down' (Interview with Kitaj), *RA, The Royal Academy Magazine*, No. 55 (Summer 1997), pp. 40–1.

23. See Richard Morphet's attempts to resolve these issues in his introduction to the catalogue *R.B. Kitaj: A Retrospective*, pp. 9–42.

24. *R.B. Kitaj: A Retrospective*, p. 45.

25. A prime source of information on Rivers is his frank confessions, *What did I Do? The Unauthorized Autobiography*, written with Arnold Weinstein (New York: HarperCollins, 1992).

26. L. Rivers and D. Hockney, 'Beautiful or Interesting', *Art and Literature*, No. 5 (Summer 1964), pp. 94–117. Rivers' letter is reprinted in *Pop Art Redefined*, by John Russell and Suzi Gablik (London: Thames & Hudson, 1969), pp. 77–9.

27. See John Kasmin and Allen Jones, 'Kasmin/Jones: a Dialogue', *Modern Painters*, Vol. 4, No. 2 (Autumn 1991), pp. 58–9.

28. *David Hockney by David Hockney*, ed. Nikos Stangos (London: Thames & Hudson, 1976), p. 42.

29. Phillips, quoted in *Retrovision: Peter Phillips Paintings 1960–82*, by Marco Livingstone (Liverpool: Walker Art Gallery, 1982), p. 17.

30. See Fine-Artz Associates, 'Visualising ...', *ARK*, No. 35 (Spring 1964), pp. 38–41; 'A Fine-Artz view of Teenage Cults', *ARK*, No. 36 (Summer 1964), pp. 39–48.

31. M. Livingstone, *Pop Art: A Continuing History* (London: Thames & Hudson, 1990) p. 168.

32. Ibid.

33. George Martin and William Pearson, *Summer of Love: The Making of Sgt Pepper* (London and Basingstoke: Macmillan, 1994), p. 116.

34. For a review of this work see Robert Melville, 'A Note on the Work of Jann Haworth', *Art International*, Vol. 15, No. 10 (20 December 1971), pp. 82–3.

35. C. Barrett, 'Jim Dine's London', *Studio International*, Vol. 172, No. 881 (September, 1966), pp. 122–3.

36. R. Fraser and J. Dine, 'Dining with Dine', *Art & Artists*, Vol. 1, No. 6 (September 1966), pp. 48–53.

37. E. Lucie-Smith, 'Flamboyance and Eclecticism', *Studio International*, Vol. 171, No. 878 (June 1966), pp. 265–7.

38. Constance W. Glenn, *Jim Dine: Drawings* (New York: Abrams, 1985), p. 47.

39. Ibid., p. 196.

40. J. Russell, 'London: Dine and the Bobbies', *Art News*, Vol. 65 (November 1966), pp. 58, 87.

41. A report of the court case with statements by Fraser and the Police is given in 'Private View', *Art & Artists*, Vol. 1, No. 10 (January 1967), pp. 68–9.

42. This show was organised by Ronald Pickvance and travelled to various places during 1974 and 1975. See the catalogue, *English Influences on Vincent van Gogh* (Nottingham and London: Fine Art Dept, University of Nottingham and Arts Council of Great Britain, 1974).

43. For more about Ono see *Rolling Stone*, Jonathan Cott and Christine Doudna (eds), *The Ballad of John and Yoko* (London: Michael Joseph, 1982); Jerry Hopkins, *Yoko Ono* (London: Sidgwick & Jackson, 1987); Jon Hendricks (curator), *Yoko Ono: In Facing* (London: Riverside Studios, 1990); Barbara Haskell and John G. Hanhardt, *Yoko Ono: Arias and Objects* (Salt Lake City: Gibbs-Smith, 1991); Yoko Ono and others, 'Is that an Apple? Yoko Ono in London', *Art Monthly*, No. 212 (December–January 1997–98), pp. 1–7.

44. J. Reichardt, 'Art is Big, Round and Good', *Studio International*, Vol. 174, No. 892 (September 1967), pp. 80–1.

45. On the visual art of Lennon see Wulf Herzogenrath and Dorothee Hansen, *John Lennon: Drawings, Performances, Films* (London: Thames & Hudson, 1995).

46. For a perceptive account of Ono, Lennon and politics see Kristine Stiles: 'Unbosoming Lennon: The Politics of Yoko Ono's Experience', *Art Criticism*, Vol. 7, No. 2 (1992), pp. 21–51.

47. Ono, quoted in, Hopkins, *Yoko Ono*, p. 94.

48. Y. Ono, *Grapefruit* (London: Peter Owen, 1970). A paperback edition was published by Sphere Books in 1971.

49. Except by the Tate Gallery, London, which at the time of writing has very little by her and nothing by Lennon. An Ono retrospective exhibition was mounted by Oxford's Museum of Modern Art in November 1997.

50. B. Rose, *Claes Oldenburg* (New York: Museum of Modern Art, 1970), p. 35.

51. C. Oldenburg, *Proposals for Monuments and Buildings 1965–69* (Chicago: Big Table Publishing Company, 1969), p. 18.

52. Ibid., p. 19.

53. C. Oldenburg, 'London: Male City', *International Times* (London) (12 December 1966), pp. 6–7.

54. Oldenburg, *Proposals for Monuments and Buildings 1965–69*, p. 19.

55. On Oldenburg's multiples see C. Oldenburg and others, *Multiples in Retrospect 1964–1990* (New York: Rizzoli, 1991).

56. G. Baro, *Claes Oldenburg: Drawings and Prints* (London and New York: Chelsea House Publishers, 1969), p. 200.

57. Oldenburg, *Proposals for Monuments and Buildings 1965–69*, p. 20.

58. See Martin Friedman and Claes Oldenburg, *Oldenburg: Six Themes* (Minneapolis: Walker Art Centre, 1975), pp. 48–53.

59. Patricia Bickers, 'Interview with Claes Oldenburg', *Art Monthly*, No. 171 (November 1993), pp. 3–11.

60. G. Celant, *A Bottle of Notes and Some Voyages: Claes Oldenburg and Coosje van Bruggen* (Sunderland: Northern Centre for Contemporary Art/Leeds: The Henry Moore Centre for the Study of Sculpture, Leeds City Art Gallery, 1988), p. 18.

61. For more on Craig-Martin see Anne Seymour, *Michael Craig-Martin: Selected Works 1966–75* (Leigh, Lancashire: Turnpike Gallery, 1976); M. Craig-Martin, 'Reflections on the 1960s and early 1970s', *Art Monthly*, No. 114 (March 1988), pp. 3–5; Lynne Cooke and others, *Michael Craig-Martin: A Retrospective 1968–89* (London: Whitechapel Art Gallery, 1989).

7   Criticism and Resistance

1. Leon F. Litwack, 'Introduction: The Nifty Fifties: Myth and Reality', in *Advancing American Art: Painting, Politics, and Cultural Confrontation at Mid-Century*, by Taylor D. Littleton and Maltby Sykes (Tuscaloosa, Alabama and London: University of Alabama Press, 1989), p. 4.

2. B. Hillier, *Austerity/Binge: The Decorative Arts of the Forties and Fifties* (London: Studio Vista, 1975), pp. 77–8.

3. M. Barker, *A Haunt of Fears: The Strange History of the British Horror Comics Campaign* (London and Sydney: Pluto Press, 1984).

4. *Arena: The USA Threat to British Culture*, Vol. 2, No. 8 new series (June–July 1951).

5. John Kasmin and Allen Jones, 'Kasmin/Jones: a Dialogue', *Modern Painters*, Vol. 4, No. 3 (Autumn 1991), p. 58–9.

6. R. Hoggart, *The Uses of Literacy: Aspects of Working-Class Life with Special Reference to Publications and Entertainments* (London: Chatto & Windus, 1957), pp. 246–8.

7. J. Kasmin, quoted in *The Young Meteors*, by Jonathan Aitken (London: Secker & Warburg, 1967), p. 194.

8. K. Vaughan, *Journals 1939–77* (London: John Murray, 1989), p. 134.

9. Ibid., p. 187.

10. Ibid., p. 205.

11. Cited in Kenneth Rexroth's article 'US Art Across Time and Space 2: Americans seen Abroad', *Art News*, Vol. 58, No. 4 (1959), pp. 30–3, 52–4.

12. G.S. Whittet, 'London Commentary', *The Studio*, Vol. 157 (May 1959), p. 156.

13. L. Alloway, 'sic, sic, sic', *Art News and Review* (11 April 1959), pp. 5 and 8.

14. Spear, quoted by Mervyn Levy in *Ruskin Spear* (London: Weidenfeld & Nicolson, 1985), pp. 33–6.

15. Heron later gave a lecture at the ICA in December 1970, in which he attacked the American penchant for symmetry.

16. Juliet Gardiner, *'Over Here': The GIs in Wartime Britain* (London: Collins & Brown, 1992), p. 61.

17. P. Heron, 'The Ascendancy of London in the Sixties', *Studio International*, Vol. 172, No. 884 (December 1966), pp. 280–1; 'A Kind of Cultural Imperialism', *Studio International*, Vol. 175, No. 897 (February 1968), pp. 62–3; 'Two Cultures', *Studio International*, Vol. 180, No. 928 (December 1970), pp. 240–8.

18. See *Guardian*, Arts section (10, 11, 12 October 1974), p. 12, p. 10, pp. 8–9.
19. On Aldrich and his collection, see John Russell, 'Collector: Larry Aldrich', *Art in America*, Vol. 57, No. 1 (January–February 1969), pp. 56–65. Aldrich was described as a flexible, fast decision-maker in both business and in art acquisition.
20. B. Riley and others, *Bridget Riley: Dialogues on Art*, ed. Robert Kudielka (London: Zwemmer, 1995), p. 69.
21. P. Fay, 'Quick Cues: Op-position', *Queen* (5 January 1966), p. 9.
22. Another American artist of the Abstract Expressionist generation Riley met in New York was Ad Reinhardt. Apparently he escorted her around in order to protect her from 'wolves'. They collaborated on the production of an issue of *Poor Old Tired Horse* published by Wild Hawthorn Press in 1965. Drawings and layout were by Riley and writings/script by Reinhardt.
23. See Alex Bellos, 'Black and White Spiral Proves a Grey Area in Harrods v Riley', *Guardian* (12 April 1996), p. 3. Michael Bracewell, 'A Plea for Painting', *Guardian* Weekend (15 March 1997), cover illus, pp. 14–21.
24. Fay, 'Quick Cues'.
25. Ibid.
26. B. Riley, 'Perception is the Medium', *Art News*, Vol. 64 (October 1965), pp. 32–3 and 66.
27. Riley, quoted in, Aitken's *The Young Meteors*, p. 196.
28. L. Alloway, 'Notes on Op Art', *The New Art: A Critical Anthology*, ed. Gregory Battcock (New York: Dutton, 1966), pp. 83–91.
29. R. Hamilton, *Collected Words 1953–82* (London: Thames & Hudson, 1982), p. 94.
30. A detailed account of the print is given in *The Tate Gallery Illustrated Catalogue of Acquisitions 1984–86* (London: Tate Gallery, 1988), pp. 371–5.
31. The statement is reprinted in *Collected Words*, p. 95.
32. However, James Aulich has expressed the opinion that in the print: 'Victim became martyr and was taken out of history. The image inspired by moral outrage, stitled by irony and mediated by process served in the end ... to extol the virtues of technology. In other words, the picture participates in the ideological base of the conflict itself.' 'Vietnam, Fine Art and the Culture Industry', *Vietnam Images; War and Representation*, eds Jeffrey Walsh and James Aulich (Basingstoke, Hants: Macmillan, 1989), p. 83.
33. See P. Kennard, *Images for the End of the Century: Photomontage Equations* (London: Journeyman Press, 1990).
34. See J.A. Walker, *Art in the Age of Mass Media*, rev. edn (London: Pluto Press, 1994), pp. 109–10, 162–4.
35. On the Greenham Common struggle – which was eventually victorious – see Guy Brett, 'To rid the World of Nuclear Weapons ...', *Through Our Own Eyes: Popular Art and Modern History* (London: GMP, 1986), pp. 130–54.

The first McDonalds in Britain was opened in Woolwich, South London, in 1974. Millions of Britons and their children now eat at branches of McDonalds. Morris and Steel, two members of London Greenpeace, were taken to court by the fast food chain for libel, that is, for handing out a factsheet (which they had not even written) critical of its burgers, advertising, employment policies, environmental effects, etc. Two poverty-stricken anarchists with no legal aid or experience took on the might of a corporation with an annual turnover of billions of dollars. In 1997, after the longest court case in English legal history – it lasted several years – the judge (there was no jury) found for McDonalds on several counts but the British underdogs had won a moral victory. Furthermore, they and their supporters promised to continue to exercise their right of freedom of expression, their right to criticise supranational corporations whose wealth exceeds that of many nation states. For an account of the case see John Vidal, *McLibel* (London and Basingstoke: Macmillan, 1997).

George Ritzer, an American sociologist, is the author of *The McDonald-ization of Society: An Investigation into the Changing Character of Contemporary Social Life*, rev. edn (Thousand Oaks, California: Pine Forge Press/London: Sage Publications, 1996), which analyses the history and success of the fast-food chain. Ritzer also uses its name metaphorically to describe 'the process by which the principles of the fast-food restaurant are coming to dominate more and more sectors of American society as well as the rest of the world' (p. 1). These principles include: calculability, control, efficiency, predictability, rationalisation and standardisation. Ritzer provides an illuminating critique of 'an icon of Americana' and he does cite various critics of McDonalds but he makes no mention of the British resistance fighters Morris and Steel.

8   The Decline of American Influence and the Rise of BritArt

1. A. Searle, 'When Mr Gloom Came to Play', *Guardian* (14 May 1996), pp. 10–11.
2. See 'Robert Morris: A Dialogue between David Sylvester and Michael Compton', *tate: the art magazine*, No. 11 (Spring 1997), tate Extra, 8 page supplement.
3. See Burgin's remarks in *The Impossible Document: Photography and Conceptual Art in Britain 1966–76*, ed. John Roberts (London: Camerawords, 1997), pp. 80–1.
4. The history that follows is heavily indebted to Charles Harrison's and Fred Orton's, *A Provisional History of Art & Language* (Paris: Editions E. Fabre, 1982).
5. J. Roberts, 'Photography, Iconophobia and the Ruins of Conceptual Art', *The Impossible Document*, p. 41.
6. Art & Language, 'Moti Memoria', *The Impossible Document*, p. 55.
7. Art & Language (UK), 'The Worst of All Allies', *The Fox*, No. 3 (1976), pp. 78–9.
8. Harrison and Orton, *A Provisional History of Art & Language*, p. 20.
9. Ibid., p. 19.
10. Ibid., p. 50.
11. Ibid., p. 63. See also Art & Language, 'Portrait of V.I. Lenin in the Style of Jackson Pollock', *Artforum*, Vol. 18, No. 6 (February 1980), pp. 34–7.
12. See the letters published in 'Signing Off', *tate: the art magazine*, Nos 11 and 12 (spring and summer 1997), pp. 80 and 88.

13. A. Bowness, 'The State of British Art: A Debate, Session 3: The Multinational Style', *Studio International*, Vol. 194, No. 989 (February 1978), p. 103.

14. P. Fuller, 'The Visual Arts', *Modern Britain: The Cambridge Cultural History of Britain*, Vol. 9, ed. Boris Ford, paperback edn (Cambridge: Cambridge University Press, 1992), pp. 144–5.

15. P. Fuller, 'Against Internationalism', *Art Monthly*, No. 100 (October 1986), pp. 12–14.

16. P. Fuller, 'The Eastward March of Civilisation?', *Art & Design*, Vol. 3, Nos 9–10 (1987), p. 25.

17. It could be argued that during the 1960s the North Vietnamese army and people succeeded in resisting and defeating the American armed forces stationed in South Vietnam but this was achieved at incredible cost and it is also the case that the Americans held back from using the most powerful weapons in their armoury – nuclear bombs.

18. M. Corris, 'Yet Another Palace Revolt in the Banana Republic?', *The Fox*, No. 2 (1975), pp. 143–53.

19. Liz Jobey, 'Tate Expectations', *Guardian* (10 February 1996), pp. 12–13.

20. Norman Rosenthal and others, *Sensation: Young British Artists from the Saatchi Collection* (London: Royal Academy of Arts, 1997).

21. R. Hughes, *American Visions: The Epic History of Art in America* (New York: Alfred A. Knopf, 1997), p. 620.

22. See Anthea Gerrie, 'BritArt makes London World Culture Capital', *Observer* (20 July 1997), p. 16. For a suitably shallow account of the shallow London art scene see Matthew Collings, *Blimey! From Bohemia to Britpop: The London Artworld from Francis Bacon to Damien Hirst* (Cambridge: 21, 1997). For a more thorough account see Bernice Murphy (ed.), *Pictura Britannica: Art from Britain* (Sydney: Museum of Contemporary Art, 1997).

23. In 1997 Tony Blair, the new Labour Prime Minister, recognised this by hosting a reception at 10 Downing Street for Britain's designers, film-makers, etc. See T. Blair, 'Britain can Remake it', *Guardian* (22 July 1997), p. 17.

24. D. Puttnam and Neil Watson, *The Undeclared War: The Struggle for Control of the World's Film Industry* (London: HarperCollins, 1997), pp. 353–4.

25. Andrew Graham-Dixon, *A History of British Art* (London: BBC Books, 1996), p. 10.

26. For example, Anish Kapoor (b. 1954 in Bombay) was trained at Hornsey College of Art and is now a noted Anglo-Indian sculptor. British artists such as Howard Hodgkin and Deanna Petherbridge have spent time in India and their work has been influenced by exposure to India and its visual culture.

Index

gun culture, of America, 196
Guston, Phillip, 44, 60, 62, 66,
    75, 110, 118, 180, 211
Guttuso, Renato, 56–7
Guyana, South America, 161

Habitat, 25
Haley, Bill, 91
Half-a-Wind Show (exhibition),
    193
Hall, James, 177
Hamilton, George Heard, 141
Hamilton, Richard, 19, 21, 29,
    30, 31–2, 33, 34, 35, 43, 68,
    73, 76, 77, 86–8, 102, 111,
    115, 141–4, 151, 157, 163,
    166, 167, 178, 185, 188, 191,
    211, 223–4, 233, 239
Hamilton, Terry, 19, 32, 43
Hamilton-Fraser, D., 72
Hammarskiöld, Hans, 198
Hammersley, Frederick, 80
Hampson, Frank, 209
handicraft, 183
Hanson, Al, 192
Happenings, 73, 125, 186, 197
Hard-Edge painting, 73, 98
Haring, Keith, 242
Harkness Fellowships, 104, 112,
    124, 148, 233
Harlow, Jean, 90
Harrison, Charles, 124, 232,
    234, 235, 236
Harrison, Wallace K., 38
Hartigan, Grace, 44, 70
Hartung, Hans, 45
Harvard University, Cambridge,
    Mass., 23
Harvey, Marcus, 244
Haunt of Fears, A (book), 209
Haworth, Jann, 91, 101, 145–6,
    169, 183–6
Haworth, Ted, 145, 183
Hay, Alex, 234
Haynes, Brian, 111
Haynes, Jim, 169
Hayward, Susan, 61
Heartfield, John, 225

Heath, Adrian, 22
Hebdige, Dick, 232
hegemony, 53
Heller, Preston, 232
Henderson, Nigel, 7–8, 19, 20,
    24, 25
Hepworth, Barbara, 14, 81, 170,
    211
heraldry, 152
Herbin, Auguste, 122
heritage, 210
Herman Miller Furniture
    Company, 25
hermaphrodite figures, 159
Heron, Delia, 121
Heron, Patrick, 5, 28, 48, 49,
    53–6, 63, 73, 76, 78, 79, 82,
    86, 117, 121, 122, 170, 172,
    176, 214–15, 238
Hess, Thomas B., 17
Heston, Charlton, 87
Hicks, Alistair, 176
hierarchies, in culture, 36, 42
high culture, 36, 39, 42
Hill, Anthony, 58
Hiller, Bevis, 207, 208
Hiller, Susan, 169
Hilton, Roger, 48, 52, 54, 67, 73,
    76, 170
Hilton, Tim, 176
Hirst, Damien, 202, 244, 245
history, of art, 39
history-painting, 173–4, 177, 238
Hitchcock, Alfred, 4
Hitchins, Ivon, 56, 63
Hitler, Adolf, 177
Hockney, David, 3, 66–7, 68, 73,
    86, 99–101, 111, 118, 119,
    127, 128, 133–41, 148, 149,
    159, 161, 163, 166, 172, 173,
    180, 181, 205, 211, 239
Hodgkin, Howard, 148, 176, 205
Hofmann, Hans, 123, 124, 179
Hogarth, William, 133, 239
Hoggart, Richard, 210
Holland, Van Dutch, 149
Holly, Buddy, 91, 94
Hollywood, 8, 43, 77, 87, 90, 95,

Santa Monica, California, 22, 24, 135, 146
Sargent, John, 169, 176
Sartre, Jean-Paul, 77
satellites, 3
satire, 87
Saturday Evening Post (magazine), 12
Savage Eye, The (film), 128
Schaefer, Bertha, 170
Schapiro, David and Cecile, 72
Schapiro, Miriam, 63
Schermer, Betsy, 88
Schnabel, Julian, 243, 244
Schneede, Uwe M., 21
scholar-painting, 172
Schonzeit, Ben, 150
School: of London, 176; of Paris, 9, 10, 45, 52
Schwitters, Kurt, 111
science, 19, 246
science fiction, 10, 32, 36, 37
Scientific American (magazine), 29, 98-9
scientists, 168
Scotland, 10, 154
Scott, James, 203
Scott, William, 48-9, 52, 54, 76, 85, 170, 171
Scottish art/painting, 10, 46
screenprints, 21, 223
sculpture(s), 17, 18, 21, 81, 84, 85, 101, 124, 131, 129, 142-3, 153, 154, 155, 183, 184, 197, 200-5, 208, 223, 231
sea travel, 104, 106, 107, 118
Seago, Alex, 104
Seagram Murals, 171
Searle, Adrian, 228
Second World War, 3, 4, 5, 39, 207, 214
Segal, George, 116, 231
Seitz, William C., 124, 125, 126, 170, 219, 221
Self, Colin, 127-33, 141
Self, Robert, 235
Selz, Peter, 116
semiotics, 23, 50, 232

Senegal, Africa, World Festival of Negro Arts, 162
Sensation (exhibition), 243
sensationalism, 177, 221
Sergeant Pepper (LP), 91, 185, 186, 194, 240
Serota, Nicholas, 242
Serpan, Jaroslav, 49
Serra, Richard, 231
Seven Year Itch, The (film), 32
Sewell, Brian, 110
sexist art, 156, 177
sexual: imagery, 190, 194, 199; liberation, 200; subject matter, 157
Shahn, Ben, 17, 60, 66, 89
Shannon, Claude, 29, 43
shaped canvas, 93, 151, 157
Shaped Canvas (exhibition), 116
Shapiro, Meyer, 17
Sharkey, John, 192
Sharrer, Honore, 89
Shearer, Moira, 172
Sheffield, 68, 231
Shepherd, Sam, 92
Shepperton Film Studio, 88
ships, 106, 107
Shirelles, the, 115
shopfronts, 7-8
Sickert, Walter, 105, 239
Siegelaub, Seth, 235
signs, 50
silk-screen painting, 164
Sinatra, Frank, 90
Siquerios, David Alfaro, 227
Situation (exhibition), 76, 77-8
Situation 'group', 78
Situationists, 77
Skidmore, Owings and Merrill, 22, 23
Sleigh, Sylvia, 37, 78
Slowinski, Ron, 113
Smith, David, 15, 81, 82, 84, 85, 132
Smith, Jack (American), 164
Smith, Jack (British), 56, 57
Smith, Leon, 80
Smith, Matthew, 56